the Idler

ISSUE 26 | SUMMER 2000

First published in Great Britain in 2000 by
Idle Limited
Studio 20, 24-28a Hatton Wall
London ECiN 8JH
Tel: 020 7691 0320
Fax: 020 7691 0321
e-mail: admin@idler.co.uk

ISBN 0-9536720-1-8

....

Editor: Tom Hodgkinson
Creative Director: Gavin Pretor-Pinney
Deputy Editor: Matthew De Abaitua
Designer: Liz Harris
Researcher: Dan Kieran
Literary Editor: Tony White
Contributing Editors: Greg Rowland, Joshua Glenn
Sports Editor: John Moore
Editorial Assistant: Sam Jordison
Cover painting: Mark Ryden (www.markryden.com)
Advertising: Jamie Dwelly at Cabbell 020 8971 8450

"THE MIND IS ITS OWN PLACE,
AND IN ITSELF CAN MAKE A HEAVEN OF HELL,
A HELL OF HEAVEN"

JOHN MILTON

FREE ABSINTHE

Our last absinthe competition was a great success. We had nearly as many entries as prizes. The following Idler readers were the deserving winners of a bottle of finest Hill's Absinth.
Kevin Foxall, Hull; Tim Footman, Surrey; Richard Lewis, London, NW5; Benedict Baldwin, Oxford; Gareth Evans, London, E5; Steve Timms, Oldham; Brian Whitmore, Lancashire; Anna Battista, Italy

We have decided to repeat the experience. This time, we want you to write a piece on why absinthe should be banned. The article should be no longer than 300 words. The ten best-written and most persuasive tracts in the entirely subjective view of a carelessly selected panel of amateurs will win a FREE bottle of Hill's Absinth.

SEND YOUR ENTRIES TO: The Idler, Studio 20, 24-28a Hatton Wall, London EC1N 8JH
Or e-mail them to: admin@idler.co.uk
The closing date for the competition is 31 August 2000. We can't wait!
Please note: you must be over 18 to enter this competition. Winners' ages will be verified
before delivery.

HILL'S ABSINTH
. . . .
WWW.EABSINTHE.COM
CREDIT CARD HOTLINE: 01992 511445

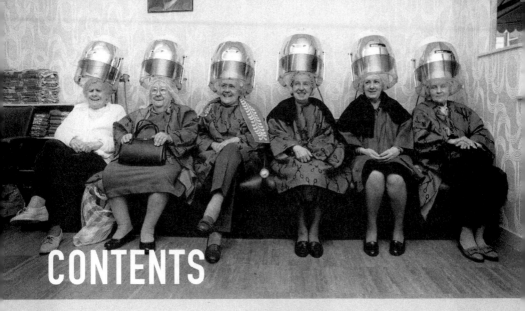

CONTENTS

DAVID SOLOMONS

Grand Order of Idlers

SUBSCRIBE NOW AND GET A FREE BOOK WORTH £10
IT COSTS JUST £20 A YEAR

When you subscribe to the Idler, you become more than just a subscriber. You become a member of the Grand Order of Idlers.

Once you have joined this august order, you will be entitled to these benefits:

Two issues of the Idler sent to your door every year
A free Idler snail tattoo
A Grand Order of Idlers membership certificate
Occasional mailings
Invitations to Idler events and parties

To join The Grand Order of Idlers, simply send us a cheque for £20, made payabe to "The Idler", and a note reading "I want to join you!"

Our address is:
The Idler, Studio 20,
24-28a Hatton Wall, London EC1N 8JH
Or go to our website at www.idler.co.uk

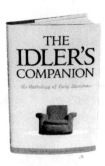

Send your cheque before 14 July and we'll send you a FREE copy of The Idler's Companion, the indispensable anthology of idle writing through the ages, worth £10.

JOIN US IN THE STRUGGLE AGAINST TOIL

CONTENTS

DAVID SOLOMONS

LETTER FROM THE EDITOR

After a winter in hibernation, we blink our eyes open and start looking around. The last issue of the *Idler* – Man's Ruin – gazed into the gutter. This time, we turn our attention to the stars, with a special issue dedicated to paradise. While others scurry about worrying, consumed by anxiety, we have been thinking about utopia. Up here in Idle Towers, we take the time to wonder, with William Blake, was Jerusalem builded here, on England's green and pleasant land? Is it possible to create a heaven in your own mind? Can we build Eden in our backyard?

We have gathered together our usual motley crew of seekers after the truth for your entertainment and edification.

The English pastoral is explored by John Nicholson, who argues that the notion of a lost England of merry peasants, milkmaids, geese in the yard and chocolate box cottages is a myth, invented by writers working in the destabilised period following the Great War.

On a more practical tip, we offer handy hints on how you can create a paradise in your own backyard. Our Tiki Special section investigates the legacy of Hawaiian holidays and Easter Island icons on the modern leisure culture.

We've pulled together some great writers. Jonathan Coe meets David Nobbs, the novelist and writer of the *Fall and Rise of Reginald Perrin*. Nicholas Blincoe reveals Sherlock Holmes to be an idler *par excellence*. Steve Beard discusses colonialism with Michael Moorcock and Tony White takes Iain Sinclair on a trip on the millennium wheel.

Uri Geller, no less, has kindly solved the world's mysteries for us, to save you the effort. Adam and Joe reveal both Ken Korda's vision of paradise and the true story of what really happened to the Bounty Hunters, the apparently idyllic community that lived on Bounty Bars and appeared in TV ads from the Seventies onwards.

As our last book-style issue was a success, we have decided to go ahead and publish it twice – yes, twice – a year. To get future issues sent direct to your home, join the Grand Order of Idlers. It costs just £20 a year. See page four.

Not only that, but, believe it or not, we have finally got round to producing a website. Idler.co.uk will publish fresh *Idler* material with an extensive archive, provide chat rooms for idlers and a shop to buy *Idler* merchandise and hard-to-find magazines and books.

With your help and the support of our advertisers and sponsors – Channel 4, Hill's Absinth, Absolut, Canongate and American Spirit – we will not cease from mental fight, nor shall our swords sleep in our hands.

Write to us at our new office: 24-28a Hatton Wall, London EC1N 8JH, or e-mail to admin@idler.co.uk

Finally, I'd just like the world to know that I had a baby. Arthur was born on March 9. Aaaah.

TOM HODGKINSON, April 2000

NOTES FROM THE COUCH

IDLER'S DIARY

The latest occurences in the world of loafing

IDLER TAKES EXERCISE, NEARLY DIES

In a moment of madness, while holidaying on the relaxing Isle of Skye, our hefty deputy editor became a victim of the X-treme sports lifestyle. He rented a mountain bike with the absurd notion that this might lead to "kicks" and "adrenalin". He raced down a hillside, failing to take into account that his recently increased mass would supply him with far greater momentum than he'd ever previously experienced. He shot off road, vaulted a small brook, and was flung headfirst over the handlebars and into a peaty bog. It was like a Pepsi Max ad gone wrong.

....

THE WAGES OF SIN

"Brown wages war on workshy" was the brilliantly alliterative headline in the Daily Mail one sad day in April. The idle were also described as "feckless", a curious archaic word meaning feeble or irresponsible. Its use caused us to reflect on what a "feck" is, and why it's supposed to be good to have a lot of it. Anyway, Daily Mail readers, that feckful bunch, who contribute so much to society through their jobs in middle management and their posts as magistrates, have always hated the idea of other people enjoying their lives. And Gordon Brown knows well how to court them with his anti-idle pronouncements. However, we know deep down that idlers are wily, resourceful creatures — perhaps because they have so much time to think — and so will always find ways to avoid losing their dignity entirely to the world of work, as it is conceived by Brown, Blair and the whole damn crew. They can feck off.

....

IDLER ON THE WEB

Like many others, we have been feeling disdotcombobulated over the last few months. Why were we not worth $40 million on paper? Where were the venture capitalists beating a path to our door? Thankfully, the dot com bubble has burst. Disgruntled investors, duped by the hype, have been left wondering whether to cash in their shares or hope for an upturn. Anyway, that brings us to the subject of the Idler website, a project first mooted in 1994 when we bought our first modem. So it's taken us seven years, but finally we have got round to creating a website. www.idler.co.uk will offer fresh editor-

THE DAILY MAIL: ARROGANCE IN DEFENCE OF IGNORANCE

DJ LE CREUSET AT THE FOUNDRY

ial content, community chat rooms and a shop selling Idler merchandise, books and other hard-to-find magazines and products for an idle life. Subscribers to the site will be sent irregular e-mails, which will provide an oasis of calm and sanity in an insane world

THE FOUNDRY OF ALL REASON

To The Foundry in London's Shoreditch for the launch of Idler contributor Mark Manning's first collection of memoirs, CRUCIFY ME AGAIN. The Foundry is a superb bar which is run by Gimpo, adventurer and former KLF roadie. In stark contrast to the unwelcoming concrete modernism of other drinking places in the area, The Foundry (which actually was a foundry) is dark, amateurish and comfy. The Foundry is occasional home to David Kirby, aka DJ Le Creuset, who mixes up great tunes and wicked hot food simultaneously (see picture above). And on Sunday nights Gimpo runs an open mike poetry event. Yes, that's generally my idea of hell too, but this one is different. This one has poet fights, tequila and lots of shouting. Plus some surprisingly good poetry. Check it out.

PENSION PROVOCATEURS

The Idler has long taken a somewhat lateral line of resistance to some of the more tiresome social systems. So it is gratifying to see the torch of rebellion has been handed up a generation, to a growing band of oldsters who, frankly, will take no more. This issue, we lift the lid on this phenomenon in our Grey Panthers feature. Certainly we can expect further rumblings from the older quarters, particularly against a recent government report recommending that benefits be stopped to those who retire before sixty-five. You'd think that, by then, most people would have grown out of work. The case of 89-year-old widow, Jessie Bonner-Thomas, who gave the chief executive of Barclays a good old dressing down for his company's hypocrisy, is a sign of things to come.

THE GRAND ORDER OF IDLERS

Ordinary magazines ask their readers to subscribe. At the Idler, we ask you to join the Grand Order of Idlers. Being a member costs just twenty pounds – and entitles you to two issues of the magazine sent to your door every year. You will also be notified of Idler events, receive the occasional free gift, AND get a specially designed certificate of membership. The struggle against work is a tough one, but we can help your mental fight. ☯

SKIVERS & STRIVERS
More whimsical and arbitrary plaudits and damnations

THE SKIVERS

TALCUM POWDER After a bath, we used to pat its chalky scent in our armpits, along our thighs, up between the legs. But no more. Why has the chalky scent of talc fallen from British life? Goddammit, why would someone secretly muck about with reality like that?

JILL DANDO Seems to have taken the entire year off.

REPRESSION In steep decline since 1979, the last two decades saw an astonishing increase in the amount of things we decided to get out in the open. Once awkward fumblings have transformed into hearty, shame-free rogerings. Now, an eight-year-old can listen to boy bands called Boyparts or Back Passage Lads without even blushing. While such cultural exhibitionism has had its upside, the IDLER can't help but feel a certain naive yet naughty charm has left British culture. Remember when a mere hint of on-screen sex would cause the entire family to shuffle around the television like it was a fart? Remember and weep.

SNOW All the snow has been taken away from Britain because the Man decided it caused a drop in productivity. Also, disrupted the so-called education being doled out in schools. Also, snowballs competed with the powerful military-industrial-videogame complex.

COMEDY SONGS Ali G's persistent refusal to cut a novelty rap record surely signals the demise of this comedic genre. Which is a shame, as the comedy song — from Noel Coward to The Bonzo Dog Doo Dah Band — is as English as estate mums. True, it was also the preserve of winsome students with an acoustic guitar and a bag of double entendres and — yes, hands up — it did give us Richard Stillgoe and — OK — the SPITTING IMAGE songs did get tiresome. But still.

LIZA TARBUCK On a day in which it was discovered that the universe is flat, not curved, and that Noel Edmonds declared that the BBC paid him a hefty sum for doing nothing for an entire year, between these two revelations, great and small, the IDLER had a third: that Liza Tarbuck is the sauciest, sharpest woman around. She took the morning by the scruff of the neck, she rolled her eyes across a rolodex of innuendo, she filled a blouse like a good woman should. Faintly fearsome, definitely gorgeous, surely she can't keep getting up that early for long?

THE STRIVERS

THE BIG Os A brand extension in which the humble potato snack, the hula hoop, has been blown up into a much bigger hula hoop. Where once you nibbled a hula hoop off your little finger, a big O – being about the size of a cock ring – suggests more erotic play. Especially when combined with the nudge-nudge Sixties Cosmo orgasm reference of the name. The gulf between the outrageous promise of a giant orgasm and the big fat zero of fried spud has been causing outbreaks of bathos in dilapidated boozers all across the land.

....

WANGST New term for self-pitying display of introspection indulged in by men in their twenties. Often caused by Russian novels and an inch of extra girth. Especially prevalent in boom times when peers seem to be so much more successful.

....

MARTHA LANE FOX The face of Lastminute.com, who briefly became the poster girl for get-rich-quick dot com mania. Now the paper millions have gone up in smoke and everyone has been left holding equity options that condemn them to years of torment at the hands of demanding venture capitalists and angry shareholders. The dot com millionaires have been compared to the Great Gatsby, but now it seems like Dr Faustus is their true antecedent.

....

LARA CROFT Dear Lara is selling out all over the place these days. She appeared in a Dreamcast ad with a different voice and different animated appearance. This is not the real Lara. The IDLER thinks that digital figures who want to become real and earn even more money are like those Scouse entertainers who got rich and started voting Tory – just like that loveable gap-toothed stand-up Dennis Skinner, whom we all enjoyed in EASY RIDER but who is now the military dictator of Finland.

....

WALLPAPER MAGAZINE The Kays catalogue with delusions of grandeur.

....

ALDERSHOT Can anyone explain to the IDLER the arbitrary dress codes of provincial nightclubs? Don't you realise, sir, that I am known in all the important private clubs in the Western Hemisphere? Yet you stand there and question the cut of my trousers and the shape of my boots? You, with your pig head and proposterous puffa! Ow.

....

JOB OUTLOOK BLEAK FOR PESSIMISTS

Employers are using emotional intelligence tests to weed out "negative" candidates

People who believe things will turn out for the worst are finding it increasingly difficult to get employment. Recent research by the American Institute for Social Policy on social security claimants found that 78% of unemployed white collar workers were rated as pessimistic under the now-commonplace Emotional Intelligence scale, or EQ.

Emotional intelligence was the name coined by Peter Salovey of Yale University and John Mayer, of the University of New Hampshire, for the collection of personal, emotional and social abilities that they were studying. But it was only with the publication of David Golemen's book, EMOTIONAL INTELLIGENCE, that algorithms to calculate the emotional intelligence of prospective employees began to seep into the candidate screening techniques of personnel departments across the USA.

Emotional Intelligence is composed of two "intelligences": intrapersonal, which is the ability to manage ourselves by knowing and understanding our desires; extrapersonal, which is our ability to read other people's emotions and psychological states. It is in the "intrapersonal" intelligence that pessimism firsts manifests itself, primarily as a doubt that our needs will ever be fulfilled, and that desires will always be frustrated. This affects motivation over the long term, and impedes the worker's ability to fix goals or indeed, develop a groundbreaking vision.

Emotional intelligence tests benefit employers by ensuring a lower rate of staff turnover. By enabling a company to match the personality of candidates to the "emotional profile" of a position, they ensure a character is suitable for the job, so avoiding wasting money training a sourpuss.

An unexpected social consequence of this practise, however, has been effectively to screen out individuals with pessimistic tendencies from the world of work. Jenny Batemen, 28, was a product developer for a major media owner until a staff reevaluation revealed her EQ to be high in negativity. "They told me to clear my desk," says Jenny, now back living with her parents in Wisconsin. "My manager explained how I tested positive for pessimism. I've always tried to conceal it. My employers never knew about all the food I had stashed for the millennium bug, or how everytime I pick up the phone I'm sure it's going to be Mummy telling me Daddy's had a heart attack. In the modern workplace, pessimism – or even realism – is career poison. In such a forward looking company, committed to innovation and dedicated to a vision of the future, the pessimist is – in the long term – counterproductive."

Jenny Bateman is just one of an estimated 350,000 people who have been eased out of employment due to "optimism impairment". The Social Policy pamphlet contains testimonies from over a dozen of such individuals. Peter Hinde, 32, was working as a marketing executive in an internet start-up company until one fateful after-hours social drink. "I was having a few beers with a colleague and I confessed that as we were losing two million dollars a week I was worried that the chickens might eventually come home to roost. That

was it. I was out."

Peter Hinde's case is far from unique, with new media companies and internet start-ups particularly keen to avoid having any pessimists on the payroll. "Our industry is dependent on positive perception," said Anthony Green of the Institute of New Media, "it doesn't matter if you're losing a fortune and you will clearly never make a profit. As long as everyone keeps their chin up and a positive vision of the future, the company will go from strength to strength. A few stray remarks from a pessimist such as 'it'll never work' or 'surely an internet site committed to selling sheds is overvalued at four hundred million dollars' can send everyone's stock price plunging."

So, as long as the economy runs on the fumes of positivity, the outlook is bleak for pessimists. When the Idler spoke to Peter Hinde and Jenny Batemen, it turned out that they have since met up with some of the other cases detailed in the social policy pamphlet. Peter Hinde said: "I got together with the other pessimists to see if there was any way we could legally combat this unfair prejudice. But we all agreed it was hopeless." ◉ **MDA**

DAVID SOLOMONS

SECTION 29: THE SEXUAL DISINFORMATION ACT

The latest government initiative to cut down on the rampant sexual activity of teens is the so-called Sexual Disinformation Act, a clause that recommends sexuality must always be promoted in schools in a misleading and slightly scary manner. The Idler has obtained some of these "sex lies", drawn up by a parliamentary advisory committee to delude the irrepressibly horny kids.

1.1 During five minutes of robust analingus, you take in vitamin C equivalent to 400 oranges.

1.2 Cinzano is the Italian word for clitoris.

1.3 "Hugh Scully" is a euphemism for vigorous auto-eroticism.

1.4 Old men grow a decorative plume of pubic hair from the eye of their penis.

1.5 Sperm burns like acid.

1.6 They've got teeth up there, you know.

HOW FAT LES BUILT JERUSALEM

ALEX JAMES on Blake's great poem and thoughts of God

You'd think I got up in the morning wanting to write football songs.

There was the irrepressibly up-for-it Keith, saying "we've gotta do another one". Telstar Records were pencilling in release dates. Pretty soon I was waking up thinking I'd better write that tune.

"Vindaloo" was easy, believe me. Roast potatoes take longer than that did. Half a terrace chant and "we're gonna score one more than you" – all on one note.

There aren't many places where people all sing together, like they do at football matches. Terrace chants are a kind of folk music. My favourites are the "son of the father" one about Teddy Teddy Sheringham, and the ones about Loverly Wolver-ham-per-ton.

I was getting quite knotted trying to write an all-embracing elegy to La Patrie when I realised someone had done it already.

The poem "Jerusalem" had it all: authority, the weight of history, majesty, epic grandeur and a great tune. What dignity, what power. Sorted. This isn't just a football tune, this is the new national anthem. As ennobling and invigorating as a spiritual sauna.

And so it was two weeks later we were in a cathedral in Hampstead making the most expensive single ever. An 85-piece orchestra, five choirs, drummers everywhere, programmers, arrangers, conductor, engineer, producers, Michael Barrymore even.

A bigger cast than Songs of Praise.

How nice it must have been for Mr Blake to invoke the deity and be taken seriously. The song got me thinking about God again, which is something I've been putting off. Only wackos talk about God, usually after a spell in rehab. I can only sense a femimine presence that manifests itself in the harmony of things. We embraced old school authority – I mean, it's my old school song – we embraced it, and it became our own and God's on our side. We will not be able to live in the present again until England win a major football tournament.

Then we can forget the Sixties and its shite architecture and be free to roam the here & now. ☜

SING-A-LONG TO JERUSALEM

And did those feet
In ancient time
Walk upon England's mountains green?
And was the holy Lamb of God
On England's pleasant pastures seen?
And did the countenance divine
Shine forth upon our clouded hills?
And was Jerusalem builded here
Among those dark satanic mills?
Bring me my bow of burning gold
Bring me my arrows of desire
Bring me my spear!
O clouds unfold!
Bring me my chariot of fire!
I will not cease from mental fight
nor shall my sword sleep in my hand
Till we have built Jerusalem in
   England's green and pleasant land

THE TEMPLE GAME

JOHN MICHEL has found the lost temple of Solomon

This was first written in the old walled city of Jerusalem, a labyrinth of ancient alleys, strange and confusing at first but so holy, and with such a golden atmosphere of peace that you feel peaceful even when people are grabbing and screaming at you. It is here that they play the Temple game, and I went there to play it. My host, Dr Isaac Hayutman of the Jerusalem Academy, is a well-known player, specialising in the regathering of the Twelve Tribes of Israel, a phenomenon that goes with the recreation of the Temple. The object of the game is to discover the lost site of Solomon's Temple and to identify the ten lost tribes who, according to the Bible (the rule book of the game) are scattered among the "nations of the world". Already in Jerusalem are two of the tribes, Judah and Benjamin, plus a certain number of Levites, who are the present Jews.

It is not for me a dangerous game because when you are old and of no importance you can say what you like. But it is taken very seriously indeed, and one false move by the fanatics who are drawn to it could start off a cataclysmic war. The history of the game begins in the tenth century BC, when Solomon built the Temple at Jerusalem, using

a plan passed on to him by his father, David, who was given it directly and in writing by God. As long as the Temple stood, the tribes of Israel enjoyed a golden age, as if under divine governance. When it was destroyed and the Israelites were carried into captivity, the world fell apart and nothing has ever gone right since. At about the time of Christ, King Herod built a new temple, probably on the site of the first, but it did not last long before the Romans demolished it, so thoroughly that even the place where it stood was forgotten. This is one thing that stands in the way of its would-be creators. There are many of these, because religious Jews are strictly bound by their law to rebuild the Temple as soon as they can. They point out that David and Solomon were mythological creatures, and there is no solid proof that there ever was a temple on the Mount. Rebuilding it, they imply, is an unhealthy Jewish obsession, which should not be encouraged.

Some years ago the site of the Temple was discovered by a native of Scotland, Rabbi Kaufman. But that did not settle anything, because other players in the game have their own favourite Temple sites, and the matter is complicated by the biblical record that Solomon built other temples at Jerusalem, dedicated to the pagan deities worshipped by his wives and concubines. But I do not doubt that Kaufman is right, because the implications from his discovery are so staggering, yet so simple and obvious, that as they occurred to me I was thrown into amazement, awe and delight and perceived the workings of divine providence. That is why we play the Temple game. As St John

found, it induces revelations, and at Jerusalem a great revelation is taking place, nothing less than the appearance of that Temple for all people that Isaiah prophesied, perfect in scale and complete in all its measures and proportions. No one has to build anything or disturb anyone else, because the Temple has miraculously appeared. Its twin pillars are two rocks, the rock of Golgotha where Jesus was crucified, and the newly discovered Rock of Foundation in the Temple's Holy of Holies. You can see I am excited, and if any reader wants to share that state, write to me at the IDLER. Or you can write to Isaac Hayutmen, PO Box 8115, Jerusalem 91080, whose Academy of Jerusalem web site deals with new ideas and discoveries in the Holy Land. ◉

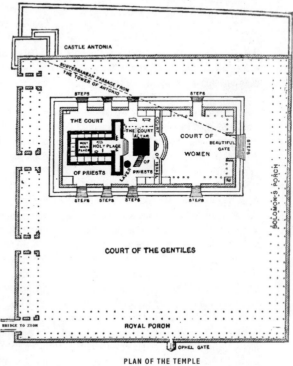

PLAN OF THE TEMPLE

GREY PANTHERS

As the young embrace materialism, it is left to the old to voice dissent, says WILL HODGKINSON

Britain's power base has shifted. For most of the last century, control of the country lay in the hands of a wrinkled élite, protecting their own interests and those of their peers, who held the means of production and most of the wealth. But these days the country is run by men who only develop grey hairs after they take office, and financed by an affluent youth happy to support multinational conglomorations by accepting that they must have the trainers/interiors/lifestyle that capitalism wants them to have. Most company executives meanwhile, are barely out of nappies. Which begs the question: where lives the voice of dissent?

The answer is, of course, in retirement homes. Increasingly alienated from the forces that drive commerce, pensioners are the only true rebels left. Richard Farnsworth's 75-year-old, crossing America on a lawnmower in David Lynch's THE STRAIGHT STORY seems far more revolutionary than today's teens-in-trouble fare; and a widespread dislike of CCTV amongst seniors who regard it as a facet of intrusive authoritarianism makes the rest of us painfully aware of our own blind acceptance. In America there's already a name for these ageing insurrectionists: Grey Panthers, people of a pensionable age who have organised themselves to fight against what they dislike. Their website, Third Age, reveals a mistrust of big business (Microsoft is particularly odious), a frustration at declining sexual abilities (recent newsletter topic: I can't get past first base with men), and most importantly, an overriding concern with the disintegration of democracy through an increasingly centralised government; a concern that is being acted upon effectively. In Miami in 1998, 82-year-

old Grey Panther David Samson succeeded in turning the small retirement home of Sunny Isles (pop: 14,000) into an independent city, of which he is now mayor, and relatively free from intervention by Washington executives.

The Grey Panthers are yet to make their mark in England, but a post-war generation who fought against the excesses of capitalism in the Fifties and Sixties are now reaching pensionable age. Gwen Evans, 63, is an ageing insurrectionary par excellence; filled with righteous anger at our young government's behaviour and at duplicitous big business practices. "Companies are interested in the people with spending power, which tends to be the young. When it gets to the elderly there isn't much you can market, apart from holidays, with beautiful grey-haired people skipping about on the sand. I tend to go into a trance when I see those ads." Gwen's concerns are the facts of modern life that most of us take for granted. "I don't like supermarket reward cards, because they monitor everybody so that they can feed you back what they think you already want. The government does this as well. And the government have access to the information on reward cards, which they can use for tax investigation, which is outrageous. Nobody tells you about that. The Big Brother aspect of the current government is more obviously manipulative than with the Tories, who generally didn't bother with anyone. These days there are endless focus groups constantly trying to predict what we don't like."

On this point, Richard Neville, founder of Oz magazine and now 60, concurs. "Sometimes I do find Generation Xers exasperating because of their constant obsession with

GWEN EVANS IS THE FUTURE OF REBELLION

brand loyalty and their general acceptance of the corporate agenda. Even the corporatisation of education, culture, rock and sport has been accepted without question."

The aged are in a good position to be revolutionary: many have more time on their hands to devote themselves to fighting the power, and it's far harder for the state to slap the hands of those with the grand bearing of age. Gwen's own twelve-point statement of what she dislikes about contemporary British authority illustrates perfectly how the future of dissent is grey.

CYCLING ON THE PAVEMENT

It is currently illegal if you're under sixteen, and in fact it's the under-sixteens who knock you over! People of my age cycle very slowly and we're forced onto the road, which is outrageous, so I do cycle on the pavement. This old lady gave me a look which I knew was going to be a reproach, so before she said anything, I said "Shut up, you silly old bitch," and carried straight on.

EROSION OF DEMOCRACY

You should have the right to choose a representative to go to the House Of Commons and speak on your behalf, but now the person who is your MP is not selected by you, but by their party loyalty and obedience to Blairite law. And once they're in parliament, there's an enormous amount of thuggery to get them to conform. So they're not there for you at all.

"THANK YOU FOR NOT SMOKING"

"Thank You" means "you have to". It makes me want to do whatever they want to "thank me" for not doing.

IDLE PLEASURES:
JUST LOOKING ANDREW MALE

GED WELLS

It used to be called browsing. But browsing implied a freedom to roam with no obligation to buy. "Just looking" is different. Your entry into the shop has aroused expectation in the Armani-clad assistant. You are his ticket to a sale, an extension of the brand. A well placed "just looking" shifts the power balance. Pick some things up and put them back down again. Shop rents are so high that every minute you're "just looking", you're also shop-lifting – stealing attention, space and valuable "brand-time". You are a flâneur dwelling within the the flow of the shop but individual, unchallenged. Everyone else is a consumer. You're "just looking".

CHARITY

We should help the poor by tax, not by charity.

CATASTROPHIC DRUG LAWS

As long as we have criminalisation of drugs, there's no stopping all the criminal activity that goes with it. The police want this as well. Far more people die of drink than heroin.

THE NUCLEAR POLICY

Nuclear companies BNFL and Lockheed-Martin are taking over Aldermaston, which is so shocking. Lockheed-Martin's record is of making local inhabitants sick time after time, and denying that they have anything to do with it.

SO-CALLED PUBLIC LAVATORIES

These new single ones are awful because they might open up at any time. You might step out and meet somebody you wanted to impress, and – as you know – it's very difficult to impress anyone when they know you've done a poo.

MOTOR TRAFFIC

We've completely eradicated natural dangers and replaced them with a system that is so dangerous that you can step out of the house, take a false turn and you're dead.

CHRISTMAS

I'm not a Christian, but now I have to go and buy presents. I'd rather someone came up to me in June and said, "buy me a garden fork".

THE FUTURES MARKET

How can anybody expect to run a business when it's such a butterfly organisation, which has nothing to do with the firms themselves?

CCTV

When I park my bike outside Sainsbury's something gets nicked off it, so I asked the security guard if I could put my bike where there are cameras. He told me that they're only dummies, which is quite normal apparently.

THE FINE LINE BETWEEN

GAMEBIRDS & PORN STARS

GAMEBIRDS	PORN STARS
The longer they are hung, the better they get	The longer they are hung, the better they get
People shoot them	They shoot on people
Twelve bore shotgun	Double anal, double vaginal
Startled out of bushes	Startling bushes
Kept in protected reserves	California

◄———| GAMEBIRDS |———●———| PORN STARS |———►

GAMEBIRDS	PORN STARS
Picked up by dogs	Will do it with dogs when hopelessly addicted to smack
Find flying a struggle	Find acting a struggle
Peck at seed	Lick at seed
Gamekeeper	Sugar Daddy
Beaters	Fluffers
Tasty birds hunted for sport	People who have sex on film for money

EARS, GOODBYE

They threatened to break every bone in his body.
But STEVE AYLETT has no fear

I have spoken before* on the matter of every bone in my body being broken. Having once again been threatened with this treatment, I find I must elaborate, for the feeble-minded, upon the concept's inadequacies as a prospect to fear.

There are 206 major bones in the human skeleton – time-consuming and challenging enough – but what concerns us here are the thousands of tiny cartilaginous ones in my ears. Any man reckless enough to threaten me will have these little beauties to contend with. Is he really committing to break each of these individually, like the bladders in a sheet of bubble-wrap? Can he make the massive investment in time required?

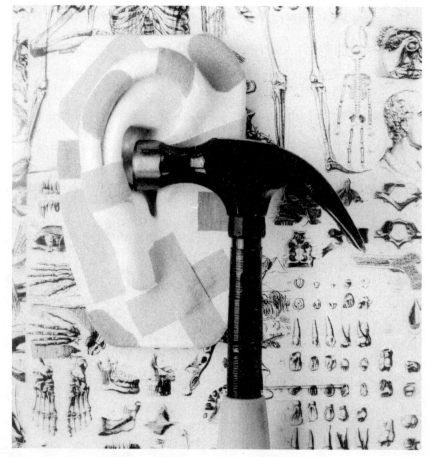

CHRIS DRAPER

But let's assume there's someone out there with the logistical skills to fulfil the contract. He wouldn't be able to carry it out at the time – each ear would take several months to break completely – so he'd have to kidnap and convey me to some isolated site, such as a country cottage, and keep me fed and relatively healthy during the procedure. This would all cost, so he'd have to go out to work during the day. I'd sit watching daytime TV and eating Turkish Delights; in the evenings he'd come home to have a go at my ears and all would be well in the world.

But life is not directed by the living. In the first six months all the bones in the first ear would be broken, at which my captor would move on to the second. By the time he'd finished breaking the second ear, the first would have mended. After re-breaking the first ear, the second will have healed and need attention again, and so on. This merry dance would continue for the rest of my life, during the course of which I would be living in relative luxury. Is this really what you bastards expect me to fear? Oh spoil me. Bring it on. 🔊

* The Crime Studio, 1994

WHO STOLE ALL THE FUN?

Right now, you feel like you are missing some fun in your life. You used to have it, now it's gone. The Idler discovers who is having your fun.

MDA

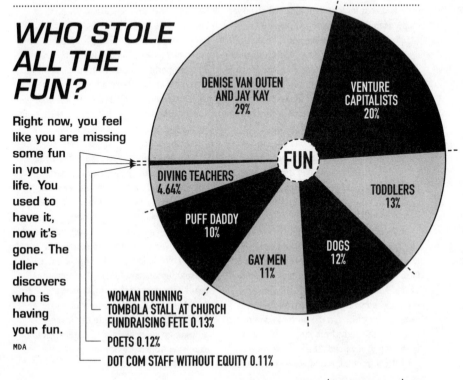

DENISE VAN OUTEN AND JAY KAY 29%

VENTURE CAPITALISTS 20%

FUN

DIVING TEACHERS 4.64%

TODDLERS 13%

PUFF DADDY 10%

DOGS 12%

GAY MEN 11%

WOMAN RUNNING TOMBOLA STALL AT CHURCH FUNDRAISING FETE 0.13%

POETS 0.12%

DOT COM STAFF WITHOUT EQUITY 0.11%

A SECOND BITE OF THE CHERRY

A short story by STEWART HOME

Julia was nineteen, Irish and blonde. She was naturally blonde but dyed her hair black. Julia lived at 24 Bassett Road, just off Ladbroke Grove. This was a few years ago, when individual rooms in what is now a swanky town house were being rented out as bedsits. Today the address would be unafford-able to someone like Julia – who'd been in The Smoke for a couple of years working as a child minder. Julia was five feet four and a half inches tall. She was smartly dressed. Her skill at needlework meant that the clothes she wore had cost far less than a casual observer might imagine. Julia made her own outfits.

Julia lay me down on the bed. She picked up a piece of cloth and threw it playfully over my head. I giggled and Julia whipped the cloth away. She stood up, walked across the room and pulled a Charlie Parker album from a pile of records. Julia was just about perfect and she'd have been inhuman if she hadn't had a fault. In my eyes, her fault was a liking for modern jazz. Rebelling against her strict Catholic upbringing, Julia had got into sounds that she viewed as seriously cosmopolitan. Her father, who worked as a docker, shared my dislike of this type of music.

Sunlight filtered through a dirty window. The room was clean, the window was grimy on the outside. It was the landlord's responsibili-ty to keep the exterior of the building ship-shape. Julia picked up the off cut she'd dis-carded when she'd walked across to the record player. She ran the bottom edge of the cloth over my body, from the tips of my toes to the top of my head. She ran the edge of the off-cut from the top of my head to the tips

of my toes. Back and forth went the cloth as I giggled and finally grabbed it. Julia held out her hand and I played with her fingers. She put two of her fingers in my mouth and I sucked them.

Julia lay down beside me and we gazed into each others eyes, deep blue eyes. I swam in the ocean of her deep blue eyes. I smiled. Julia smiled. I giggled. Julia grinned from ear to ear. I threw my head back. I could smell the fragrant flowers that stood in a vase on the window sill. Yellow flowers. Julia smelled of hyacinths, her prefume discreetly applied. These smells covered the reek of boiled cab-bage that permeated the hallway. Other ten-ants were cooking Sunday lunch. It was anoth-er, more perfect world in our room. Julia kissed me on the forehead and I imagined myself branded with a red faint "O" from her lipstick. She kissed my left cheek, she kissed my right cheek, then she kissed me on the forehead again.

I gurgled. Julia smiled. She caressed my cheek. I cried and Julia bared a breast. Pushed a nipple into my mouth. I sucked her sweet milk. My sweet mother's milk. When I'd finshed Julia put me over her shoulder and belched me. She put a towel on the bed and removed my soiled nappy. "What a clever boy," Julia burbled, "you've got a present for mummy!" More than thirty-five years have passed since I was first praised for taking a shit. Looking back on those first idyllic weeks of my life can make growing up seem like a slow but irrevocable expulsion from paradise. ☙

FRANCOISE LACROIX

LOUIS THEROUX'S UNFINISHED JOKES

But is there more to the butcher than eyes the meat?
(Does it have to be a butcher?)

....

Message to Rolf Harris: Didgeridon't!

....

Installation idea – you pay a guard from the Tate Gallery to "guard" you as you go about your daily affairs; and he keeps people away if they touch you or get too close.

....

I'm a cereal monogamist.

....

Eagle-eye Cherry – is he the first pop star who, like Action Man, comes equipped with a switch at the back of his head so you can toggle his eyes back and forth? (this would work better as physical comedy)

....

Million pound business concept (more my girlfriend's idea than mine): The Draft Dodger. It's one of those sausage-like draught excluders except it's in the shape of Bill Clinton (could also do a George W. Bush one, for bi-partisan appeal).

PET DEATHS

They just come apart in your hands

I bought four budgerigars to keep me company, but one of them turned out to be a real bastard. It kept pecking at the others. So when I was drunk, I took it from the cage and strangled it.

My four year old nephew was very excited when I bought him some goldfish and a bowl. Whenever I went to see him, we would feed them together. My sister told me how much he enjoyed watching the fish, and how excited he'd get when I came over. Anyway, one day I went over and he was in a real hyperactive mood. We were all sitting having tea in the lounge when suddenly the nephew ran in, and starting shouting "Fisheee Fisheee" while tearing the fish in half. He shredded the lot of them. God knows what was going on his mind.

My auntie told me a story about her chihuahua. It was a very greedy dog. One day she found it with its head wedged in a large tin of cat food. It had suffocated.

I was teaching this primary school class when the class hamster died. I found it in the morning and slung it onto the skip round the back of the dining hall. When the children came in, I told them the hamster had died and gone to heaven. But during playtime, one of the kids saw its stiff legs jutting out of the top of the skip. They were all very upset.

When I was nine, I was a peripheral squad player in the school football team. On the day of the big final, the coach told me I wasn't going to be playing. I walked home stifling the tears. When I got home, my mother told me that they'd had to put the bassett hound down. Thing is, I didn't care for the dog, but it gave me an excuse to let out all those tears I had been holding back.

PET DEATHS NEWS

Two cultural forces are conspiring to increase fatalities amongst metropolitan pets. Firstly, the boom in gardening has led to the installation of ponds and bird tables. Secondly, double income couples are raising cats rather than kids in the metropolis, as cats don't have to go to those terrible schools. To protect their gardens from the booming cat population, people are putting down barbaric traps. In one recent case, plumber Edward Masters set a wire noose, planted 8-inch shards of glass in his flowerbed, and attached spiked carpet grippers to the top of a gate. An unfortunate cat called Jude fell foul of Masters' macabre assault course. Her owner said "I last saw Jude sunning herself on the window. The next morning I found her hanging by her neck in the hedge."   MDA

AT LEAST YOU'VE GOT YOUR ELF

Strange tales of elves from Iceland.
By MAGNEA ORVARSDOTTIR

"I remember when I was a kid I lived on a road called Álfhólsvegur (Elfhillroad). The road was still being built at that time, and a hill, that is supposed to be an inhabitant of elves, was in their way. There was a political argument on what to do in the situation. Those who believe in the existance of elves saw angry and unhappy elves around the hill. The final decision was not to upset the elves and build the road around the hill." DÍSA

"I don't remember any elf stories right now. I just remember friends and relatives telling me very personal stories on sentimental moments. When they look you deep in the eyes, tell you about some weird figures they have seen. And they wonder if you believe them or not." BJÖRK

"I remember as a kid being at my grandparents when I heard of the mysterious elf hill in the middle of my grandpa's homefield. A farmer friend of his was cutting the grass and cut the grass on the elfhill, a couple of days before. All his horses died the day after. A few years later my farmer uncle cut the grass on the elfhll. The morning after, he woke up and his body was covered with spots and sores. Doctors believed the elves were punishing him. MAGNEA

"I only remember the folk stories. At Christmas everyone went to a mass apart from one person, usually the maiden. When they came home from mass an elf had come for a visit, either to give the family fineries or to steal from them, the maiden or anything else." ANNA JÚLÍA

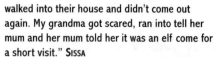

"My grandma told me a story. She had seen an elf, a tall, thin woman dressed in black. She walked into their house and didn't come out again. My grandma got scared, ran into tell her mum and her mum told her it was an elf come for a short visit." SISSA

"I lived next to a street called Álfhólfsvegur (Elfhillroad) and I remember the road being built around the hill. They had to decide whether to move an elf rock or not. They didn't take the risk so the road was built a round it. I think elves are just so stuck in people's minds, since the olden days. But I've never seen one." KRISTJÁN

BILL & ZED'S Bad Advice

"WE'VE FUCKED UP OUR LIVES, NOW IT'S YOUR TURN"

Dear Bill and Zed,

I have just become a Dad. Could you two offer any advice on how I can make sure my little boy grows up strong and free?
New Dad, SHEPHERDS BUSH

{Zed} Heh heh. Well, the fun starts here. Not. Only joking, friend. A serious answer to your exciting new situation. Although my colleague and I disagree on certain details on the rearing of strong and free youngsters, our attitudes are very similar.

Whilst agreeing on an extremely vigorous regime of ruthless and often horrific discipline, I still prefer the traditional birching for the mildest transgression of domestic rules, while Bill insists on thrashing the child with a large bunch of Scottish thistles. And again for more serious offences I prefer the more lenient diet of stale bread and brackish water for a year or two. Bill feels that the wicked child should eat nothing but stinging nettles and traditional Scottish Habenero chillies for at least a decade.

Punishment should start as soon as possible. I recommend a firm, savage thrashing from the age of three, every day, whether the young scamp has performed any miscreant behaviour or not. Because believe me, my friend, children do bad things every day. Just because he wasn't apprehended should be no excuse.

Again, on the issue of sexual abuse, Bill and I differ even more strongly.

I think a child should be at least allowed to reach puberty before being turned over to the local paedophile gang. Bill suggests it should be at around two or three. Either way, I hope you enjoy fucking up your kids. Good luck to the three of you.

{Bill} Congratulations. My advice is simple. Every time you change his nappy (and I hope you're not shirking your new man responsibilities) imagine he is going to grow up to be the new Peter Sutcliffe or Dennis Nilsen. The vibes you will be vibing out to your bonny baby will ensure he will grow up to be as strong and free as a man could want to be.

....

Dear Bill and Zed,

I am an emotional cripple. While I am capable of feigning sensitivity to the problems of my friends and lovers, when it comes down to it, I have to admit that I really don't give a shit. In fact, when friends start to talk about their real problems, I'd prefer not to see them again. I understand the lack of empathy is a psychopathic trait – yet I have no violent urges towards others. Just an indifference to their problems. Can you recommend some mental exercises to improve this lack within my soul?
Yours with trepidation,
E. McDowell, TRING

{Zed} Actually, Mr Tring, what you describe is not a psychopathic trait, it is in fact sociopathic. Which, in a nutshell, means that you would make an excellent murderer.

Psychopaths are generally very messy at deathwork, and in nearly all cases leave the most ridiculous clues and are almost always apprehended. Whilst the icy nature of a sociopath enables him to – by mimicking his friends and neighbours – become an excellent serial killer. Of course, I am not suggesting that you go out and try your hand at serial murder, but, so I am told, this exotic caprice can become a rather exciting hobby. Outwitting the detectives, sending them cryptic notes and nervous breakdowns. And if nothing else it would almost certainly alleviate the tragic ennui that most of us sociopaths suffer from.

{Bill} Yes, I can recommend some mental exercise but in deference to my fellow Zen Master's advice to your problem, there was a time a few years back when Zed and myself were considering on embarking on a career as mass murderers. The prospects looked good. Instant tabloid fame, artistic fulfilment and a fortune to be made from the memoirs. The only problem seemed to be which photo of ourselves we would want used to establish our iconic status as the most evil men in the universe. We were never able to agree. It got to the point when on one drunken night Zed kicked the shit out of me, so I sent him a letter via my solicitors saying, that's it, it's off. You can go and find somebody else to be your mass murdering partner. Of course, I knew he wouldn't and would come crawling back begging forgiveness. Anyway, enough of our tiffs. Back to you. Your friends and lovers are just feigning as well. They don't give a fuck about you. Just keep feigning it and that will be all the mental exercise you need.

....

Dear Bill and Zed,
I am worried that the youth of today will be so go-getting and materialistic that my lazy, liberal ways will see me on the scrapheap before the end of my thirties. How can I stave off the threat of these whippersnappers?
With angst,
Peter P, SUNDERLAND

{Zed} In most of India there is a tradition known as Sadhhu – or "turning Sadhhu" to be more correct. This involves the period of a man's life when he feels he has provided for his family: his children have grown up and he has left enough money for his wife. He simply walks out of the home with a big stick and wanders off, never to return. He takes off all his clothes when they are worn out, never buys any to replace them, grows monster dreadlocks and heads off to the mountains to smoke dustbins full of dope with other naked Sadhhus. Occasionally hundreds of these naked holymen venture into villages and small towns to collect alms. Understandably, the villagers want these naked fuckers out of town as soon as possible, so they give them as many rupees as they can afford.

These Sadhhus are often ex-heads of banks, political dignitaries and so on. It just hits them one day. "I hate that fucking nagging bitch and her crappy chapatis. I'm out of here. I'm turning fucking Sadhhu and you'll never see me again, you sharp-tongued sow of the fields!"

The reason I offer this obscure information is because we have a similar tradition in Britain. This could be the solution to what seems to be your problem. There are many Sadhhus here in our own country. Although they refrain from nudity because of our climate, they too wear dreads and sit around together, except they don't smoke barrels of herb. Their drug of choice is Tennants Super and they're called dossers. Just an idea.

{Bill} A rather negative bit of advice from

Zed, don't you think? And anyway, Tennants Super leaves such a bad aftertaste. The trouble is that all that talk of mass murdering has got me in a nostalgic mood. We should never have let our petty differences get in the way of such a promising career. Still, there is no need for you to let such opportunities slip by. I recommend you give yourself a definite clear and achievable goal. Select seven dot com millionaires under the age of 30 and set about murdering them all by Christmas. You will undoubtedly become a national hero. You can then slip back into your lazy, liberal ways as you spend the rest of your life basking in the glory.

Dear Bill and Zed,
I haven't taken significant exercise for a decade. Am I going to die soon?
Concerned, SOMEWHERE IN LONDON

{Zed} How the fuck does anyone know when they will die? My only advice is to enjoy life while you're alive, because it's a lot harder when you're dead. Take myself as an excellent example. I smoke, drink like a fucker, shag ugly women and I'm as happy as a pig in shit. Life is what kills you, you lily-livered dwarf. Unhappiness kills you. A job you hate, a wife you loathe, kids you wish you had thrown in the canal at birth. That's what kills people. Not all this ridiculous cancer shite made up by quack doctors wearing blinkers like carthorses. Go and get laid you miserable cunt. Get stoned, get pissed. Destroy!

{Bill} I have reason to believe that you are a virtual teenage dot com multi-millionaire and yes, you are about to die because there is this mad, bitter nutter who is out to get the likes of you. His name is Peter P and he lives in Sunderland. You have my permission to go and kill him before he kills you.

Dear Bill and Zed,
What would you say was the minimum amount of sexual partners that a man should have in his lifetime?
Yours – not committing myself either way,
P.Bettany, CAMDEN

{Zed} They're all fucking cunts.
{Bill} Ditto.

Dear Bill and Zed,
Recently I had a good idea for a dot com start up. When I say "good", I mean that with a bit of work it might attract a decent amount of venture capital. But I'm worried that if I leave the safety of regular employment to pursue the project, I might come a cropper. Do you think it's risky to get involved with the internet at this delicate stage, or would I be a fool to miss out?
Yours,
DR, CLERKENWELL

{Zed} You poor fuckers that worry about money. Don't fret about security and all that bank-sponsored mind-rape. Worry, worry, worry, echoes the mantra of those cosmosodomistic institutions, raining down on evil surfboards riding black radiowaves. Just do it, friend. If it fucks you up you can always turn Doshu with Mr P.

{Bill} Yes, you would be a fool to miss out. Start by dumping your crappy idea and start up www.massmurder.com. Then go and murder every sexual partner you have ever had. Then post the pictures of the evidence on your site. This will attract a lot of media attention. You can then go and sell your dot com for a fortune and retire. Job done. ☻

CONVERSATIONS

YES, JC

JONATHAN COE, author of the seminal satire of the Eighties, What A Carve Up! meets DAVID NOBBS, author of the seminal satire of the Seventies, The Fall and Rise of Reginald Perrin

My train is running twenty-two minutes late: a source of irritation at first, but in the end I don't mind because I realise it gives me the perfect opening line when I see David Nobbs waiting for me at Sheffield station. "Morning, David," I say. "Twenty-two minutes late: defective junction-box at Chesterfield." He recognises the catchphrase at once and smiles.

Nobbs is used to having his own jokes quoted back at him. *The Fall and Rise of Reginald Perrin* had a startling influence on the national psyche: not just the name of the central character but even whole chunks of dialogue have become lodged in the public consciousness.

In Plymouth, for instance, there is a restaurant called "Veggie Perrin's" which boasts "no cock-up on the catering front" on its premises. As we pound the streets of Sheffield looking for a suitable interview venue, I tell him that in the Landmark Trust holiday properties to which I periodically retreat for writing purposes, they have log books in which people are supposed to record their impressions: the last one I visited contained the simple entries, "Great – Tony Webster" and "Super – David Harris-Jones".

But Nobbs's writing is more than just the sum of his catchphrases. He is also a novelist of enormous distinction; a fact which his publishers' thumpingly jokey covers and his high reputation as a TV gag writer tend to obscure. Nobbs's early novel *Ostrich Country* is an absurdist gem which also manages to satirise the Nineties fads for nouvelle cuisine and food-combining thirty years before they came to pass, while his later books have a tenderness and an eye for detail and a range of human sympathy that is notably lacking from the work of some Booker prizewinners.

When David Nobbs wrote to me a couple of years ago and asked if he could adapt my own novel *What a Carve Up!* for the screen I could hardly believe my luck. Other novelists have to make do with fly-by-nights like Stoppard and Pinter adapting their books, but I'd got the real thing. The *mélange* of comedy, melancholy and social comment I'd attempted in that novel owed its existence to him, if anybody. Who better to dramatise the tragi-comic excesses of the Thatcherite Eighties than the man who had caught the spirit of another era - the *weltschmerz* of the Seventies suburban commuter — with such lethal accuracy?

COE: *The Fall and Rise of Reginald Perrin* seems very much of its time. TV comedy of the late Sixties and early Seventies is obsessed with notion of the commuter, the little man in his bowler hat and his pinstripe suit, getting on to the same train every morning and living a rather dull, circumscribed life. You find that figure in Monty Python and you find him in Marty Feldman. Have you any idea why that was?
NOBBS: A lot of people were doing it and they were all so clearly identified visually: the rolled umbrella; the way they dressed. But there's no City look any more and I think that's one of the reasons that *Reginald Perrin* seems to be so of its time. However, seeing it again, it was extraordinary how very relevant and up to date a lot of it was: all about Euro rhubarb and the fact that country people aren't living in the country because they can't afford it. Other things, certainly, are dated. The behaviour of his wife, for example. Her peculiarly bland and servile attitude, just being there to cook meals and never complaining about anything: that struck one as much more extraordinary now than it would've done in 1976.
COE: In the second series, though, she became his business partner.
NOBBS: Somebody did attack me for the attitude to the wife and then, of course, later on it all changed. They

should wait till they've seen the whole thing really.
COE: Have you been following the stuff in the papers about internet companies floating on the stock market? There's a parallel there with what Reggie was doing with Grot. In both cases people are making huge amounts of money by selling something which isn't really a product.
NOBBS: I think there is a parallel. It's interesting. I hadn't thought of it until you mentioned it, but it's nice when you do an interview and you learn something [laughs]. I think the funny thing about satire is that it's very difficult to get beyond the real thing, and if you wait twenty years you'll be behind the real thing as the world gets more and more absurd. It's a very interesting parallel, yes it's extraordinary how much money they're making, and extraordinary how much money Reggie made.
COE: Are you on the Internet?
NOBBS: I'm not on the Internet. At the moment I'm a Luddite through laziness.
COE: Did you know there's a Reginald Perrin page?
NOBBS: Yes I do, and it's very nice to know there is.
COE: But it's American, strangely.
NOBBS: It gets shown on public service endlessly in Boston and New York and one or two places. I met a man in a bar of a London Hotel - from Idaho, I think - and I said my name was David Nobbs and he said "Not *the* David Nobbs?" He said, "I didn't get where I am today by being in a hotel in London with The David Nobbs." It turned out all his students did these catchphrases, and

there was this little pool of fans somewhere in mid-America.

COE: What do you think of British TV comedy today?

NOBBS: It's a very difficult question for me to answer. I have to be careful because I don't watch a lot of television. I find the constant rudery depressing, and I find the shit and fart jokes endless. I find too much sex, I find these things not put in a particularly funny context. I always say farting isn't funny in itself, but it's funny in a wedding reception, or a dinner party or in church. I watched an episode of *The League of Gentlemen* but I watched one that was particularly revolting, with exploding dogs and everything. I couldn't quite take it. People tell me if I'd watched any other episode I'd have loved it.

COE: Comedy these days has lost its inclusiveness. Anybody between the ages of eighteen and 65 can sit down and get something out of *Reggie Perrin*, whereas something like *The League of Gentlemen* will only appear very funny to a rather restricted age group. And it's kind of baffling and unpleasant to anyone older. One of my happiest memories of *Reggie Perrin* is watching it with my grandfather when I was fourteen or fifteen and he was in his seventies.

NOBBS: That's absolutely right, and I think it rather reflects life. There's a great gap between the youngsters in their café bars and the older people in their pubs; the youngsters in their clubs and the older people in sedate hotels in the Cotswolds. There's the series with Geoffrey Palmer and Judi Dench on Sunday evenings which

"TV COMEDY OF THE LATE SIXTIES AND EARLY SEVENTIES IS OBSESSED WITH NOTION OF THE COMMUTER, THE LITTLE MAN IN HIS BOWLER HAT AND HIS PINSTRIPE SUIT"

goes on forever and is loved by old people and is very successful. No young person would watch that and old people wouldn't watch the other ones. I think that is a shame. But repeats of *Dad's Army* still cross that divide brilliantly.

COE: The generation gap and the disenfranchisement of the older generation was a theme you took on in *The Legacy of Reginald Perrin*. How did you feel that series worked out?

NOBBS: It didn't work out. We had great fun making it, it had a marvellous point to make along the way but it just got to it too slowly. I think I overestimated – not for the first time – the strength of my characters. I didn't think I needed a particularly strong story. I'm sad about it because it did build to a marvellous climax with the old people's march. And of course it was a terrific gamble without Leonard Rossiter. It was a cheek to do it and it didn't come off.

COE: *Reginald Perrin* is full of character actors who probably can carry a series by themselves. Geoffrey Palmer, who is a bit player in the first series of *Reggie Perrin*, went on to become one of the biggest sit com stars.

NOBBS: Yes. It would be nice to think one pushed him on a little bit. Of course I took him on myself into a starring role in a thing on Channel Four, called *Fairly Secret Army*. Another cult show, but a smaller cult [laughs] and the sad thing with that was that I loved the character and the way he talked so much that I didn't give him enough story line in the first series. I had a strong story line in the second series, but it was a bit late.

COE: Reggie is someone that young people today feel drawn to and feel sympathetic towards. There is a tremendous "fuck you" attitude about him.

NOBBS: Absolutely. There is a moment where he's going to give a speech at the British fruit seminar and this chap talks about how British food can be no more or no less competitive than the society in which it is raised, and he looks at him and gives a little laugh and says, "really, that is uninteresting," and he did it brilliantly. That is saying "fuck you", but I hope it's saying "fuck you" more wittily. I love saying "fuck you", but I don't want to say it just as "fuck you" every time.

COE: I love your feeling in *Reggie Perrin* that there's something magical about trios of lines. There's a moment where CJ is pitching terrible ideas at Reggie, and with each one Reggie sits there thinking to himself, "Oh my God," but what he says out loud is "Wonderful, CJ," until the third one, when he thinks to himself, "Wonderful CJ" and out loud says "Oh my God."

NOBBS: Someone at the BBC said, "You can't do that, it's just too complicated" and then somebody else said "well, we can dub those things on later" and Leonard Rossiter wasn't having any of that. We had endless trouble at the beginning of the series with the timing of the hippopotamus going across the screen. He refused to have it cheated or edited in, he said the look on his eyes must entirely reflect what he had seen and he must see it. He was a perfectionist. They had to announce its start about eight seconds before it came on. It had to be perfectly timed, and it always was.

COE: Was he a demanding person to work with?

NOBBS: He was a demanding person to work with, but not so much for me because... it sounds immodest, but it was a pretty good product. Once he said, "this scene doesn't work at all." And we all sat round and I said, "We're not going to rewrite this scene in committee. I'll go home and deliver you a better scene tomorrow." He was quite frank about the scene not working. I once criticised him, I said, "Leonard I don't think you're saying that line quite right," and he said, "Oh. How would you like me to say it?" I told him, and he said "well, your fervour impresses me. I'll do it the way I want it." And he did it the way I wanted it and there was an enormous laugh, and I said to him, "I was right wasn't I?" and he said "No, you were wrong and so were the audience." That was his attitude [laughs].

COE: Which, would you say, gives you more satisfaction as a writer: the pleasure you give to readers of novels, or the pleasure you give to or have given to television viewers?

NOBBS: The great thing about giving pleasure to viewers is that you actually hear the laughter so I suppose that is more instantly rewarding. I once read that my books are very embarrassing to read on public transport because you roar with laughter. So imagine my joy at seeing someone on the Northern Line reading one. I stayed on long beyond my stop to hear him roaring with laughter. He

"I LOVE SAYING 'FUCK YOU', BUT I DON'T WANT TO SAY IT JUST AS 'FUCK YOU' EVERY TIME"

never did. He got sunk in deeper and deeper gloom [laughs].

COE: But they are melancholy books. The ending of the first series of *Reginald Perrin* and the novel is quite downbeat. Elizabeth and Reggie are together again but he visits his ashes and has to wipe a tear from his eyes.

NOBBS: Yes, it all comes out like that. There is a lot of sadness in the world, obviously, but I do get great pleasure from life, and sometimes I think it would be nice to write something of total pleasure and optimism. But it just doesn't come out like that. I don't think it ever will.

COE: Was the process in the Seventies of getting an idea from the page to the screen easier than it is now?

NOBBS: It was so much easier that it's almost impossible to talk about it. You didn't have the layers of command, so you actually saw the person who made the decision. That's the key factor. Now you just don't see the person who has the say so, and you don't really know why they say yes or why they say no. They issue edicts, they'll say they don't want period pieces. My edict would be "we don't want any bad stuff", and then I would try to look for good in every area. Everything has to go through the ITV network centre. They have an enormous amount of work, they take time, then the decision has to be relayed back by which time the writers are doing something else and the actor isn't available. I long for the simplicity of the old days.

COE: Your creative efforts are being thwarted or held up by exactly the sort of bureaucracy that Reggie Perrin was satirising.

NOBBS: I suppose that's one more irony in a very ironic world.

COE: Your new book is called *Going Gently* and it's published in July by Heinemann. To me, it sounds very different from anything you've done before.

NOBBS: The first great difference is that it's about a woman, which intrigued me enormously. When I told the publisher it was inspired by being present when my mother died, that didn't make it sound like the road to hilarious comedy. But it was. I saw my mother die very peacefully at a very old age. I had not been sure how much she was able to understand in her hospital ward and this gave me the idea for a book about a woman who relives her whole life in order to escape from the mad, bad and sad old women in her ward. She goes back over her rich and varied life which is also - to some extent - the life of the 20th century, It's not a millennium book, though. It's more of a rattling good yarn. I find I get more and more interested in the process of telling a story, and I want to lead the readers up the garden path and then surprise them. I don't think I was bothered about story when I was younger. Perhaps you don't respect the reader as much when you're young.

COE: What were you more bothered about as a writer then? Getting the jokes in?

NOBBS: Getting the jokes in and showing people how clever I was and therefore occasionally failing to be clever most dismally.

COE: I was re-reading your very first novel the other day, *The Itinerant Lodger*. It's very different from the rest of your work. Were you a Beckett fan at the time?

NOBBS: I was a Beckett fan at the time and I wrote plays, I was into NF Simpson and the theatre of the absurd, and I think it shows. I think the book stands up moderately well and that I did manage to show some of my own voice. I wished I'd shown more but it was a first novel. The publisher's reader actually recommended that it should not be published because it was a load of drivel, but they ignored Alan Coren's advice.

COE: Has he ever spoken to you about that?

NOBBS: I've never spoken to him. I admire him and think he's terribly funny, but we've never met.

COE: At that time you were also writing for *The Frost Report* and other BBC comedy programmes.

NOBBS: I started out on *That Was The Week That Was*. That led me on to *The Frost Report*, and that led on to *The Two Ronnies*. There were also diversions to write for other stand up comedians like Tommy Cooper and Ken Dodd. I did a long stint with Barry Cryer, writing for Les Dawson. Some very enjoyable times. You might say that, from one's own career point of view, it was a waste of time but then there's a great deal beyond one's own career. It was a great pleasure to work with some of these people.

COE: It does seem to me that TV

comedy was at its best in the late Six-
ties through to the mid Seventies.
Was it just good fortune that there
was a good generation of writers
around then?

NOBBS: I would slightly dispute your
dates. I think it went on into the
Eighties. I think there was more
understanding on the part of the
people running television. I think it
was the fact that they allowed the
people whose speciality was comedy
to make the decisions. Comedy is
very difficult to read on the page. I
think it's very difficult to judge a
script. I can't believe there aren't the
writers around, I think there are.
Sometimes the wrong decisions are
made.

COE: Do you think that if you pitched
the *Fall and Rise of Reginald Perrin* today as
a six episode comedy drama about a
man having a nervous breakdown
and faking his own suicide, it would
get made?

NOBBS: Well, it's very difficult to say.
Probably not, and I'm sure that's the
answer you want me to give, and it's
the most interesting answer. Things
are made that are unusual and off the
wall, but it's much harder.

COE: I suppose you'd have to make
sure you had someone like Leonard
Rossiter attached before they took
any interest.

NOBBS: Well, exactly. They want to get
people attached and I write the other
way round. I like to write from the
café and the pub and on the train
and on the bus and the various
places I go. I get ideas from life and
then think: who would be good for
that? But they do say "will you write
something for so and so" and some-

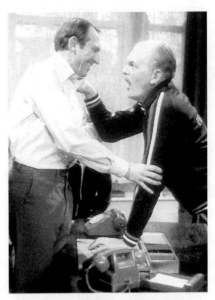

**"I LIKE TO WRITE FROM THE
CAFE AND THE PUB AND ON THE
TRAIN AND ON THE BUS AND
THE VARIOUS PLACES I GO"**

"BY THE VERY NATURE OF HIS REFUSAL TO ACCEPT THE CONVENTIONAL VALUES OF CAPITALISM, REGGIE COULDN'T POSSIBLY BE A CONSERVATIVE"

times I find that difficult. You're dredging around for something for them rather than letting your imagination run free.

COE: How does it feel to be named by the *Times* as one of the top ten cult TV shows of all time?

NOBBS: Well, it feels very good, and then I remind myself that it's just somebody's view. I looked in a history of television in the library and found a very snide comment about the whole of *Reggie Perrin*. You have to bear the two together. When I started out, I just had my own idea of what was funny. I think that's the thing about young writers. You don't question what you find funny, and then you constantly come up against people who just don't find some of these things funny. I mean, *Reggie Perrin* had a big audience but it didn't have a *huge* audience because it was not for everybody. *A Bit of a Do* was more for everybody and had a much bigger audience. You mentioned Beckett; well I think Beckett is a minority taste, but a huge minority of fans and brilliant stuff, so I'm very happy with that. Quite a muddled answer to your question, but never mind.

COE: I should ask you something about *What A Carve Up!* What has it been like working on that for the last couple of months?

NOBBS: I bought your book really because you'd written such a nice comment on the cover of mine, I thought I must read one of Jonathan's. I was riveted by it. I thought it was a marvellous book and, as you know, I asked you if it was being adapted and now I finally have the chance to adapt it. I've enjoyed doing it enormously. I think it's very punchy, I love the anger and the drama as well as the marvellous jokes, and I just hope somebody makes it, and makes it soon and makes it well.

COE: It might have been a strange experience reading it for you because so many passages are full of your comic rhythms. There's a scene where Michael visits his publisher and is told to put more sex scenes in his books, where the rhythm of the exchanges there is pure Reggie and CJ. I know I'd been re-reading the Reggie Perrin books just before I wrote that scene.

NOBBS: Well I didn't know that of course, so I wasn't looking out for it. I haven't used that scene because, on television, you can't use everything. We have to concentrate on the hard hitting central story line.

COE: I remember *Reggie Perrin* was re-run exactly the same time as the BBC was showing *Gormenghast*. I realised that I first read Mervyn Peake in the Seventies, and that at the same time I was watching *Reggie Perrin*. Suddenly it seemed perfect serendipity to me. Put *Reggie Perrin* and *Gormenghast* together and you end up with *What A Carve Up!*

NOBBS: [laughs] I certainly hadn't thought of that. *What A Carve Up!* is a book with an enormous range of emotions, and styles. Yet, I think, all held together by the passion about the story line. But I'm not familiar with Mervyn Peake's work. I've never got on with these fantasy worlds. It may be my loss.

COE: There are lots of echoes of *Reggie Perrin* in *What a Carve Up!* I was thinking again of the central motif of the book, the scene where Kenneth Connor is waiting for Shirley Eaton to come into his bedroom. When she finally does come, he's embarrassed and horrified and has to run away. It's just like Reggie lusting after Joan for months and months and when she finally turns up at his house and throws herself at him, he can't wait to get rid of her.

NOBBS: These are the kinds of things that actually define the modern audience. I suspect that large numbers of people in the audience would find that disappointing, they would rather that he just went through with it. I think that's very funny, and I think more discerning lovers of comedy would see that as the true joke, but that's where you can't please everyone. I can see all those echoes where you mention them.

COE: Something that's always intrigued me, who do you think that Reggie would have voted for? Was Reggie a socialist?

NOBBS: I don't know, I've never thought about it. It's a very good question...

COE: He kind of goes beyond politics, doesn't he?

NOBBS: I suppose by the very nature of his refusal to accept the conventional values of capitalism he could-

n't possibly be a Conservative. That's certainly part of the baggage he was getting rid of so I would think he would've voted Labour or Hairy Monster Green party or something, as part of his rebellion.

COE: I think he'd have voted for Ken Livingstone in the mayoral election rather than Frank Dobson.

NOBBS: I suspect Ken Livingstone is a bit of a Reggie Perrin, so I think he might see an echo there [laughs].

I switch off the tape recorder and we go looking for lunch, finally settling on an inexpensive pizzeria where, in tribute to Reggie, I am sorely tempted to order ravioli, followed by ravioli and ravioli. It wouldn't be the first time, David Nobbs tells me, that a fan has carried his devotion that far.

Relieved that the formal interview is over, he radiates the quiet contentment of a man who is now enjoying a happy second marriage, a well-earned tranche of repeat fees from the BBC, and the gratifying sense of having created a fictional character who is still, almost thirty years on, well-known and well-loved by the British public. Not many writers can boast as much.

Two weeks later I am back in a Landmark Trust property on the South Coast, wrestling with a new novel and, of course, the even more challenging task of writing something memorable in the property's log book. A quick flick through the previous entries and I see that somebody has got there before me: "I didn't get where I am today by writing in log books..."

SUMMER 2000 | THE IDLER | 47

LONDON, I

Who better to take on a free ride on the London Eye than writer Iain Sinclair, magus of the metropolis? By TONY WHITE. Photographs by SARAH AINSLIE

I arrive slightly early outside County Hall on the south bank of the Thames next to Westminster Bridge. It's sunny, but roll-ups are impossible in this wind, and the Costa Coffee concessions on the newly-paved section of Jubilee Gardens at the foot of the wheel — sorry, at the foot of the British Airways London Eye — are still under construction. Like the saloon bars and livery stables of a Western film set, they're all frontage and signage. Glassless windows. No coffee, then. Looking up at the vast weight of steel above me I feel slightly sick — pre-emptive vertigo — but I grin and bear it because what brought me here was a flash of inspiration that's worth suffering the odd stomach-churning dizzy-spell for. Who would be the tour guide of choice, I thought, for a press freebie on the London Eye? Why not Iain Sinclair, the novelist, satirist and psychogeographer, who's taken his occult-obsessive explo-

rations of the Capital into the best-seller lists. He hadn't, I discovered, been up on it yet. So I made him an offer he couldn't refuse.

Sinclair (and, for some reason I'm sticking to the surname protocol that surrounds him like an aura) arrives bang on time. A wave in the crowd and there he is; taller than I'd remembered, big black waxed coat[1], bag slung over the shoulder. He looks around. "Fabulous day. You managed to blag it, then?" he asks, gum stretched between teeth and tongue. He'd relocated his meeting for a "Shakespeare's London" radio documentary to the South Bank so he could stroll along The Embankment for this. "Shakespeare's London?" I ask. Curtain Road? Southwark? Coaching inns? "Yes. A chance to wander around, talking to people." I draw out an anecdote about the artist Jo Joelson, who does lighting design on the side, and tell Sinclair about her work in Tokyo last

---

[1] "Christ!" he says, when I show him the photos, "I look like Doctor Dee! That coat!"

year on an indoor replica of London's own replica Globe Theatre...

"Artificial London light? Didn't realise until I started working with Marc[2] how many different kinds of London light there are. There's the dull grey that everyone expects, but that can change spectacularly in seconds. London's prey to all these wildly contrasting micro-climates at any one time. The weather can just sweep in and suddenly bathe everything in clear light. Like it is now, and then, just as suddenly, it's gone. Something else entirely. Since I've been doing the M25 work I think that Heathrow has an effect too. Must have. All those jets constantly coming in. It's like they create their own weather: a kind of Ballardian microcosm." He looks up at the wheel. "Should see a fair bit of it from up there."

I mention the work Sinclair did in the novel *Radon Daughters* on Luke Howard, the East End chemist who corresponded with Goethe, and developed the cloud classification system that's still used today[3]. I'd read somewhere recently that vapour trails have now joined Cumulus Nimbus etc as a bona-fide cloud form.

"Atkins," he says, "has a thing about vapour trails which form an 'X'. Where two cross over. They're everywhere. These bloody great alphabetic signs in the sky."

We're due to rendezvous with "Atkins" next to County Hall in ten minutes or so — he's going to be doing our pictures today. I'm straining my neck to keep an eye out for him — I have no idea what he looks like.

"Don't worry," Sinclair says, "You won't miss him, he's about six foot eight." He looks at the slowly descending capsules between us and the river. "Wonder how long till someone does a remake of *The Third Man*," he offers.

In fact, Atkins doesn't show. At the press office, a woman asks me if I'm from the *Idler*. "Marc can't make it," she says, "So he asked me if I could come down instead. I'm Sarah." BA took so long to confirm our tickets that Marc had assumed it was off.

As we walk across The Embankment and get waved through security it starts to rain; a sudden shower that magnifies the Sun's glare off the river in every drop. Sarah marvels at the light, and Sinclair starts telling her about the Tokyo Globe. He does introduce it as my story, to be fair. It's unassimilated as yet. The press officer looks as solemn as a pre-teenager at a wedding. He shakes our hand and promises to catch up with us when we get off.

"The suit! The handshake!" Sinclair roars, when the press officer has gone. "Were they tough about letting us on?"

"The tough bit was talking to someone," I tell him. "Spent the

[2] Marc Atkins, the photographer — Sinclair's long-time collaborator

[3] See *Radon Daughters*, Granta 1998, p33, and *Lights Out for the Territory*, Granta 1998, pp93-94, if you want to know more. Marc Atkins, incidentally, appears in *Radon Daughters* as "Axel Turner": "some gaunt acolyte, a ceiling-scraper... Another bonehead: a Futurist whose future is all used up." They're still friends.

"THEY LOOK STRANGELY SINISTER, DON'T THEY? AS IF YOU'D GET SEALED IN THERE AND GASSED OR SOMETHING"

best part of a week phoning the press office at half-hourly intervals."

"It was the same with the Dome," he confirms. "Bloody impossible to get through. Especially once my first piece came out. Had to leave message after message after message. They only let me in, eventually, because they thought I was from the London Review of Bricks[4]." A uniformed usher signals us out onto the platform with an almost imperceptible eyebrow movement. "Thought I was from some building magazine – 'course they let me in."

He points at one of the capsules. "They look strangely sinister, don't they? As if you'd get sealed in there and gassed or something. Then sucked out through those big vents under the seat."

"Have you seen the hatches on the bottom?" I ask, pointing at two trap doors.

"Yes, look," he says. "I'm sure that one was full a second ago."

Our capsule glides slowly along next to the asphalt. I'm expecting us to have to break into a run, to make a leap for it at some critical moment, but boarding the Eye is less dangerous than – though comparable to – jumping onto the running board of a big bubble car that's doing one mile an hour.

As the doors close behind us, Sinclair takes the bag off his shoulder and squats down to retrieve his

---

[4] Published as "Mandelson's Pleasuredome" in London Review of Books, Vol. 19, No. 19, 2nd October 1997.

WE'RE AT BOMBER HEIGHT. BEST VIEW OF LONDON YOU'LL GET WITHOUT GOING BACK IN TIME AND JOINING THE LUFTWAFFE

Super 8 camera. "Thought I may as well," he shrugs, switching it on and nestling the finder against one eye. He points it through the glass and fires a burst of frames at the Palace of Westminster opposite.

"So why has no-one else invited you up here, then?" I ask.

"Well it's not that no-one's asked, actually. A few people have, but I've been so furiously busy finishing the book [5] that I haven't wanted to do any journalism. And, of course, now, the film [6] has taken up the whole of the last two or three months. You're lucky, you timed it right."

I remember that I'm supposed to be interviewing him. That was the original idea – how I swung it. Doesn't work in practice. I'm not stupid

---

[5] A novel called *Landor's Tower*, due out in spring 2001. I asked Sinclair to talk more about the book: "It's a fairly complex thing," he tells me. "What it is, it started out to be a sequel to *White Chapell Scarlet Tracings*, my first novel, which is obviously set in London, and which was projected as this sort of four part work. And a lot of the same characters are in it, at earlier or later stages in their development. And it's essentially... It discusses ways of setting up alternative communities to living in the metropolis. Is it possible to live out in these fringes? Because so many groups over the years attempted to live in this one valley, where Walter Savage Landor had bought an old Augustinian priory and tried to build a kind of sanatorial estate around it, which was a total disaster. And then, a man called Father Ignatius who was a religious nutter of the Corvo type – a kind of self-invented Prelate – tried to buy it to set up his own community, and then Eric Gill and David Jones, again in the Twenties, and then right through into the Seventies and these various communes. And this is quite near Hay-on-Wye, coincidentally. So the middle part of the book takes segments of this experience and slices it up with an ongoing narrative which is to do with this paranoia and conspiracy theories and someone who starts off in the first part of the book investigating these Marconi suicides in Bristol, where a whole load of Sikhs and Indians from London take off to Bristol and kill themselves in apparently strange ways. There's twenty-seven deaths – all people who worked on these big defence

enough to fire questions at him and stick a microphone under his nose. I'd rather let it all sink in. I'm playing with fire here, anyway — I'm well aware of this. Christ! Look at Atkins. If that's how he describes one of his friends in a book, how would someone who really pissed him off fare?

"Let's play this by ear," I suggest, "then meet up in a week or so when the ideas have settled a bit."

"Closer to home. Yes, all right."[7]

I look down at an oil slick spreading along the river between a string of orange pontoons and Hungerford Bridge, then turn to look west. I nod in the direction of Vauxhall. It's too far away to see whether he's at home, but we know that Jeffrey Archer's place is there, and we're approaching penthouse-altitude.

"Should be entering the Archer-

---

contracts. But most of the Indians who went out there, they tried to say they were part of some kind of cult. One guy jumps off Clifton Suspension Bridge; one man ties a rope around his neck and ties it to a tree and then drives off, puts the car into automatic and strangles himself; one fills up the back of the car with petrol and bangs into the wall of a Happy Eater. It's like Seventies TV – like it's come out of some strange, paranoid TV programme. And then the English people all seemed to be S&M victims, supposedly. And killed themselves that way when they start to go mad. And the whole thing builds up, incredibly. There's a book called *Open Verdict* by a guy called Tony Collins; I mean it's unbelievable. Well, anyway this one character starts to chase this story to the West Country and he sees that so many of the cases that he's previously been interested in London, with time they kind of filter out west. So the first part of the book is a series of fragmentary journeys west which never get to the community. Theoretically he, the narrator, is trying to write a novel, gather material for a novel about this collapsed utopian community, but actually never gets anywhere near it because he keeps getting deranged because of this other stuff on the road to Bristol. And by the second part of the book the narrator has been fitted up for one of these murders, and he's in a kind of asylum, etcetera, etcetera. And eventually kind of ten or twelve different narratives do come together. And this is twelve years... I mean, I hadn't written anything until September '99, so it's been written quite quickly, but the gathering of material has been going on, I suppose, for twelve years. But in part two you get either true, or bent, or adulterated autobiography, because I grew up in South Wales, a bit further on. And little bits of this are seeded throughout the book. In the final section that becomes more important. But all of these fantastic secret state contracts which all sort of went down to Bristol, and all of the listening stations in Cheltenham and all of that. There's quite a lot of weirdness out there. And by the same token, people who'd been writing about dubious, gothic crime in London – Jack the Ripper murders and so on – also shot out to the same part of the world; people like Dan Farson and Colin Wilson. And Jeremy Thorpe plays quite a big part in the book. There's that comic-tragic killing of the dog on the hill, and hiring the people to do it – they were the most outrageous bunch – a lot of them from South Wales. These guys from like carpet warehouses and slot-machine arcades get weaved up with big cheeses in Liberal politics. It's an unholy stew of a wonderful kind. And all these trails get charged after by all these people who may themselves be deranged. And one of the characters keeps sending these tapes back; he just records strange accounts of these versions of this at night, and it's like Donald Crowhurst – you don't know if at some point he's given up on the real investigation, he's just making it up off the top of his head while he sits in a boarding house in Minehead. Like so many of these pulpy conspiracy books it's all just hideously recycled. Anyway, that's the basic pitch of the book. I'd like also to do some kind of little booklet that went with it, that just outlined its various stories, with photographs and drawings and things. What's really nice about this, this other strange element about the book, is that numerous key points in the book are also key points in the film, but with a totally different meaning. In that Mike Moorcock criss-crosses through the book, and this poet Ed Dorn gives a reading in Bristol just before he dies, and that's in the film and in the book. You hear a different part of it. So it's again like alternative worlds; the same elements are there, but they mean something else entirely. And some of the characters have the same name. So these two versions of the story which go in absolutely the opposite directions exist at the same time. The film is part of the guide to the book – and vice-versa."

[6] *Asylum* (or, *The Final Commission*) is a film about Michael Moorcock which Iain Sinclair and Chris Petit have directed for Channel Four. I asked Sinclair to tell me a bit more about the film towards the end of our second meeting. But unfortunately I'd only brought one hour's worth of micro-cassettes with me, and the tape finished just as he started talking. *Asylum* is due for its first screening on Channel 4 in May 2000, and some stills are used elsewhere in this magazine to illustrate Steve Beard's interview with Michael Moorcock. Apologies, then, dear reader, for not being able to reproduce Sinclair's lengthy explanation here. It's my fault; I shouldn't have got him started on the Post Office...

[7] We meet about a fortnight later. He's already corrected some of my wayward bibliographic references by letter, and he invites me round for tea, and to do some more taping, at his place.

sphere any second," I suggest.

I get a laugh. "That's a good name for London; the Archersphere. Would have been, any way. It's amazing, you know. There was a review in the paper today — another book of some sort. Did you see it? The thing is, I think Archer only ever had enough ideas, or energy — or enough *material* — for maybe one book. At a pinch. But he can't stop writing the things. I just don't know why he's got this compulsion to write more and more books when he's got absolutely nothing to put in them." He nods at County Hall, obliquely invoking last year's disgrace. "Bound to be doing loads of them now."

It's destined to become a truism, but this wheel fucks your sense of direction. The river seems to be spiralling around us. Chelsea's there? I look towards what I think is the east — I'm way off, Canary Wharf is practically behind me. Planes for Heathrow seem to be going north. Sinclair has the same problem.

"Look at that insurance building, the kind of Egyptianate one, in Finsbury Square. Amazing."

He lines up his fore-arm with the Telecom Tower.

"See the Post Office Tower. Now go along three, below and to the right of that green one."

"Ah. So what's that dome thing below it?" I ask. (I notice that we're both saying "above" and "below" as if we're looking at a picture.)

"Must be Smithfield. Yes, it's Smithfield, I'm sure of it."

Wait a minute, I think. Then it dawns on me. "Christ, no, it's the

British Library reading room."

"What? Oh, hang on." He squats down to rummage in his bag again, and comes up with a pair of glasses. "That's better. Yes. So that must have been the Senate Building."

I turn and try to take a bearing from the three towers of the Barbican, to try and find Smithfield. But I can't.

We're not the only ones who are confused, though. At that moment the Stewardess comes over. A couple of the other passengers are asking where Buckingham Palace is. "Look," says the stewardess, "you see the river?" She's not pointing at the river. She's Australian, and every sentence is a question. The couple both nod. "Follow the river up? You see, there? Follow the river up until you see a kind of gold thing?" They nod again. "Behind the gold thing? That's Buckingham Palace."

Sinclair and I exchange glances and raised eyebrows. What kind of disinformation is this? That's not the river, for God's sake. It's the duck pond in St James' Park.[8]

"Buckingham Palace," Sinclair says, taking his cue. "Look at it. Don't know what the Queen was complaining about. Can't see a thing. Makes you wonder whether she came up to check."

"Perhaps that's why she sent Fergie," I suggest, remembering one of the earlier press photos.

"That's what the trap doors were for." He points and shoots.

"Look at that," he says, nodding down at Whitehall. "Vast amounts of real estate. It's hard to visualise just how much of it they own. But up here you can see it all. It's the best view of it I've ever had. See that?" He's pointing at the Shell Building now. "Used to be able to go up there. Had to pay. No point now." He turns and shoots another few 8mm rounds. Tracer fire invisible but implied. We're at bomber height, and Sinclair's still got Big Ben in his sights. Best view of London you'll get without going back in time and joining the Luftwaffe. A small storm is coming in over — what? — the Berkshire downs? Can we see that far? It's changed the light, though, already.

A defunct office block beyond Waterloo carries a banner offering apartment conversions, which could only be seriously visible to passengers on the Eye. Reminds me of that Saatchi & Saatchi advert back in '89: "First over the wall". Six months, I think, and every roof will carry a hoarding for this captive audience. I'm glad we're on it now, when rooftops are just rooftops, not advertising opportunities.

"It's a leap of the imagination compared to The Dome," I say. "You don't have to fill it with something, because there's all this stuff,"

[8] I tell Sarah this story when I go to pick up the contacts from her studio. She tells me that she heard the stewardess telling one of the other passengers that before the Eye she was working as a "greeter" at Eurodisney. I tell this to Sinclair.

"So they're not people who've failed the audition to become real stewardesses, then?"

"No. They're these kind of itinerant theme park 'greeters'."

"The perpetual trade show circuit. They had a kind of fixed look about them didn't they? Hadn't quite worked up to the full beam sort of smiles and stuff yet. Mind you we were on a freebie, so they didn't need to bother!"

I wave my hands in the general direction of outside, "already here."

Sinclair starts waving his arms around too. "What's great[9] about this is that it has absolutely no agenda. You can't impose what people will see.[10] It's up to you; completely open. And it seems that people have completely accepted this. They should have just left the dome empty — just come and see this space, this great thing — instead of filling it with loads of tat. I haven't been on the Jubilee Line yet, but that's part of the problem. I mean there's no interest in useful tube lines, the Hackney tube extension, say — and that area of London's crying out for it — but they'll build the Jubilee Line extension to make it easy for people to get to where they don't want, or

[9] Sinclair qualifies this later on: "Well it's pushing a really low-key idea. I mean it *is* Blackpool front in the Forties or Fifties; it's a miners' outing. But the grotesque thing is that it's been placed in this piece of real estate which supposedly represents every American's vision of London. It's just the Houses of Parliament, the river, and now you've got this gigantic bicycle wheel which is the highest thing you can come up with; to be spun around on a nebulous tour, with a couple of "ooh aah" moments. But because it's not actually, actively bad we've all said it's wonderful. But I don't think it is that wonderful; it's pretty banal, but it just isn't actually tragically awful or a total scam in that they're paying for it themselves. This is an airline doing this — an airline with a bad press to say the least — offering you flights that don't go anywhere. So it's the equivalent of the Gatwick experience of being on one of those shuttles that go backwards and forwards, without the horror of the flight at the end of it. You know, you pay to wait and have a bit of a view. But really, to me, it's no better than the train we got going out to see Mike Moorcock. We spent time laid up in Chicago airport, and there's this shuttle service train that just goes three or four stops out past the Hilton Hotel and gives you a fabulous view over parked cars and bits of the airport and then it comes back from where it started from. And that's free as well. And the Eye is kind of the same experience, except you go up into the air."

[10] "Be quite dramatic if it went down under the ground, I was thinking, though," Sinclair says from the safety of his sofa. "If it actually took you down into the bowels of the Earth, and the

"BIT OF A TERRORIST TARGET, I SHOULD THINK," SAYS SINCLAIR, HOLSTERING THE CAMERA FOR A SECOND. "DIDN'T SEARCH US OR ANYTHING DID THEY?"

need, to go. The best thing would be if you just got off the Jubilee Line and there was a staircase up into the Dome and then you turned around again and came straight back home."[11]

He turns and shoots more footage of the Houses of Parliament as we approach the apex of our revolution. From this angle it feels as if we're on a rollercoaster; a curve of track above us, and beyond it the void. I almost expect the car in front to disappear, but gravity has no special claim on them, or us. Sinclair looks back at the car behind us.

He laughs out loud. "Even up here, look! Even up here people have got to be on their mobiles!"

We both laugh "I'm on the wheel!" we say together. It's tagging — microwave tagging.

"Bit of a terrorist target, I should think," says Sinclair, holstering the camera for a second. "Didn't search us or anything did they."

"I know, since they're calling them 'flights' you'd think they might have some of those airport scanners or something," I say.

Sinclair mimes frisking me with an airport metal detector. "Not making very much of the British Airways franchise at all, are they? We've got our stewardess, I suppose, but you'd think they'd be handing out brochures."[12]

"Giving away flights!" I say. "Branded souvenirs. Well, they'll get their logo in half the photo albums in the country." I nod at the writing on the glass.

"Yes it's well placed isn't it. D'you think Virgin'll want their own wheel on the opposite bank? You know Ayling's involved with the Dome as well. Good publicity. Sweeps away all that 'dirty tricks' press doesn't it?"[13]

I'm looking down the chimneys of County Hall, the former GLC HQ, as we talk — surprised by the bland, hospitalesque architecture — all white-tiled atria and pre-fab flying corridors — that's behind the imposing facade.

"Went in there, years ago,"

sewage system, and you confronted the horrors and then you went up into the sky. I mean, it's not too scarey at the moment is it? I mean, you with your vertigo, you didn't find it too unpleasant, did you? No. It'd be quite good if people were having full-blown panic attacks; pressed up against the window, screaming as it went round. You could sit in one of the other capsules and watch people freaking out above you. It's all very calm. Bit too calm. I mean, I don't think it's got piped music yet, but you get the feeling that it may come to that."

[11] "Interesting that they're trying to scam a double ticket," Sinclair adds in his note. "Tempting the Eye punters to make the ride downriver to Bugsby's Marshes." I've missed the papers over the past week, so when we meet for a cup of tea in his Hackney drawing room I ask him more about this: "It's because the wheel is a success, they're trying to get you to buy a double ticket, and if you didn't know London, you'd do the wheel and then you'd get a boat trip that took you down to the Dome, and it all becomes part of a single package. But by the time you've done the wheel and then the boat trip you're not going to have a lot of time left for the Dome anyway. So then you'd probably have to stay over night in the Holiday Inn on Bugsby's Marshes. That's the way to do it — a triple package. And a free ride back on the Jubilee Line! And London becomes a kind of pleasure dome: the Jubilee Line — sponsored by Derek Jarman! It's gonna be quite strange, cos I think the whole South Bank is going to be themed up to the eyeballs with every possible delight and then on the other side the underground's going to slip into the dark ages. It's going to be like going back to those films where they were haunted by the undead. So you'll go down the Central Line and spend forty-five minutes in a tunnel, sweating in a cattle car, while on the other side you're swooshed through beautiful stations going nowhere."

[12] "The concessionary aspect doesn't really seem to have got into its stride, yet." Sinclair says. "What about T-shirts! You know; 'I experienced the Eye'."

Sinclair says, following my gaze. "Amazing inside. Third Reichian architecture. These great, sweeping staircases. Now it's all burgers and fish." We look down at the piece-meal conversions, the London Aquarium; the tourist attractions and watering holes that are bringing people back to this forgotten part of the river. "Shame they're not going to use it for...?"

"The Mayor's office? No. I think they've confirmed that it's going to be that 'headlamp' thing by London Bridge," I say. There's a long pause as we continue our descent — twenty-past... twenty-five-past... — at twice the speed of the minute hand on the opposite bank.

"Christ!" Sinclair says, eventually. "What are they doing to our river?"

As we approach the platform, I can't believe the ride is over. "That was the fastest half-hour of my life."

"Was it really half an hour?" Sinclair asks.

We should have stayed put — gone around one more time. But for some reason it doesn't occur to us to chance it. The press officer is nowhere to be seen. At the exit is a booth selling computer generated images of punters in the capsules. It's unstaffed at the moment, so we both take a "British Airways London Eye"-logoed mini-carrier bag from the pile on the counter instead.

"A souvenir!" I say.

"Yes," says Sinclair. "Should give these out before you get on. Look," he opens it and mimes puking, "British Airways sick bags!" ➷

Iain Sinclair's novels include Radon Daughters, Downriver *and* White Chapell Scarlet Tracings. *His non-fiction work,* Lights Out for the Territory *is published by Granta. Iain Sinclair and Marc Atkins'* Liquid City *is published by Reaktion Books, price £14.95. All are highly recommended. An audio CD of Iain Sinclair reading from* Downriver *is published by King Mob.*

"Yeah, or like [I lift my jumper to reveal a Carnaby Street tourist purchase] 'Some idiot went on the Eye and all I got was this lousy T-shirt!'"

"Surely they've got to get people coming round with trays of souvenir drinks in miniature bottles with the logo on them."

"Duty frees," I say.

"Duty frees, as it were. And then gradually the area around it's got to turn into an airport concourse, those little shops that sell underwear, you know, cigars, so it builds up and up and up, and then you have this flight, and come back into this zone as if you've been somewhere. But you haven't been anywhere, you've just been around in a circle, and had glimpses into bits of stuff they don't want you to see. People in MI6, or the MOD, trying to pull their desks away from the windows."

"Yes, so you can't lip-read conversations about how the British Army's rifles aren't working."

"Or catch a glimpse of Jeffrey Archer's latest attempts to become a second hand car salesman on the net. He's bought a franchise that's basically just selling second hand motors but through the net."

"Like 'Would you buy a used car from this man?'"

"Yes, well they've done all those stories in the papers, all those gags, yes."

"Is that going to be his slogan, then?"

"I think it is, yeah," says Sinclair, laughing.

"Well if Norris has kind of vacated the car salesman role...'

"He's left an empty chair, yeah. And Ken has lost his building [County Hall] to the Eye, which is sort of gloatingly sliding past his windows, with a basement full of sharks! Great! It's perfect! Crazier and crazier!"

[13] Readers may care to note that the original interview took place about ten days before Bob Ayling and British Airways parted company in March 2000. "Shame," we both agree. "Unable to enjoy his one success!" Sinclair adds.

SAGE OF EMPIRES

The Grand Old Hippie of English letters, Michael Moorcock, talks with STEVE BEARD. Pictures taken from Asylum (or the Final Commission), a film by Chris Petit and Iain Sinclair

The Royal Overseas League in the ritzy bit of London's West End is a grand old duffer of a building which still flies the flag of the Union.

Old school British scientific fantasy novelist, bohemian man of letters and retired rock'n'roller Michael Moorcock became eligible for membership in 1994, when he quit England for Texas to be closer to his American wife's family. It has been his English base of operations ever since.

A stone plaque on the front of the building indicates that it is dedicated to the "citizens of the British Empire" who died in the first inter-imperialist war. It strikes me as an appropriate introduction to a man whose work — whether in the avant pop Sixties novels dominated by counter-cultural dandy Jerry Cornelius, or in the later Oswald Bastable future Edwardiana novels — has been consistently fascinated by the signifying practices of high imperial culture. The renaissance of English republicanism signalled by the emergence of political groups like Charter 88 has reminded us that, in a multi-national state governed by a monarch, we are all technically quasi-feudal "subjects" rather than enlightened bourgeois citizens. And yet here is a pointer to a slightly different way of looking at things.

I am ten minutes early for the interview but my subject is already waiting to greet me at the front door. He is a generous host. We wander disconsolately through the building's warren of sitting rooms and waiting areas looking for a good place to do the interview. Moorcock kvetches about the increasing number of business people who have started to invade his inner sanctum and pauses only to show me a ritual instance of Blighty as it should be — a recess full of snoring clubmen and brightly chatting ladies. Eventually we settle in the dining room and he treats me to the full cream tea.

MOORCOCK ALSO FOUND TIME TO BECOME AN HONORARY MEMBER OF HEAVY METAL BAND HAWKWIND

"I was always looking for representations of colonial England in my novels," he says as he tucks into some tea and toast. "I didn't know about the Royal Overseas League in those days. There certainly would have been a lot going on here if I had known about it."

What he did know about is enough to have filled huge numbers of science fantasy novels. Moorcock started out as a juvenile prodigy on the pulp mag *Tarzan Adventures* in the late Fifties, and has written the odd collection of letters, political pamphlets, critical studies and — increasingly from the eighties onwards — a sequence of more obviously literary novels like *Mother London* and its current follow-up *King of the City*. In the Sixties, he edited the science fiction magazine *New Worlds* and introduced an avant-garde agenda, mixing social comment and collage with speculative fiction by American young turks like Harlan Ellison, Thomas M Disch and Samuel R Delany as well as British postmodernists like Barrington J Bayley, M John Harrison and JG Ballard. He also found time to become an honorary member of heavy metal band Hawkwind. He fed the band his Elric of Melniboné sword'n'sorcery mythology soon after it was formed on his London manor in Notting Hill during 1969.

Moorcock is full of stories from this period of his life. He tells how he first commissioned the imagistic fragments which went on to make up JG Ballard's masterpiece of condensed mediagraphic surrealism *The Atrocity Exhibition*: "I demanded them. I put them all over the covers of *New*

Worlds." He then told me how American beat savant William S Burroughs first developed his obsession with human culture as a virus: "Barry Bailey had a story called 'Star Virus' which Bill Burroughs actually ripped off for his key notion that we are the virus. Well he didn't rip it off... he said, I'm gonna have it... and Barry said, sure mate yeah, very proud, happy to oblige."

There were many such cultural crossovers in the pages of *New Worlds*. Moorcock identifies their importance in hindsight: "Postmodernism was in science fiction mags twenty years before it arrived elsewhere in the culture. Ballard and me were doing it without really having a name for it. We just knew we didn't like modernist fiction and it didn't describe our experience. Coming from backgrounds where we didn't recognize the established forms of cultural continuity, we were forced to invent a lot of our own culture. Ballard took a lot from American culture, as did I, because that was quite as strong as our own culture. Long before people started to discuss these things, we were already there."

With his cosmopolitan political instincts and easy London charm, Moorcock is a deep-frozen hippie geezer from a sixties Notting Hill bohemia of freaky-deaky communes, radical publishing collectives, part-time MI6 agents, groovy drug dealers and failed urban terrorists. The fact that he refused to thaw out in the hothouse economic climate of the Eighties like so many of his peers

is testament either to a stubborn integrity or a radical naivety. His latest novel, *King of the City*, belatedly reckons with the long march of Thatcherism through the institutions of civil society. The novel's considered rage veers between bitterness and tenderness.

Moorcock is more sanguine on the subject during our interview: "When I was in Fleet Street in the fifties, journalists — financial journalists in particular — were forever talking (you know how they love to bullshit: they prefer bullshitting to actually working)... but they were forever talking about how the economy had to expand into two new areas — the domain now marked out by globalisation and the domestic public sector. So the plans for Thatcherism were in place and had been discussed for about as long as Lenin and Trotsky had been discussing the revolution. They had been blocked by various social institutions but deregulation and union-busting helped to get them going. When Thatcherism came into place it came in fast 'cos the power structures which were gonna get it moving had already been tested."

Later in the evening, on the same day as our interview, Moorcock shuffles on stage at London's Conway Hall to read from *King of the City*. He is on the same bill as London magus Iain Sinclair, conceptual punk novelist Stewart Home, theatre clown Ken Campbell and rock-star-turned-poet Nick Cave, all promoting a series of spoken-word recordings released on the King Mob label. Before we parted company in the

Royal Overseas League, Moorcock had enjoyed a moment of self-disparaging irony when he referred to himself "opening for Nick Cave". Yet, it is his voice — with its quiet authority and melting passion — which dominates the night's proceedings.

Moorcock's heyday may have been in the sixties, but it was his childhood experience of London during the Second World War — with its wild enemy bombing runs, new forms of industrial mobilisation and spontaneous acts of popular sovereignty — which deformed his political imagination. As he writes in *King of the City*: "Only rarely do people come together at their very best against tyranny and brute evil. Londoners seem to do it more often than most. At least on their own behalf. It helps you remember that there... can be a world... where mob rule means the rule of common law and mutual respect."

Moorcock was born in Mitcham in the Home County of Surrey in 1939 and soon after moved to the South London suburb of Norbury. His upbringing was unconventional. He was part-raised by gypsies: "Although I wasn't raised by gypsies I was babysat by gypsies. My mother worked and in Mitcham there was a camp of settled Romanies. They were there 'cos of the fairs and used to use their horses to go totting round the streets. Part of my early childhood was spent fairly intimately with this gypsy family. They used to take me to Brixton, which was their big treat. They loved jellied eels, which I used to hate." Meanwhile his guardian was a Jew: "He was just an ordinary businessman but he went in and out of Germany and Austria buying Jews. He pulled out as many as he could. People have told me stories — I never heard it from him — of meeting him at the Pyrenees and getting out through Spain."

This cosmopolitan background feeds into all his fiction and allows him to confront with equanimity the liberal middle-class ideology of laissez-faire calculation which has dominated modern British culture. Like many of his fellow speculative fiction writers, Moorcock has refused the easy temptations of the North London adultery novel and the Anglo-Catholic novel of intimate manners. He has exited the élite philosophico-liberal tradition of the oedipal novel, which begins with Henry James and joins E M Forster, Virginia Woolf, Evelyn Waugh, Kingsley Amis, Julian Barnes and Michael Bracewell together in an unbroken continuum of aesthetic good taste. In his Jerry Cornelius novels, he discovered a more hybrid domain of letters capable of mixing technical fiction with newspaper reports, sampled quotes and ad straplines. He repudiates the inward liberal sensibility which is so perpetually riven by cynicism and sentimentality. Instead he turns back to the expansive colonial rim of the old British Empire.

This position delivers its own paradoxes and they bleed into the text of the semi-autobiographical *King of the City*. Stoned and isolated at Christmas, the narrator finds himself responding unexpectedly to the ritual broadcast of the Queen's speech: "I was moved to tears and found myself bonding with the entire British Commonwealth. It was like the last scene from *Nineteen Eighty-Four*. I was weeping with love for Big Brother." Meanwhile Boulting Brothers movies and Ealing come-

"ONLY RARELY DO PEOPLE COME TOGETHER AT THEIR VERY BEST AGAINST TYRANNY AND BRUTE EVIL. LONDONERS SEEM TO DO IT MORE OFTEN THAN MOST"

"A LOT OF PEOPLE WERE EXTREMELY SENSITIVE TO OTHER CULTURES. SO IT'S NOT THAT SIMPLE. IMPERIALISM IS NOT THAT SIMPLE."

dies on late-night or afternoon television exert a strange fascination: "I studied those movies the way a Mexican might study Mayans. They promised clues to my obscured and revised past."

There is a typically quixotic passage in Moorcock's 1977 Cornelius novel *The Condition of Muzak* where his Notting Hill anti-hero is crowned King of London. Moorcock relishes the pageant in which "the mandarins of Liverpool and Morecombe... the blazing flags of New Trinidad and Old Jamaica... the green-kilted warriors of Eire and Cymru... the Scottish Mounted Rifles, Australian Light Horse, Canadian Artillery... Iceni... Mercians and Northumbrians" come together to celebrate Jerry's coronation from the edges of ancient myth and the ends of the British colonial territories.

Under the influence of Mervyn Peake's *Gormenghast* trilogy, Moorcock presents the whole event as a Harlequinade characteristic of the posh Covent Garden pantomimes of eighteenth century London. In an appendix to the novel he describes the Harlequinade in the following terms: "at a moment of tension in the plot, the characters would be transformed magically into members of the Harlequinade to act out their parts in a fantastic, musical, satirical and symbolic manner and bring the whole entertainment to a satisfactory resolution." This implicit ideology of symbolic compensation contrasts with a passage elsewhere in *The Condition of Muzak* where Moorcock quotes venerable British surrealist Herbert Read on the "shock therapy" delivered to society by "insurrection".

What is the moment of social tension which inspires Moorcock's consoling mythology of high imperial romance? I suggest that it is the period between the 1880s and 1914 when the British ruling élite was split by the issue of Empire (much as today it is split by the issue of Europe). The climax of this period was marked by reforming Birmingham radical Joseph Chamberlain's political campaign in the early 1900s to displace the liberal economic orthodoxy of free trade with a colonial protectionist policy designed to build a tariff wall around the British Empire. The free trade practices of the liberals emerged victorious from this struggle and went on to morph into the neo-liberal capitalist programmes we are more familiar with today. However Chamberlain's eclipsed policy of "Imperial Preference" sunk deep into the popular imagination where it has perhaps remained ever since.

Moorcock seems to agree with late Victorian novelist Joseph Conrad that what distinguished British imperialism from its rapacious European competitors was that there was "an ideal at the back of it". He belongs to a generation which can still get misty-eyed about the burdens weathered by the national colonialist apparatus as it got down to its self-appointed task of civilizing the natives. Moorcock gestures around the dining-room of the Royal Overseas League: "Half the people here are or used to be the kind of people who dedicated their entire lives — often without any great reward — to

some small country. Admittedly there might have been an element of paternalism involved but surprisingly there wasn't always. They're people who just got caught up in the notion of helping another country to do its stuff without any real sense of interfering with that culture. A lot of people were extremely sensitive to other cultures. So it's not that simple. Imperialism is not that simple."

It's no wonder that Moorcock started out as a writer on Tarzan, adding to the repertoire of noble savage imagery associated with Lord Greystoke of the jungle. Tarzan creator Edgar Rice Burroughs was originally a disciple of H Rider Haggard and it is perhaps here that an origin point for Moorcock's own imperial mythology can be discerned. Haggard delivered his first novel *King Solomon's Mines* in 1886 and remained hugely influential right up until the eve of the first inter-imperialist war. The tropes of his speculative romances — primitive rituals, lost worlds, alien ruins, cosmogenetic entities — are shared by other late Victorian men of letters like Rudyard Kipling and Arthur Conan Doyle and go on to define a popular anthropo-colonial tradition of the novel which links HG Wells, Aldous Huxley, William Golding, JG Ballard, Iain Sinclair and Alex Garland.

Moorcock of course is right at the heart of this tradition. In fact what is extraordinary is the way his work implicitly historicizes it by going back to its origins and hooking them up to the Sixties, at the same time as they are being rediscovered by the counter-culture during the moment of decolonization. He has a rationalization for this process: "In about 1970 I decided I could only really cope with going back a hundred years 'cos that still gave me living memory and I didn't want to go past the place where I couldn't check my work in various ways. 1870 was my cut-off point for going back. All the repetitions are there, everything that had already happened was still happening, and the language was almost the same. You have the same kind of racism (with Jewish immigration beginning at that time), the same combination of optimism and pessimism. You've got the middle classes with disappointed hopes who start reading *The Time Machine* by HG Wells 'cos they're disenchanted with the machine that's supposed to have made them rich and so start to become socialists."

Moorcock goes on to tell how the popular tradition of Haggard and Wells was delivered to him in its original, highly impure form by the Norbury second-hand bookstore Jennings and the back pages of *Exchange and Mart*. It was here as a child that he was able to get hold of bound volumes of the old illustrated fiction magazines which had started out in the 1880s and in many cases kept going up until the early Fifties (when they were forced out of business by a combination of paper rationing, declining sales and the emergence of television).

He looks back on his literary education with fondness: "I used to buy bound volumes of *The Strand*, *Windsor* and so on because nobody wanted

them in those days and you could get them for pennies. I read *The Time Machine* first in serial form in *Fortnightly Review*. Conrad appeared mostly in *The London Magazine* (not the same as the current title), together with Wells, Kipling and so on. Hardy was in *Harpers* and pretty much everybody was in *The Strand*. *Pearsons* ran a lot of Wells and specialised in science fiction, whereas *The Strand* specialised in detective fiction. My own belief is that this catholic kind of fiction publishing came under attack when Eng Lit got politicised by Leavis."

Moorcock has placed his finger on something here. Embattled Cambridge liberal humanist FR Leavis professionalized the discipline of literary criticism in the thirties but it was actually in the crucial period between the 1880s and the first inter-imperialist war that the proponents of Eng Lit had to fight for it to be taken seriously as an object of academic study. It was first institutionalized in the working men's clubs and lecturing circuits as a poor man's version of the Classics (much as Media Studies today is regarded as an inferior version of Eng Lit) and only later made it into the universities of Oxford and Cambridge.

What remains interesting is the ideological work Eng Lit was expected to perform. Victorian sage Matthew Arnold identified long before Leavis the need to hip the emergent industrial middle classes to the liberal values of the ruling élite so they might be better placed to do their job of pacifying the restless working classes below them. Instrumental to this invention of tradition was the process of canon formation. The fact that the liberal tradition of EM Forster, Anthony Powell and Michael Bracewell has been automatically included within the canon of Eng Lit while the popular tradition of HG Wells, Michael Moorcock and Stewart Home has been branded with patronizing designa-

"IN ABOUT 1970 I DECIDED I COULD ONLY REALLY COPE WITH GOING BACK A HUNDRED YEARS"

"ONCE VESTED INTERESTS HAVE BUILT UP THEIR OWN PATRONAGE SYSTEM THEN YOU'VE GOT THE NEED TO ESTABLISH AN ORTHODOXY IN ORDER TO MAINTAIN CAREERS."

tions like "pulp", "genre fiction" and — most tellingly — the "novel of ideas" is the result of a social hierarchy being able to take itself for granted. Or as Moorcock puts it: "Once vested interests have built up their own patronage system then you've got the need to establish an orthodoxy in order to maintain careers."

What remains inspiring about Moorcock is that he has remained unscarred by the cultural exclusions he has suffered, and has resisted the lures of envy and resentment. When he talks about his American old school comicbook creator buddies Howard Chaykin and Walt Simonson, it's possible to catch a glimpse of his own trenchancy: "They're both smart and both well-read even though they're both determinedly working in the popular arena. They had the choice and they know what choices they're making. These people aren't fools and they know when they're being condescended to too. There's no question of it. They've learned in a sense like black people to shrug it off a lot of the time or form an idea whereby in some way it doesn't bother them."

So what do we have here? A grand old man sympathetic to the white man's burden of Empire and an enfant terrible who feels like an oppressed black man in the dominant neo-liberal culture of his day. The cultural contradiction is productive rather than disabling and finds its greatest literary expression in the "Colonel Pyat" quartet of novels which Moorcock began in 1981 with *Byzantium Endures* and is due to finish soon with *The Vengeance of Rome*. Colonel Pyat is a minor character from the Jerry Cornelius novels whose White Russian background allows Moorcock to take the full reckoning of Empire – colonial exploitation, institutional racism, structural genocide – which his earlier work had shied away from. (Pyat comments on the difference between the Russian and British Empires: "They said Britain was the New Rome. All she inherited was the patrician. Moscow inherited the priest.")

Moorcock plans to dedicate *The Vengeance of Rome* to his guardian. He says of the sequence as a whole: "I was trying to deal with the whole twentieth century and how the Holocaust could occur in that historical context of North Africa and the West. So the same interest is there: I'm looking for evidence but trying to turn it into entertainment as I go along. *The Vengeance of Rome* is a hard one to write. I won't take anyone else's experience of the camps as fiction because the idea is disgusting to me. I've had to invent a camp, make it fictitious. I just can't stand the idea of getting even close to someone's real experience and messing with it. Iain Sinclair gave me the ending to the book. He took me to Princelet Street. That gave me a better, a quieter ending than the camps." ❧

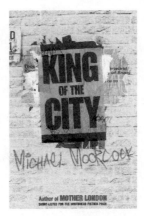

King of the City *(pbk, £9.99) and* Mother London *(pbk, £6.99) are both published by Scribner UK.*
Asylum (or the Final Commission) *directed by Chris Petit and Iain Sinclair for Illuminations Films and Channel 4, is due for its first screening in May 2000.*

FEATURES

KICK BACK

ROBERT NEWMAN went to Seattle for the protests against the World Trade Organisation

Never before in history has there been anything like the protests in Seattle. Never before have so many different movements from all over the world all united in one mass-action in one place.

I was very excited to be in Seattle during WTO-week, too. First time I've ever been at a bit of yer actual, real, proper history. I was especially pleased about this, because I'd just been reading Eric Hobsbawm's history of the twentieth century, *Age Of Extremes*, before I left. If you've read it you'll know it makes you feel a bit inadequate and unlived, 'cos Hobsbawm's been everywhere and he keeps popping up in person at major events in world history. You get stuff like: "As Fidel Castro announced to a crowded, thronged square in Havana that the revolution had been victorious, this author remembers that the atmosphere was electric." He's so

cool, I mean, he's everywhere, man. The L.A. Riots: "Such was the people's control of the streets, I myself carried a Nicam Digital Stereo three blocks back to my hotel!"

They came from factories in Mexico and South Korea, from rural family farms in Iowa and Bangalore. Ethiopian economists, Harvard lawyers, direct action networks and French academics, the Raging Grannies and the Zapatistas. Cab drivers in Seattle had been giving out anti-WTO leaflets for weeks before and went on strike in support. Every dock and port along the West Coast of America from Alaska to Los Angeles and Hawaii was shut down.

How was an obscure outfit like the World Trade Organisation able to arouse such passions and mobilize the biggest, broadest citizen's alliance in history? Maybe the offi-

cial Chinese observer in Seattle for the WTO got nearest the mark when he commented: "This is as significant for the West as Tiannenmen Square was for us..." His comparison is right on the money. Seattle was above all else a pro-democracy protest. But, unlike Tiananmen Square, a global one.

Just why the Battle of Seattle was a pro-democracy protest becomes clearer when you look more

closely at the WTO (World Take Over) itself.

In 1816 Thomas Jefferson warned of "a single and splendid government of an aristocracy founded on banking institutions and moneyed incorporations" which would mean "the end of democracy and freedom". By 1999 his worst fears had come true and the line No Globalisation Without Representation was on banners and placards all over

Seattle. Jefferson, however, was only thinking of the United States, not the world.

"The WTO is writing a constitution of the global economy," declared ex-president of the World Trade Organisation, Renato Ruggiero. The constitution of this "single and splendid government" makes scarey reading.

Here's a snippet:

"Each Member [nation] shall

YOU MAY THINK THAT WHEN YOU GO INTO A POLLING STATION YOU CAN VOTE FOR WHICHEVER MANIFESTO TAKES YOUR FANCY – YOU CAN'T. YOU MAY THINK YOU LIVE IN A DEMOCRACY – YOU DON'T

ensure the conformity of its laws, regulations and administrative procedures with... WTO objectives."

Meanwhile all existing or future laws of member nations can be challenged, says the constitution, if "the attainment of any WTO objective is impeded."

You may think that when you go into a polling station you can vote for whichever manifesto takes your fancy – you can't. You may think you live in a democracy – you don't.

The WTO even bans certain objectives from domestic legislature. These include subsidies for energy conservation, sustainable agriculture and alternative technologies.

The people of Massachusetts, to give another example, passed laws identical to the old anti-apartheid legislation, banning state procurement from the military dictatorship in Burma. The WTO over-turned the democratic rights of these US voters in favour of the anti-democratic rights of Myanmar generallissimos.

But is this quite "the end of democracy and freedom" which Thomas Jefferson predicted? Our media comissars have put the case that the World Trade Organisation enhances global democracy. But how democratic is the WTO itself?

The dozen members of the WTO's trade disputes panel are unelected. All documents, transcripts and proceedings are secret. There is no required disclosure of conflict of interest. No media and no citizens can sit in and observe the proceedings. And there is no outside appeal or review available. Or to put it

another way, in the words of WTO president Michael Moore: "The World Trade Organisation is about as democratic as it gets."

The WTO lowered El Salvador's minimum wage fom 60 cents an hour to 36 cents an hour (at the request of a very famous high street clothing brand). If, however, the WTO really is "about as democratic as it gets", then we must assume that El Salvadoreans voted themselves a near 50% cut in wages. Probably they were dizzy with all the silly money and experienced Dave Stewart-type "paradise syndrome" problems. Perhaps, just one too many El Salvadoreans had woken up in a jacuzzi, stared dejectedly at empty champagne bottles bobbing on the foam, at the coked-out supermodel slumped across their satin sheets, and yearned for the simple life they used to know before the sixty cents craziness years. And so, smiling as they changed from Armani sharkskin suits into the dear, old overralls they used to wear, the people of El Salvador heard the polling day church bells ring... and each knew what to do.

Yeah, that's probably it.

On November 30, the aristocracy of banking institutions and moneyed incorporations were in town having bankrolled the WTO Seattle ministerial. In return the WTO's Seattle Host Organisation had promised them "the greatest possible interactions" with decision-making. The moneyed incorporations each had specific policies in mind when they bought a seat at the table. The American Electronics Association (AEA) for example — whose members include Microsoft, Intel and Motorola — wanted the WTO to ban an EU proposal to control electronic pollution. (When computer equipment is chucked out its toxic components leach into groundwater and are hard to store safely in landfills). The EU proposal suggested three things:

1. A modest 5% recycled rule for plastic components.

2. A ban on lead, cadmium, mercury, hexavelent chromium and halogenated flame retardants in computers.

3. The computer companies should pick up some of the cost for the pollution.

The AEA were pretty confident too. In its five year history the WTO has overturned every single environmental law that has come before it. Every single one. (By the way, the WTO is based in Geneva on a legal technicality: its courts would be illegal in London, Paris, Berlin or Tokyo because there is no public disclosure).

Well, the AEA didn't get what they wanted because the delegates couldn't get to the Convention Centre. The roads were blocked by heroic young women, old Quaker ladies and grown men dressed as turtles who held their ground in a hail of CS canisters and rubber bullets. Many received head wounds from baton-wielding soldiers and several small children were injured as I clambered over them to run away from the tear gas.

Inside the Four Seasons Hotel,

THE ROADS WERE BLOCKED BY HEROIC YOUNG WOMEN, OLD QUAKER LADIES AND GROWN MEN DRESSED AS TURTLES WHO HELD THEIR GROUND IN A HAIL OF CS CANISTERS AND RUBBER BULLETS. MANY RECEIVED HEAD WOUNDS FROM BATON-WIELDING SOLDIERS AND SEVERAL SMALL CHILDREN WERE INJURED AS I CLAMBERED OVER THEM TO RUN AWAY FROM THE TEAR GAS

Bill Clinton was telling the TV cameras of the world's biggest media corporations: "I wanna hear the views of those protestors." Outside the Four Seasons Hotel, there was a dawn-to-dusk curfew, No-Protest-Zone, lock-down of all public meetings, and suspension of civil liberties with martial law declared, and troops and tanks on the streets. This was all done so that the man whose middle name is Jefferson could talk about

"learning the lessons of the fall of the Berlin Wall". But he was very selective about which lessons to learn from the rotten collapse of the Soviet Union. He excluded, for example, the main one. The main lesson from the fall of the Berlin Wall is, clearly, that economic centralisation is both environmentally and democratically unsound. And yet what is corporate globalisation other than an attack on democracy and the environment in

the name of economic centralisation? (Check Ceefax for latest mega-merger). Well, OK, it's also an attack on the poor. The UN calculates that since the WTO was set up the least developed countries have lost $2 billion dollars in trade to the rich countries.

Never mind that. Still our pundits lapped up Clinton saying that taking global economic liberalisation to the max leads to freedom and democracy. This from the man who in 1994, while on a visit to China, ended the historic link between a country's human rights record and its favoured trading status. But then in 1995, after a threat to property rights – McDonald's leases and Mickey Mouse's royalties – Clinton's administration threatened China with $1 billion of trade restrictions. The Chinese government changed its policy to enforce intellectual property rights.

The night before in a packed Seattle Symphony Hall, Professor Susan George got to the heart of this contradiction: "If the Cold War was the Third, this is the Fourth World War, and it's a war being fought between private power and civil society."

Institutional corporate bias, however, made the news media unable to twist its melon round the idea of single issue movements finding common cause and realising that all our social and ecological problems have their roots in corporate globalisation. The news commissars' fixation on the small picture instead saw the WTO crisis in terms of different countries wanting different things. That was the problem. Nations squabbling. That's what it was all about. G&T anyone? If these cunts ever did their fucking job they might have got round to reading the WTO's own brochure on the benefits of joining the organisation which states:"Quite often governments use the WTO as a welcome external constraint on their policies: 'we can't do this because it would violate the WTO agreement'."

Hence, Desmond O'Rourke, President of Washington's Trade Department saying at a meeting of the Business Roundtable of CEO's in Seattle:

"We usually invite the Japanese to challenge one of our laws as a trade barrier, and they invite us to appeal against one of theirs."

They might even have read the director of Washington's Centre for International and Strategic Research put it another way:

"Nation states have already lost their role as meaningful units of participation in the global economy. In the final analysis what matters is how effectively the surrender of governments to the global markets is carried out."

And it was all looking like such a shoe-in to them as well. But standing on a dumpster in the middle of the 3rd and Pine cross-street, a headscarfed Puerto Rican B-girl leads a couple of hundred of the fifty thousand people on the street in a chant. "Ain't no power like the power of the people, 'cos the power of the people don't stop!"

The brilliant, millennial, epochal, Age of Extremes significance of Seattle was the emergence of a transnational resistance. Or "a resistance as transnational as capital" as the People's Global Action slogan goes.

And yet here in Britain we are still behind France, India, US and the rest of the world in mainstream public recognition of corporate globalisation as the biggest threat to democracy and human rights since the Second World War, of how it is the rollback of a century of social progress. But this, too, is beginning to change and change fast. (After all, what was the battle between Dobbo and Ken really about if not corporatism versus democracy? A choice between being subject or citizen?) As one Republican Senator who had previously been a WTO supporter said after meeting protestors in Seattle; "This is what democracy looks like."

But even though this rollback destroys lives, jobs, environment and human rights in the Northern Hemisphere, the suffering this system inflicts on the South is incalculable and incomparably worse. And we have a moral duty to bring about change through non-violent direct action and campaigning.

The next ten years are, I believe, the most crucial in human history. Across the world people are waking up to the fact that that even in the face of imminent ecological collapse capitalism cannot change its ways. We are poised between two choices.

Moby — corporate placeman and ugly poshboy — tells the world's interviewers that the World Trade Organisation is marvellous and the CEOs know what's best. Accept. Consume. Obey. Egyptian activist and writer Nawal El Saadawi is a woman who describes the alternative path:

"My cousin Zeinab looks old and sick, when I hold her hand I can feel horny knots and cracks caused by long years of labour with a hoe. She whispers: 'When I was a child I dreamed of escaping from this awful life but now I've lost hope. Now there are no jobs, and our debts keep growing. Now we eat fava beans canned in California instead of growing enough ourselves.' I see her eyes questioning... Can I tell her that 443 people (men) own as much wealth as half the people of the earth?... Can I tell her that the peoples of the world are learning how to work together and that many Seattles everywhere, in the North and South are my wish, and my hope?" ◉

THE NEXT TEN YEARS ARE, I BELIEVE, THE MOST CRUCIAL IN HUMAN HISTORY. ACROSS THE WORLD PEOPLE ARE WAKING UP TO THE FACT THAT THAT EVEN IN THE FACE OF IMMINENT ECOLOGICAL COLLAPSE, CAPITALISM CANNOT CHANGE ITS WAYS

RIGHT TO MOAN

Behind the glibly positive PR speak of modern
companies lies a reality of drones and sweatshops.
But, says BRIAN DEAN, the future really could be bright.
Pictures by MAX REEVES

Office work brings out the com-
plainer in me. The pointless
meetings, the unrealistic dead-
lines, the team-bonding horse-
shit, the long hours and lack of time
off — all fuel for my endless carping
and growing resentment. Most com-
pany managers, unfortunately, are
prejudiced against complainers; they
think we should be more grateful.

Their prejudice is due to a fear of
what we represent: the inevitable
collapse of the corporate manage-
ment worldview. The complainers,
you see, represent the future, where-
as those favoured by management —
the grateful and obedient — belong
to a sinking past. Company execu-
tives are fond of talk about "vision",
but the real vision is in employee
disgruntlement. Deep down, the
managers know this — that's why
they're afraid.

Complaining is taboo in backward societies, authoritarian regimes and modern corporations. Most well-informed people understand that complaints have a positive social function, and that dissent should not be buried. Employee discontent should be treated as a valuable resource. Instead, it's automatically dismissed or frowned upon. The reflex management response to staff disgruntlement is: "you should be glad you have a job". This is the medieval logic of lower expectations: no complaint is valid, since things can always be worse than they are, and we should always be grateful.

The lower expectations culture — working longer, for less pay, and being grateful — though encouraged in every corporate slave galley, is conspicuously absent from corporate public relations. The PR imagery, in fact, communicates utopian higher expectations, as expressed in slogans such as "we're aiming higher", "now even better", "the future is bright", etc. The company directors believe their own PR, and ignore rumours of discontent. Their boardrooms are cheerful places — full of optimistic talk, high-tech perspectives and futuristic management buzzwords.

But behind the executive vanity and PR cosmetics, industrial-age hierarchical bureaucracies and Fordist production-line methods continue to operate. Desks are still lined up in rows. Workplaces are still bleak, centralised production hives, and workers are still treated as insec-toid units of productivity. The high-pressure, traffic-jam work culture looks more like hell than utopia, but "business leaders" and politicians have no plans for change.

In November, 1999, call centre workers held a nationwide strike in protest against "a 19th century management style, impossible targets, stress and overwork". Protesters were particularly unhappy with the threat of disciplinary action against workers failing to complete calls within 285 seconds. The *Guardian* quoted a London School of Economics researcher as saying, "the possibilities for monitoring behaviour and measuring output in call centres is amazing to behold — the tyranny of the assembly line is but a Sunday school picnic compared with the control that management can exercise in computer telephony".

TV commercials give a false picture of call centres — they show relaxed employees taking customer calls in pleasant surroundings. The reality is thousands of workers packed together in giant sheds, relentlessly answering telephone calls to predetermined scripts. The term "sweatshop" comes to mind. Visits to the lavatory are rationed and monitored. One of the software packages commonly used by call centre managers is marketed as "Total Control Made Easy".

As we zoom into a bright new future, traffic congestion and parking space are becoming difficult problems. One far-sighted solution, devised by leading government thinkers, is to advise employees to give each other lifts to work. This lets the government off the hook, and dodges important questions such as:"must we always travel to work?", and: "must we always work?" A nationwide survey revealed that 60 percent of workers see their work as being of no use to society — so why not pay people to stay at

ONE OF THE SOFTWARE PACKAGES COMMONLY USED BY CALL CENTRE MANAGERS IS MARKETED AS "TOTAL CONTROL MADE EASY"

home enjoying themselves? Think of all the public benefits — less traffic, less stress, less pollution, lower medical costs and more people enjoying life.

The usual argument against utopian social policy is economic rectitude — that, as a society, we can't afford it. Buckminster Fuller, the utopian polymath, claimed that this economic argument is just a convenient excuse for government and corporate apathy. Fuller argued that the dominant economic worldview — that of "not enough to go around for everyone" — is seriously flawed, due to being based on outdated inventories of world resources.

In 1798, Thomas Malthus predicted that since world population was growing faster than known resources, poverty was inevitable for the majority of humanity. Malthus' forecast of ongoing scarcity and starvation had an enormous impact on economists and politicians. For many years, his prediction was cited as a reason not to give welfare to the poor — all attempts to remove poverty were seen as futile. Malthus was later discredited — his forecast was incorrect — but his gloomy influence left economics with a nickname: "the dismal science".

Fuller claimed that the Malthusian ideology of "lower expectations" still pervades mainstream politics and economics. Politicians continue to remind us that we must "make sacrifices", "cut back", "tighten our belts". Of course, it's always the poor people who make the sacrifices, not politicians or the well-off. Malthusianism shames the poor into accepting their situation with stoic resignation, rather than raising their expectations. If there isn't enough to go around, then you should be grateful for what you already have. Understandably, Malthus was very popular with the ruling classes.

Fuller spent much of his life challenging the Malthusian notion of "not enough to go around". He documented the technological trend of extracting more and more life-supporting wealth from less and less raw material. For example, he compared a modern communications satellite, weighing a fraction of a ton, with the 75,000 tons of transatlantic cable that it replaces and outperforms. This process of "more from less", he said, is accelerating faster than population growth and is removing scarcity from the planet.

Over the last few decades, Fuller's claims have been scientifically vindicated. Current inventories of world resources show overwhelming abundance of sustainable life-enhancing wealth — enough to maintain a high living standard for every person on the planet. Scarcity now has to be artificially induced to preserve an obsolete system of "haves" and "have-nots". Most people suspect as much when they hear that, for decades, governments have been paying farmers not to grow food.

Fuller regarded the "us versus

them" paranoid-competitive business world as a highly destructive combination of Malthus and Social Darwinism. Humanity's real mission, as he saw it, was not to fight competitors, but, "to make the world work for 100 percent of humanity in the shortest possible time through spontaneous cooperation without ecological offense or the disadvantage of anyone." In 1980, Fuller asserted his confidence in the practical realisation of this utopian vision:

POLITICIANS CONTINUE TO REMIND US THAT WE MUST "MAKE SACRIFICES", "CUT BACK", "TIGHTEN OUR BELTS". OF COURSE, IT'S ALWAYS THE POOR PEOPLE WHO MAKE THE SACRIFICES

BUSINESS PEOPLE THINK THEY HAVE THE "BOTTOM LINE" IN HARD-NOSED REALISM: WE MUST ALL COMPETE FOR SURVIVAL BY PECKING EACH OTHER TO DEATH LIKE DUCKS

"For the first time in history it is now possible to take care of everybody at a higher standard of living than any have ever known. Only ten years ago the more-with-less technology reached the point where this could be done. All humanity now has the option to become enduringly successful."

Meanwhile, back in bureaucratsville, Fuller's message is yet to be heard. Our reflexes have been conditioned to dismiss utopia as synonymous with the unrealistic or impossible. Corporations see technology as just another way to gain competitive advantage. Business people think they have the "bottom line" in hard-nosed realism: it's a brutal world and we must all compete for survival by pecking each other to death like ducks. And the function of advertising and PR is to put a warm, friendly gloss on all this, so the consumers don't die of fright before they get a chance to buy the products.

Fortunately, a minority of economic commentators are starting to echo Fuller's arguments. Charles Hampden-Turner, in *The Seven Cultures of Capitalism*, notes that "we, in the English-speaking economies, are still at war with each other, fighting for scraps of wealth in a scarcity contrived by our own beliefs." Hampden-Turner then suggests that we redefine capitalism as "a function of evolving co-operation, which spreads outward, pushing competition to its own boundaries" — a notion very much in tune with what Fuller was saying half a century ago.

Perhaps, as Fuller claimed, humans have a habit of trying all the stupid approaches before hitting on the intelligent ones. Unfortunately, this seems to be a slow process, with a time-lag of decades or centuries before stupidity is acknowledged. Those who plan to accelerate this process — the complainers, the dissenters — should be honoured, as they may be our best hope. ◉

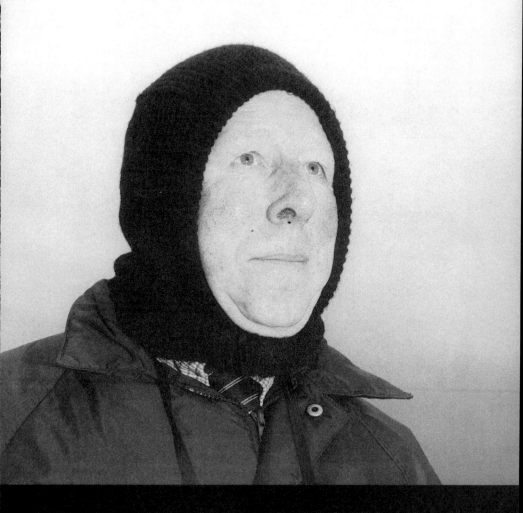

PLANE SPOTTERS

Photography and interview by **ADAM BROOMBERG**
and **OLIVER CHANARIN**

ROGER SEAR, 62.
RETIRED ENGINEER FROM RUGBY

IDLER: What is it that you find appealing about plane spotting?

ROGER: We Brits have always had a passion for collecting things. I also collect stamps, and I've got a friend who'll travel to the other side of the

earth just to find an unusual beer mat.

IDLER: What does plane spotting involve?

ROGER: There are two different types of plane spotter. Every plane has an identity number which will always stay with it no matter which airline it belongs to. Now I have my lists,   through my books, and cross out the

their chances of seeing a new one by recording the registrations.

Some spotters specialise. You get people who only collect the registration numbers of business jets, some

fascinated by all of them. Next Tuesday, I found out on the Internet that there's some Turkish fighters coming back through RAF Bildenhall in East Anglia. So I'm going over there

ROGER: Not anymore. I think with the Internet the hobby has got too advanced. In the past you just left home in the morning and didn't know what you were going to see.

IDLER: Is plane spotter a derogatory term?

ROGER: I don't think so. The sad thing is that a lot of younger people aren't taking it up because they get ridiculed for it. But it's a harmless hobby and there's incredible camaraderie between spotters.

IDLER: What does your wife think about your hobby?

ROGER: My first wife and I got

divorced on the grounds of incom-
patibility. She couldn't understand
my passion for spotting. So when I
married my second wife I offered to
give it up but she said she didn't
mind. It's just a hobby and when I
die she's going to collect all my
notebooks and bin them because

they're no good to anyone.

IDLER: Would you have liked to have
been a pilot?

ROGER: I'm colour blind. I wanted to
join the RAF but they wouldn't take
me. It's just life. ✆

*Call Aeroprint Tours 01703 610230 for info
on spotter trips to Frankfurt and Amsterdam*

Aloha!

The word "Tiki" entered common usage when Norwegian anthropologist Thor Heyerdal challenged armchair explorers with his "theories" of Polynesian migration in his book *Kon Tiki*. On his expedition of the same name he observed similarites in the stone statues of Peru and the Tiki god sculptures of the Polynesian islands. Apparently an old Marquesan cannibal related to him that Tiki – the first man – had come to them on a raft from a land far across the ocean. The Incan Sun God Kon Tiki Virakocha was hence the same Tiki worshipped by the Polynesians. As the Hawaiian islands became a tourist destination for Americans travelling by cruise ships at the turn of the last century, carved wooden Tiki god figurines along with Hawaiian shirts, ceramic hula dolls, and ukuleles captured the "aloha spirit": memories of paradise that holidaymakers took back home with them. The term "Hawaiiana" was coined.

The allure of the South Seas entered the public consciousness to such an extent that in 1934 Ernest Raymond Beaumont-Gantt – aka Don The Beachcomber – opened the first "themed" Polynesian bar. He served tropical rum cocktails, in a setting of floor-to-ceiling rattan, bamboo, and tapa cloth. Maritime junk hung from the rafters, and the walls were decorated with tribal masks and velvet paintings of semi-nude island beauties. There was even a fake tropical rainstorm which lashed down on tropical foliage at regular intervals. Bars and restaurants, following Don's blueprint, soon erupted all over America, and to a more limited extent throughout Europe and the Far East, mainly due to the efforts of Don's arch rival, Trader Vic.

By the advent of jet travel and mass tourism in the mid Fifties, the Hawaiian theme had infiltrated the American popular mainstream. The iconic Tiki god came to symbolise the culture. A figure of fun, a loose cross between the traditional Polynesian Tikis and abstract sculptural forms and cartoon characters such as The Jetsons and The Flintstones, the Tiki was a modern primitive artform. Tiki-themed motel complexes, bowling alleys, apartment blocks, and golf courses, not to mention drive thrus and boutiques, sprang up. Custom-designed Tiki cocktail mugs became the calling card for each Tiki restaurant and bar, usually given away with the house cocktail. And the Tiki image began to appear on record sleeves as new forms of music such as "exotica" and

"surf" were born. Martin Denny provided the soundtrack to the cocktail haze of many a backyard Luau, while Dick Dale and the Surfaris played wild instrumental rock-'n'roll. Tiki remains an enduring icon for surfers everywhere, representing the leisure-orientated lifestyle of the beachcomber, the quest for the ultimate wave, and an endless summer.

But by the early Seventies the Tiki wave broke on the rocky shore of an emergent counter culture, with the Vietnam conflict dampening the optimism of the Fifties and Sixties. The Tiki mugs and Hawaiian shirts were stored away in the attic. It was these curiosities which began to infiltrate my lifestyle during the Nineties. A younger generation, whose parents surfed the first wave of Tiki, now pursued a modern beachcomber aesthetic, searching for forgotten treasures of an ancient mythical religion, customising Tiki's pop heritage, and transforming it into a spirit of resistance to the manufactured slickness of contemporary consumer culture.

I have found my new God, and it's called Tiki. Enjoy this exploration of my world. ◉

CONTENTS

The Sounds of Tiki

Jay Strongman takes you on a tour of tikitastic tunes

Tiki music is a strange hybrid — an esoteric, multi-headed creature that has its origins in the lounge bars and bachelor pads of Fifties America but which has now risen phoenix-like to take on a new life in the 21st century. Tiki music was the original escapist soundtrack of the post-war era. Its primitive mix of watered down latin rhythms, lounge bar sensibilities and Polynesian percussion became the music of choice for the generation too old for rock 'n' roll but young enough to swing with Sinatra's Rat Pack. Bizarre instruments, strange chants, bird calls and the sounds of crashing surf became *de rigeur* on these "easy listening" albums as did the explicit sexuality of their covers. The exotica albums generally featured photos of pretty, nude or semi nude female models in a variety of come hither poses and against a variety of fake tropical backgrounds.

Fast forward to the Nineties and a growing number of hip young Americans began rejecting the MTV diet of house, hip hop and grunge in search of something more stylised. Although Sixties surf music attracted a completely different audience to the one then listening to exotica, by the mid Nineties it made perfect sense for the two to go together. Both were very underground and both were centred emotionally in sun, sea and surf. The Tiki Tones, The Blue Hawaiians, The Bomboras and many others began lacing their high octane brand of Sixties influenced surf instrumentals with both the imagery and the sounds of exotica. The booming West Coast lounge scene's pre-occupation with Tiki also meant that reissues of Martin Denny, Arthur Lyman, Les Baxter and dozens of other favourites began appearing in record stores throughout the US. So it was that Tiki music began its second incarnation, an incarnation that is poised to sweep the world... ◉

Tiki Tracks

EXOTICA – MARTIN DENNY

Martin Denny is the Big Daddy of Tiki music. In a string of classic albums he defined the exotica sound with his gentle Latin-inspired grooves, bird calls and an armoury of primitive persussion instruments. His cover of Les Baxter's

"Quiet Village" complete with jungle noises became a million seller in the United States and is still considered by many to be the quintessential exotica tune. His live performances in Hawaii throughout the late Fifties and early Sixties have become the stuff of legend. His other albums like Primitiva, Forbidden Island and Quiet Village are

all excellent examples of the genre vibe. A true legend, Denny is still alive and well.

>

The Lava Lounge

JOIN US IN OUR FANTASY TIKI BAR, AS WE SIP MAI TAIS
SURROUNDED BY BAMBOO AND SUNSETS. FEEL THE
STIRRINGS OF A FERTILITY GOD IN YOUR LOINS AS THE
UKULELES BEGIN TO PLAY...

ILLUSTRATION: SHAG PHOTOGRAPHY: JULIA HEMBER
STYLING: NJ HODGKINSON MAKE-UP: WENDY OLIVER
HAIR: RICHARD SCORER ASSISTED BY CHERYL POULTER

JIGGERY-POKERY: GAVIN PRETOR-PINNEY
ART DIRECTION: JONNY HALIFAX

IKI – TIKI HAWAIIAN SHIRT
FROM LA ROCKA, CONTACT
LLOYD@LAROCKA.NDO.CO.UK

RICHARD – RED CUMMERBUND,
BOW TIE SET AND ARMBANDS
ALL FROM LA ROCKA. SHIRT
AND TROUSERS, MODEL'S OWN

ZOE - BAMBOO PRINT DRESS FROM LA
ROCKA. SHOES, FLASHBACK

APEMAN - GREEN TONIC SUIT, MODEL'S
OWN. RED POLONECK FROM LA ROCKA

KAREN - PINK JUMPSUIT, MODEL'S OWN

LLOYD - SHRINER SUIT,
SHIRT AND FEZ,
MODEL'S OWN. CUMMER-
BUND AND BOW TIE SET
FROM LA ROCKA

DAN — HAT, SUIT AND
TIE FROM LA ROCKA.
SHIRT, MODEL'S OWN

JONNY GUITAR - BLACK LEVIS STA-PREST AND BABY BLUE IOLANI EXECUTIVE SHIRT, MODEL'S OWN

PRESIDENT BONGO - 3/4 LENGTH SLEEVE BABY BLUE IOLANI EXECUTIVE SHIRT, MODEL'S OWN

COLETTE - BRA AND LEI, MODEL'S OWN. GRASS SKIRT FROM FANCY DRESS SHOP

BABS – SHIMMY SHIFT BY BABZOTICA TO
ORDER ON 020 7713 0460. JEWELLERY,
MODEL'S OWN

LLOYD – BERET, BLACK POLONECK,
GLASSES AND MEDALLION, MODEL'S OWN

RICHARD – LILAC TIKI COCKTAIL JACKET
TO ORDER FROM BABZOTICA

Bora-Bora decor

HOW tO tUrN yOUr HOME iNtO a tiki WONDErLaND BY JOSH COLLiNS

Fed up with the dreaded Swedish style and techno mod? Then why not turn your own home into a south pacific paradise?

The ideal place to start is the bar area, as this is the true centre of any tiki activity (hanging around, playing ukuleles, hip waggling and drinking lots of Mai Tais). Lofts are great as the sloping rooves and beams make them easily convertible into a Tahitian coconut-thatched shack. Conservatories, terraces and patios with the addition of some palms, bamboo furniture, flaming torches and wood carvings will create your own little corner of Bora-Bora.

So with imagination, a few readies and the following tips, create your own South Seas decor adventure.

NAUTICAL JUNK is key. Any self-respecting Hawaiian garden or house is filled with drift wood, shells, old buoys, broken surfboards, canoes, potted plants, empty bottles — basically anything that can be picked up on an island beach. A walk along the Thames always yields at least some good driftwood. The Tiki staple Giant Clams are can no longer be imported, but old specimens can still be found in more salubrious markets. Human skulls, real or fake are also a good addition.

CARVINGS and masks should adorn every available surface. London is a good source of African and Indonesian stuff, though they aren't strictly Tiki but make a good filler item. Hawaiian artefacts are more common in America and can be picked up off ebay.com or ordered direct from Oceanic Arts (the main global suppliers of Tiki stuff who've worked on Hollywood movies since the Sixties and have supplied decor to every Tiki establishment in the world).

Alternatively, passable Tiki can be carved at home quite easily. A couple of eye slits and a rough mouth hacked out of a bit of tree trunk and you're there. Or a breeze block can be carved into a Moari or Easter Island head using just a saw. Those

Tiki Tracks

BLUE HAWAII – ELVIS PRESLEY

Riding the beach movie wave of the early Sixties — awash with palm trees, Hawaiian shirts, and pretty girls — Blue Hawaii is a chesseball classic. However, the soundtrack album is a superb collection of Elvis tracks. Traditional Hawaiian melodies suffused with trademark Elvis rock'n'roll make the perfect accompaniment to the over-saturated technicolor scenes of Hawaiian paradise, American style. The album features straight up Elvis rockers alongside the classic ballad "Can't Help Falling In Love". But the real gem is the

title track, originally recorded by Bing Crosby for the 1937 film Waikiki Wedding.

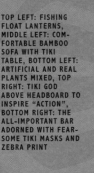

TOP LEFT: FISHING FLOAT LANTERNS, MIDDLE LEFT: COMFORTABLE BAMBOO SOFA WITH TIKI TABLE, BOTTOM LEFT: ARTIFICIAL AND REAL PLANTS MIXED, TOP RIGHT: TIKI GOD ABOVE HEADBOARD TO INSPIRE "ACTION", BOTTOM RIGHT: THE ALL-IMPORTANT BAR ADORNED WITH FEARSOME TIKI MASKS AND ZEBRA PRINT

RITUAL OF THE SAVAGE — LES BAXTER

Although Martin Denny became the biggest name in exotica, Les Baxter was the man behind the man. Denny made it no secret that he was heavily influenced by Baxter's compositions and arrangement, and "Ritual..." was the blueprint that Denny adopted as he set out to create his own sound. Using the lush arrangements that served him well in his career as a Hollywood composer, Baxter created a heady mix of soft jazz, exotic percussion and haunting melodies on this groundbreaking album. His original version of "Quiet Village" went on to become one of

the most covered somgs in history. The cover art was equally influential.

in possession of a router or chainsaw can start hacking into any bit of wood or furniture they can find to produce their own versions of South Seas art. A couple of cowrie shells for eyes and you have a fitting tribute to your honourable ancestors.

TIKI MUGS are the home of a true cocktail and no Tiki hut would be complete without a little collection of them. Coconuts, shells and bamboo sections also make fine drinking vessels witha bit of a varnish.

PLANTS Tropical plants have long been available in this country. Cheese plants, Tree Ferns, Orchids, Gingers Bamboos and Ti plants are particularly suitable. A few fake plants and plastic fruit mixed in with the real ones can help your garden bloom all year long. Similarly a bit of fake fauna can really bring a potential jungle to life, perhaps a plastic lizard scuttling across your verandah, or a beautiful butterfly alighting on your orchid? The more adventurous Tiki Fiend would consider a parrot, iguana or even some hermit crabs as suitable pets. Tropical fish tanks always look great.

LIGHTS should be plentiful. To recreate the days before electric lights reached the islands, as many low-wattage, well-shaded bulbs as possible should be used. Fairy lights hidden away in the vegetation or hung amongst the rafters are a good way of doing this. Anything glass wood or bamboo can be used as a shade, but particularly ideal are old fish traps and glass fishnet floats (Lasco £70). Even a puffer fish can be used.

BAMBOO is the staple Pacific construction material and should be used as much as possible, preferably to cover every trace of western construction material. Most garden centres supply Bamboo and reed fencing which can be easily tacked onto walls, bars and cupboards. The Cane shop on Blackstock Road stocks several types of matting and all sizes of bamboo cane, but the best approach is to order your bamboo from the Philipino centre in Romney Marsh.

DOORS should ideally be Jouvred, as this is standard in the tropics. Spotlights can be shone through them to create the illusion of sunlight streaming in. Bamboo or reed blinds also act as great dividers. ☉

Thanks to Lloyd at Johnsons, Otto at Tiki News, Oceanic Arts, Sven Tiki, Trader Vics

Tiki Tracks

JUNGLE EXOTICA — VARIOUS
The opening track of this compilation starts with crazed laughter and the menacing taunt; "I am the voice of the jungle!", followed by more lunatic laughter over what sounds like Martin Denny on industrial strength LSD

attempting the Munsters theme tune. Primitive stuff. This is a potent Latin garage rock'n'roll soul surf voodoo cocktail party, with no rules other than make it ridiculous. Psychotic bird calls, voodoo chanting, and monkey rants, in between occasional bursts of gibberish. It picks up on exotic themes explored by Les Baxter and Martin Denny and

give them a teenage mutant B-movie twist. Music to get naked and dance to.

The Dons

Tiki News magazine has single-handedly created the Tiki revival. Founder Otto Von Stroheim is a graphic designer and DJ. His partner in Tiki, Sven Kirsten, is a film maker. His book, *In Search of Tiki*, is published by Taschen.

How did Tiki News get started?

Otto: It started in January 1995 as a newsletter. Sven had his book formulated but was having a hard time publicising it. So we made a deal that he would write for *Tiki News* and I would print anything he wrote.

Is Tiki News a lifestyle magazine?

Otto: It is now, as a lot of readers are creating their own in-house Tiki bars and wearing Tiki fashions, having Tiki weddings, throwing Tiki parties, making Tiki art. For decades this sort of activity had ceased to exist.

Sven: I call Tiki one of the last unexploited facets of American pop culture. I think the enduring qualities of Tiki style are its weirdness, its sense of humour, its "bad taste" power, its irreverence and perceived political incorrectness. All of these have a liberating and thus inspiring effect on creative people.

Is it your aim to make Tiki fashionable, or does it need to remain marginal to retain its appeal?

Otto: While we will ride the current Tiki wave to its crest, we'll also be there in the soup when it crashes a year later.

Sven: Tiki deserves to join the gallery of pop culture icons, and once its discovery has been celebrated enough, it will settle in, but the world will be a richer place.

Does Tiki today have anything to do with the South Seas Islands?

Sven: Well, more with the South Sea Islands of the mind. Polynesia is an enduring metaphor for paradise on earth, and although we know that this does not exist, we like to play with its clichés.

Go to *www.tikinews.com*

TABOO
THE LEGEND OF PELE
– ARTHUR LYMAN

Arthur Lyman was the young pretender to Martin Denny's throne. As a vibes player for Denny's original band, Lyman learned his craft from the master and then struck out on his own. Very similar in sound to Denny, Lyman had a slightly younger, more percussive approach and kept his sound closer to the Hawaiian Islands. For their covers alone these albums stand out, and the quality of the music makes them essentials for any Tiki vinyl collection. Check out the groovy version of Dick Dale's surfer classic "Misirlou" on the TABOO album  for one of the earliest links between surf instrumentals and Tiki.

Mix it up!

TOP COCKTAILS FOR RUM BUMS AND JUICY LUCYS!

MAI TAI

1 1/2 oz fresh lime juice
1/2 oz Curacao
1/4 oz orgeat syrup
1/4 oz rock candy syrup
1 oz aged Jamaican rum
1 oz Martinique rum

Serve in old-fashioned double glass filled with crushed ice and spent lime shell. Garnish with mint sprig.

MAGIC MONKEY JUICE

Invented by Dick Bradsell

25ml Wray & Nephews overproof white rum
25ml Hill's Absinth
25ml Wood's overproof dark rum
A few dashes angostura bitters
25ml lemon juice
100ml pineapple juice
5 tsp grenadine
Splash of juice from a mango, guava or similar exotic fruit

Shake like hell with ice. Strain over fresh ice. Pour. Grate a load of nutmeg over the top.

"If that won't send you mad, nothing will," says Dick.

FOGCUTTER

2 oz fresh lemon juice
1 oz orange juice
1/2 oz orgeat syrup
2 oz light Puerto Rican rum
1 oz brandy
1/2 oz gin
1/2 oz sweet sherry

Shake everything — except sherry — with ice cubes. Pour into tall Tiki mug. Add more ice cubes to fill. Float sherry on top of drink.

DREAMY WAHINE

1 oz dark Jamaican rum
1/2 oz Amaretto liquor
2 oz milk from freshly cracked coconuts
1/2 coconut cream
1/2 oz fresh lime juice

Serve in a cocktail glass with the hair of a coconut, a maraschino cherry, a pineapple slice and a grass skirt.

Cocktails courtesy of Beachbum Berry's Grog Log *by Jeff Berry and Annene Kaye, SLG Publishing $9.95*

TIM TWELVES

Tiki Tracks

EDEN'S ISLAND – EDEN AHBEZ

Eden Ahbez was the missing link between the swinging lovers of the pre-Beatle era and the flower-power of the mid-Sixties. A hippy before the word was invented, Ahbez was years ahead of his time in his rejection of materialism and embracing of the natural world. In 1946 he gave Nat King Cole a song called "Nature Boy" which sold over a million copies but then waited almost fifteen years before going into the recording studio himself. The result was the very wonderful EDEN'S

ISLAND which was released on surf label Del-Fi. A tribute to Pacific mysticism.

Tikinformer

THE BOOKS, THE WEBSITES, THE MAGS. NOW START a tiki CLUB IN YOUR OWN area!

LITERATURE

Kon Tiki by Thor Heyerdahl
In Search of Tiki by Sven A. Kirsten (Taschen)
Tiki News magazine tikinews.com
Taboo: The Art Of Tiki
ed. Martin McIntosh
Hawaiiana, The Best of Hawaiian design by Mark Blackburn
Aloha Spirit, Hawaiian Art and Popular Design by Douglas Congdon Martin
Beachbum Berry's Grog Log by Jeff Berry and Annene Kaye, 3755 Aloha Street, LA, CA 90027-3301 USA
Hawaiian Shirt Design, Nancy N Shiffer
House Industries Magazine houseindustries.com

ART

Shag shag-art.com
Watts www.illbilly.demon.co.uk / wattscandy@aol.com
Mysterious Exotica mysteriousex@hotmail.com
Mark Ryden markryden.com

MUSIC

The Temple of Denny at www.chaoskitty.com
Intoxica records Portobello Rd. London
Sounds that swing Camden Town, London
Magnum 500 magnum500.com

FASHION

Johnson's /La Rocka - lloyd@larocka.ndo.co.uk
Babzotica exoticen@dircon.co.uk / Detra Venus

STUFF

Last Chance saloon lastchancesaloon@demon.co.uk
Tiki trader tikitrader.com

BARS

Trader Vic's at The London Hilton

MOVIES

Perverella
Swingers
Blue Hawaii
Paradise Hawaiian Style
It's A Wonderful Life

TIM TWELVES

TALKING PIPES EP – MAGNUM 500

Magnum 500 rock. No messing, no frills, and taking no prisoners. Conrad, Dean, Chris, and Matt show a fondness of original exotica with their sleeve artwork reminiscent of Les Baxter's classic RITUAL OF THE SAVAGE, bearing the legend; The Forbidden Sounds Of... Magnum 500. Hawaiian shirts, Elvis hairdos, and cartoon Tikis and hotrods all play a big part in their visual melting pot – and the music: straight up psycho surf with extra flames to go. Like the soundtrack to the coolest biker flicks, and the most extreme surf movies – they even have original Sixites drag racing commentary cutting in over the music. Tunes that speak speed, excitement and danger

TIKI

REVOLUTIONARY MANIFESTO

We demand the abolition of serious culture in the name of TIKI.

We demand that all world leaders are simultaneously deposed, and that a new TIKI world order is declared.

We demand that Martin Denny be crowned King, and shall reign from Tahiti.

We demand that all world religions be abolished and TIKI becomes a universal god of fun, recreation and leisure.

We demand a TIKI based education, becoming the sole subject of study for all school children aged 12 and above.

We demand that TIKI shrines are erected everywhere for the worship of fun, frivolity and the ridiculous.

We demand free fresh fish and and fruit cocktails on the National Heath Service.

We demand the disbandment of all armies and police forces and their replacement by the Freedom loving forces of TIKI.

We demand that Tahiti be declared international capital of the world, - everyone be entitled to a free holiday there once a year.

We demand that all our demands are met.

We demand the Millenium Dome be turned into a full size Hawaiian island theme park.

We demand that Bamboo and coconut become subsidised building materials replacing bricks and mortar.

2000
JON-TIKI

URI GELLER SOLVES HISTORY'S GREATEST MYSTERIES

Conduct psychic investigations from the comfort of your armchair. Or even your bed. By **URI GELLER**

The CIA's remote viewing programme, Project Stargate, trained dozens of intelligence agents to project their minds to distant points on the globe. Reports have trickled out, detailing the kinds of tests developed by government scientists who wanted to make psi a major cold war weapon. Former American agent David Moorhouse published a bestseller revealing how remote viewing — a technique for inwardly "seeing" what exists at specific map references — was regarded by the CIA for a time as the perfect complement to satellite pictures.

In the Eighties, the Agency experimented with glimpses of the future. Instead of asking their mind-spies to focus on places like psychic satellites, they suggested a trip into the years ahead. The reports were alarming. Each viewer said the world of the future was a blackened, blasted place, in the grip of a nuclear winter or an ecological catastrophe.

The accuracy of remote viewing, when used to report on known sites in the current time-frame, has been established at around 85 per cent. We can only pray that the psi spies' vision of the future fall into that narrow band of inaccuracies. Humanity retains a 15 per cent window of hope.

The *Idler* asked me to conduct a remote viewing investigation in the other direction — into the past.

HOW DID MARILYN MONROE DIE?

The facts are simple – an overdose of sleeping tablets, a desperate phone call that was ignored, a naked and bloated body on a dishevelled bed, the sexiest icon in movie history dead at 36. The motives are anything but simple.

Los Angeles County medical examiner Thomas Noguchi recorded the cause of death as probable suicide. Marilyn, depressed that her career was fading, OD'd on barbiturates. The name of Bobby Kennedy, the President's younger brother, was being whispered long before assassin Sirhan Sirhan shot him dead. Marilyn was mistress to both JFK and Bobby – but I believe it was another of her lovers, the mobster Sam Giancana, who orchestrated her death. His hit men forced lethal doses of chemicals into her, probably while she slept under normal sedation.

Marilyn's life is a distressingly clouded story. She felt her way through every episode, responding with emotions rather than lucid thoughts and words. It is easy to share her pain, and that's a major reason why her image has always enjoyed huge appeal. But the last hours of her life are not a happy place to visit.

My mission: to solve the unsolvable, decode the indecipherable, discover the unknowable, without moving a muscle. It would be the ultimate test of the mind's superiority over the body.

Even if your psychic abilities have always lain dormant, you too can probe these unsolved mysteries. Light a candle in a quiet, darkened room, and gaze into the flame. Frame clearly in your mind the question you wish to investigate – it's no use looking for answers if you don't know the question. Now relax, and breathe steadily. Enjoy the flow of oxygen into your lungs, steady and rhythmic.

Let your mind flow out to the flame. Feel your thoughts drawn to the fire like moths. Let them flutter into the fire, and repeat that question to yourself. Watch the images that flash in your mind, but do not stop to recapture them – there will be time to go back and make sense of what you've seen later. For now, just let the past unfold in broken images on your internal TV set... and perhaps unravel an unsolved mystery.

I do not believe the CIA ordered her killing, with or without the connivance of the Kennedys. Giancana was a jealous and sadistic man, and he had motive enough to snuff out the Candle in the Wind. Bobby Kennedy, however, made certain that his own tracks were covered.

WHERE IS LORD LUCAN?

URI SOLVES IT

He's dead. But despite a High Court ruling that, after bludgeoning his children's nanny to death with a lead pipe, the ruined gambler drowned himself in the English Channel in 1974, I do not believe Lucan died till the early Nineties. I did not meet the man. But in his case, unlike Hollis', photos are easy to find. I use a traditional psychic method called psychometry, placing his picture on my desk and letting my eyes drift out of focus on it. The pictures that flicker on the TV screen behind my eyes, inside my skull, give me clues to the true story.

Lucan lived for 17 or 18 years after the murder. He planned his "suicide" in a desperate throw of the dice and then, abetted by at least two friends, fled the country. A new life in Australia failed abysmally, with more crimes committed, but his friends held good, as nothing else in his life ever had. The Englishman, unrecognisably scarred and dissipated, died a hopeless alcoholic in Canada.

WHO KILLED JILL DANDO?

URI SOLVES IT

On the day Jill died, I phoned friends and insisted: "A Balkan hit man did this." Nothing in the conflicting and puzzling evidence which has emerged has made me doubt my intuition.

Jill, with her TV appeal which helped raise £10 million for Kosovar refugees, had enraged mercenaries and fascistic hit squads. And the callousness of the shooting, with a pistol's muzzle at the back of a beautiful, unsuspecting woman's head, clearly indicates the killer was hardened to death.

This was not the act of a insane fan – a fan would have faltered and sought Jill's recognition. It was not the act of a professional – professionals do not make their escape by bus. Only a veteran of the Balkan fields of death, a killer who had blown out the brains of countless victims at point-blank range, just as Hitler's SS murderers despatched whole communities of Jews, could have done this vile deed.

DID ALIENS REALLY LAND AT ROSWELL?

URI SOLVES IT

The Roswell evidence has been frequently discredited, and yet it keeps resurfacing. It's almost as if someone wanted to smear the whole UFO movement... The alien autopsy video was definitely faked. The purported crash evidence – a spaceship, weird materials, bodies – was never put on public show. Lieutenant Colonel Philip Corso, the US government investigator, who broke cover, 50 years after the alleged UFO wreck in the New Mexico desert, died suddenly.

While we argue over a 1947 mix of myth and hokum, extraordinary findings are ignored every week. Hundreds of hours of video footage taken in Mexico City two years ago, some shot by TV crews, revealed UFOs in close-up detail. Weeks later, thousands of Arizonans witnessed a triangular craft the size of three football fields gliding silently over their homes. In

Israel, investigator Barry Chamish has collected metallic elements from UFO landing sites which are literally like nothing else on Earth. And at Harvard University, psychology professor John Mack has interviewed hundreds of alien encounter witnesses, and argues we must learn more about how the human mind perceives reality before we write off the ETs.

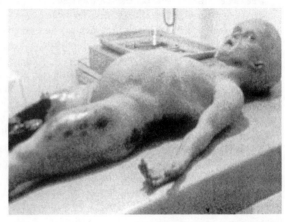

HOW DO CROP CIRCLES APPEAR?

The majority are witless hoaxes, and experienced circle-hunters can spot them immediately. The stalks are crushed, there are footprints and even cigarette butts, and the shapes are clumsy. This isn't scepticism – it is vandalism.

URI SOLVES IT

True circles are different. The stalks are weighed down, not snapped. The geometry is perfect, and the energy that bristles inside the formation can often be measured on traditional electronic equipment – it also causes many cameras and camcorders to fail. I once experimented by bending a spoon in a Wiltshire circle, and the bowl almost exploded from the handle.

Many witnesses say strange lights seem to hover over the fields, emitting a loud drone as the circles are created. This has been observed for at least 350 years, according to a pamphlet published in Civil War times, and this year circles have been found in remote Canadian wheat fields and Japanese Zen gardens. There's good reason to suppose crop circles are a natural phenomena... except for their increasing complexity. Natural forces cannot draw windmills and Mandlebrot sets, seashell whorls and religious symbols.

I am forced to the conclusion that something intelligent sometimes wields Earth's energies. Whether that intelligence is humanity's, or the planets, or belongs to something beyond the planet – I have not yet decided.

IS THERE LIFE ON MARS?

URI SOLVES IT

Certainly there is bacteriological life, surviving in frozen conditions as hostile as Earth's Antarctic. But there is also single-cell life on Jupiter's moon Europa, in the rings of Saturn and perhaps on comets such as Halley's too. The absorbing mystery is this: does Mars harbour intelligent life?

Many UFOlogists - who do not believe Mars is now inhabited - say the Red Planet must once have been the base of an advanced species. They point to the face at Cydonia, a massive construction in the shape of human – or superhuman – features. Are those landmarks arranged by coincidence or design?

Mars has been without liquid water for a billion years, and I believe it has never been properly inhabited. However, it is fascinating that four Mars probes were lost during ten weeks in 1999. Numerous videos relayed from space appear to show UFO activity, including 1996 space shuttle footage which revealed hundreds of small orbs dancing attendance on a satellite being towed on a twelve mile tether.

Our space probes appear to be attracting attention. If Nasa persists with its plans for a manned mission to Mars, we will have to find out whether these probes are being lost to accident – or enemy action.

WHAT HAPPENED TO SHERGAR?

Shergar was the tragic victim of man's tendency to despise what he cannot control. Trained to a level of perfection never attained by any other horse,

Shergar was kidnapped by IRA gangsters who thought they knew about horses. When they discovered Shergar was a very different kind of creature to the average hunter, they panicked. Shouting at the terrified animal and trying to throw a bag over his head, they drove him into a frenzy. His leg was broken in the horse box, a few hundred yards from the Aga Khan's stables on that night in February 1983. The thugs were relieved to seize the excuse to do the only thing they did efficiently – to kill.

I have always believed the terrorists were in foreign pay. This was not their usual protection-racket blundering. I feel the paymasters were probably Far Eastern gamblers, bent on subtly injuring the animal and returning him to race again well below his best.

WAS ROGER HOLLIS THE "FIFTH MAN"?

Someone tipped off Kim Philby. As the net closed on Britain's most dangerous traitor, the KGB sent an agent to Beirut to warn their mole to burrow deep underground. Philby escaped – but how did the KGB know he had been compromised?

Spy catcher Peter Wright claimed Roger Hollis, then head of MI5, was the double agent. But Wright's stories are seen mostly as moonshine – friends in Smiley's twilight world tell me the "Spycatcher" debacle was engineered by Mrs Thatcher's government, to plant false information while appearing to hush it up.

Hollis made an unlikely mole, compared to loudmouth extroverts like Guy Burgess and Donald Maclean, or sad bunglers like Anthony Blunt. Hollis was efficient, ruthless and commanded the respect of spies. And he did not lack courage – when he saw the fingers of suspicion pointed at him, he did not bluster but called in a spy catcher of his own, Ronald Symonds, to clear his name.

Photographs of Hollis do not seem to exist. But one event in 1999 has given us a clear picture of Britain's old-school-tie spies – the unmasking of Melita Norwood. Evidently a secretary can be as valuable a mole as a Director General.

Was "M" a Soviet agent? I doubt it. But Miss Moneypenny...

WHAT HAPPENED TO THE WHITE FIAT IN THE DIANA CAR CRASH?

URI SOLVES IT

There is nothing feigned in the grief of Al Fayed for the loss of his eldest son, Dodi. I have told him more than once that his determination to uncover the truth about the crash in the Pont de L'Alma tunnel could destroy him. Al Fayed's theories seem unbelievable – but not impossible. They border on obsession, though that is easy to forgive.

The British preoccupation with secrecy clouds this investigation, and makes it more painful, both for Dodi's family and for Diana's sons. Of course the British secret services were observing the Princess of Wales and the press pack that hounded her – some paparazzi were in the pay of MI5, reporting everything they heard and saw. The mystery of payments to drunk driver Henri Paul's bank account also suggests he was in the employ of someone other than Al Fayed.

Amid all this, the white Fiat is a red herring. Diana's Mercedes did clip the car in front, which was also certainly driven by a drunk driver too. That driver's reaction was understandable – even before the identity of the people in the Mercedes were released, the Fiat had been dumped in a field 250km away and burned to a shell. The wreckage was towed and crushed within a week.

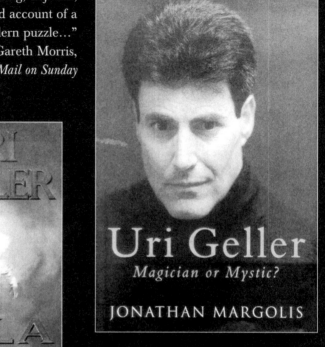

WHAT IS BIGFOOT?

URI SOLVES IT

It seems impossible that humanoids could live without detection in the mountains of America and China, because we urban humans regard ourselves as so utterly dominant on Earth. Yet we have built our towns on just a fraction of the planet's surface. The vast woodlands of America are unmapped and featureless, as any Blair Witch fan knows.

A nocturnal, intelligent ape which had learned to fear man over tens of thousands of years could probably elude capture — especially as there are no official programs to snare or even trap the Bigfoot. Game hunters report sightings ten or twelve times a year, from Florida to Alaska, and the beast's call was recorded in Columbiana County, Ohio, near the Ohio River.

The 1967 film shot by Roger Patterson at Bluff Creek, California, of a female Bigfoot lop-

ing away from the waters edge has frequently been dismissed as a hoax, though sceptics are at a loss to explain away Patterson's plaster casts of her deep footprints. Hollywood special effects artist John Chambers, who created the ape men of Planet of the Apes, has studied the footage, and commented on the natural ripple of the creature's leg muscles. Could he have faked something like this? Chambers answered: "I was good... but not that good."

Uri Geller's novels Dead Cold *and* Ella *are published by Headline at £5.99.*
Mind Medicine *is published by Element at £20.*
Visit Uri at www.urigeller.com and e-mail him at urigeller@compuserve.com

MUTANT GENIUS

GREG ROWLAND examines the early days of the Marvel misfit mutant adolescents, the X-Men

I was nine years old when my school sent me to The Society for Gifted Children. They were fed up with me finishing projects too early and correcting my teacher's numerous factual errors. My teacher, who is now dead, used to send me outside when I finished my work ahead of schedule. My mutant powers — to navigate through realms of infinite banality at super-speed — were later rewarded when I became a consultant to the advertising industry. But back in '76 I was sent outside to paint the walls. My powers were useless, as though Hinchley Wood Primary School was built of Kryptonite.

So, because the teachers couldn't deconstruct a little boy who was both bright and naughty, they tried to offload the problem on this Gifted Children society. I went along for the society's open day and quickly realised that I was seriously outclassed. A bespectacled three year-old read out the Latin names of plants from a book. One eight year-old had built a computer out of Lego. I consoled myself with the fact that they were emotionally stunted — having put all their effort into just being clever, they'd neglected all the other aspects of their personality. This was made clear to me when a

little boy asked me down from the climbing frame. "Hello," he said. "What's your gift?" For the first and last time in my life I didn't know what to say. I was just appalled. But I did remember to say to my Dad that I never ever wanted to hang out with those kids ever again.

I had been cheated really. I had in my mind an entirely different School for Gifted Youngsters. It was run by Professor Xavier and you needed to be a super-powered mutant to gain entrance. Yes, my friends, for it is true. The day I was invited to the Society for Gifted Children was the day I thought I was joining the X-Men.

I never did join the X-Men but I did give them a pretty good run for their money and often guided them telepathically with such psychic subtlety that they never even realised that I was helping them. But this summer, the X-Men leave the cultural ownership of the comic-book reading cognoscenti and meet the big bad world of corporate media hype full on. The X-Men is this year's big Hollywood movie. My psychic connection with the old gang will be well and truly severed. They belong to the world of PR and merchandising now. But once, many years ago, the X-Men were all mine.

The X-Men were born in 1963, sired by the mighty pen of he who is Stan Lee, the supreme creative genius of the superhero genre. Stan was really on a roll in the early Sixties. He had revolutionised comic books with the creation of the Fantastic Four, Spiderman, The Hulk, Iron Man, Daredevil and Doctor Strange. Yet still he strafed onwards, ever onwards. Marvel Comics was still a bit player compared to the gargantuan rival DC Comics, who owned Superman and Batman. Stan wanted to rule the comic book world. And, by the end of the Sixties, this mission was accomplished.

It didn't take a marketing genius to realise that teenagers might be popular with comic book reading public, and that superhero teams would likewise shift pulp in a big way. The superhero team offered a clear buying proposition. You got a bunch of heroes all interacting and fighting bad guys in a single comic. It was a value for money thing. But teenagers were normally relegated to sidekick status, like Robin the Boy Wonder, Speedy (the Green Arrow's little chum who, in the more socially relevant comics of the Seventies lived up to his name by developing a serious drug problem) and Aqaulad, Aquaman's completely crap side-order of halibut. Stan Lee hated kid sidekicks, but had noticed that a DC book which united several of these, *The Teen Titans*, was selling pretty well. Marked by attempts of middle-aged writers to get "hip" to the new youth culture, it was full of crazy baddies like the Mad Mod who said "gear" a lot. But this was not Stan's way.

The X-Men were a team of teenage superheroes, announced as "The Strangest Teens of All". They were certainly strange, but, in the context of your average

NEVER HAVE YOU, THE READING PUBLIC, BEEN SO INSTANTLY FASCINATED BY A GROUP OF SUPER-POWERFUL VILLAINS AS LAST ISSUE, WHEN YOU MET MAGNETO'S *EVIL MUTANTS!* NOW, WE PRESENT THEM AGAIN... MORE EXCITING, MORE UNPREDICTABLE, MORE DANGEROUS THAN EVER *!!*

comic book reading geek, they weren't all that weird. The X-Men were superpowered mutants, whose DNA had been altered at birth to give them incredible abilities. The narrative premise was pretty deep. Unlike the Fantastic Four — Marvel's first family — or the mighty Avengers, the X-Men received no plaudits from society at large. Because they were mutants (technically known as "Homo superior") they were hated and feared by the world. The X-Men could never appear on Ed Sullivan or have the Beatles attend their big showbiz wedding (as was the case for Mr Fantastic and the Invisible Girl). The X-Men were basically as paranoid as fuck. They could be found out any minute. They were outsiders, reviled by normal folks for being strange and elevated above the masses. Again, the concept perfectly mirrors the tensions of the average teenage comic book-reader — a mix of paranoid insecurity, alienation and secretive visions of ego-warping self-aggrandisement.

So the X-Men needed a convincing front. Professor Charles Xavier, the wheelchair bound mentor of the group, who himself was a mutant with telepathic abilities, sorted this out. He set up his School for Gifted Youngsters in a big posh house and trained the X-Men to battle baddies in the specially constructed "Danger Room". Xavier built a machine called Cerebro which identified mutants. The X-Men would then have to go and get them and either

THE X-MEN SYMBOLISE THE GRIM EPIPHANIES OF PUBERTY. JUST LIKE ALICE IN WONDERLAND, THEY'RE ALL ABOUT WEIRD CHANGES TO YOUR BODY AND FEELINGS

recruit them or fight them. But, this being comics, they normally fought them, got upset and went home. The recruitment thing was a matter of some urgency as the X-Men weren't the only bunch of super-powered mutants on a mission. But before we meet the baddies, I should tell you a little more about the individual X-Men and why they were so cool.

The X-Men, you see, symbolise the grim epiphanies of puberty. Just like Alice in Wonderland, the merry mutants are all about weird changes to your body and feelings.

Cyclops (Scott Summers) is a skinny lad who has powerful energy beams that come out of eyes. This would be pretty cool, apart from the fact that he has no control over them. So he has to wear a visor or protective shades the whole time. Cyclops fancies Marvel Girl — the glamorous girlie member of the band — but can't risk snuggling up to her for fear of what his dangerous optic emissions might do. Do you get it? Cyclops emits strange powerful things from out of his body that are part fun, part pure worry. They can go off at any minute. How clear do I have to make this analogy?

But the other X-Men were fairly happy with their mutant lot. Hank McCoy, the super-agile Beast, had overgrown hands and feet and was rather hairy. So The Beast is all about those changes that boys go through that make them, rather disturbingly, look more like monkeys. But Hank is a happy soul with a tendency towards literary hyperbole that would have made SJ Perelman proud. He's a smart chap but later had a little error of judgement when he decided to accelerate his mutation with drugs. He became blue and furry, a lesson to us all.

The Angel, a handsome and rich devil who had huge white wings sprouting out of his shoulder blades really had it made. The chicks loved Warren Worthington III. Being posh, good-looking and able to fly represents the sum of any adolescent fantasy of the idealised self.

Then there's the daft Iceman, who was like a frozen version of the Human Torch, throwing hard snowballs at people. My theory flounders a bit here. But he could make icecream come out of his body, which is a useful skill at parties. But, in the end, Iceman was always a bit of shmucky kid.

Finally the token bird, the lovely Marvel Girl, was a powerful telepath and had telekinetic powers. She proved that girls really could fuck with your head.

Now the baddies. And, once again, when you dig beneath the surface, it's heavy stuff. Diametrically opposed to the X-Men is Magneto and his Brotherhood of Evil Mutants. Now Magneto is a complex guy. He's strong, having control over one of the primal forces of the universe — magnetism — but that's not as important as his political beliefs.

Because of his Romany origins, Magneto had grown up in a concentration camp. So, when he realised he was a mutant as well as being part of a persecuted ethnic minority, this sent him over the edge. Or was he really over the edge? Sometimes Magento wanted mutants — Homo superior — to take their rightful place as rulers of the world. Pretty standard super-baddie fare. But at other times his demands were more conciliatory, asking for a free independent state for mutants. Sometimes Magneto was good, sometimes he was very bad. But he was always driven by a moral vision for his people. The X-Men were all about assimilation and co-existence with Homo sapiens. But the regular folk were having none of it. They built robots called sentinels to track down and immobilise mutants, they had riots, they sent them nasty letters and insulted their hair-styles with nary a thought. The "moral" X-Men were, in the public eyes, no better or worse than the "immoral" Magneto. The reader was left in a profound moral quandary.

You can make a million analogies — Magento is Malcolm X whereas Professor X was Martin Luther King. Or that Magento was an Israeli Hawk while Xavier was an assimilatory New York Jew. This is pretty heavy stuff for your average twelve year-old. These moral questions are still being played out in the X-Men comics, over thirty-five years later. Magento currently democratically rules a newly established mutant-

nation called Genosha. It's quite nice there apparently.

The old Brotherhood of Evil Mutants had some excellent baddies, most of whom went semi-straight in later life. My personal favourite was Unus the Untouchable. Unus' mutant power provided a force field around him that meant he was untouchable, hence his name. Unfortunately it went out of control after he fought the X-Men. Just like Tantalus (so my posh friend tells me) he couldn't touch food or anything else for that matter. He was trapped by his own powers. A quick wank was therefore entirely out of the question. Poor old Unus!

But, perhaps because of the moral greyness around the original X-Men, they were never as popular as the rest of the Marvel superhero stable. The "Strangest Teens of All" struggled on with poor sales until their comic was cancelled in 1970. Cult status amongst the cooler comic geeks was just not enough.

So, the trail goes quiet until the mid-seventies whereupon the Business Manager at Marvel comics had a creative idea. It was the only creative idea that he would ever have, but it would have huge implications for the comic book world. He reasoned that Marvel sold a lot of comics outside the United States, so why not do a superhero team full of international characters? The Marvel editors, themselves second-generation fan-boys, saw this as a chance to revive the X-Men with a new cast.

So, in 1976, Giant-Size X-Men number 1 introduced the New X-Men to the world. Cyclops and Marvel Girl were still around, but the Beast, Angel and Iceman did their derring-do elsewhere in the Marvel Universe.

The new cast included a blue mutant called Nightcrawler who had a prehensile tail and could teleport. He smelt of sulphur though — there's always a downside. He was German and said "Unglaublich!" a lot. There was also Colossus, a good Russian Leninist who became a really strong bloke made out of organic steel. An image straight out of Soviet realism and the Stakanovitch cult, Pyotr Rasputin showed just how culturally and politically pluralist the X-Men had become. We also met Storm, a dazzling Kenyan beauty who controlled the weather with her mutant abilities. She also had a penchant for nude flying through refreshing showers of her own creation. This probably didn't hurt sales.

But the big draw would prove to be a character called Wolverine. He was short chap who came from the Yukon, he was older than the others and had a hairy chest and big bushy side-burns, kind of like Gaz out of Supergrass but really hard and with superpowers. And, check this baby, he was never without a half-smoked cigar clamped in his mutie mouth! Fortunately, Wolvie could get away with this as one of his powers was an incredible ability to heal himself of any ill. This was combined with a berserker battle savvy, unbreakable steel bones and nifty metal claws that came out of his wrists (with an excellent "Snikt!" sound effect). Wolverine was a different order of hero. He was nasty, capable of extreme violence and hard to control — like Vinnie Jones before he became a soft nancy actor. He was a parody of machismo but, it was later revealed, was capable of some tenderness (although I hated that particular story-line). The kids absolutely loved him. We could get psychoanalytical on Wolvie's ass and suggest that he represented Freud's fantasy of the immortality of the ego — that the body and self cannot be destroyed no matter what is done to it — but I don't think that he'd appreciate it.

The new X-Men soon gathered a head of steam under the creative stewardship of writer Chris

Claremont and artist John Byrne. Over the next fifteen years Claremont would create an unparalleled mythology around the X-Men which saw the comic book rise to the top of the sales charts, eclipsing even Spiderman and Batman.

But the real highlight of this period was the Death of Phoenix story. A few years previously the old Marvel Girl had undergone a radical transformation into Phoenix, a being of unimaginable power. At one point this all got a bit much for the poor girl. She saved the universe singlehandedly but in a lapse of concentration managed to destroy an entire planet full of peaceful people who looked like radishes. The intergalactic community were not happy about this and ordered her death, which, after a lot of fighting and intrigue, was duly meted out. This particularly upset Cyclops, who had, after thirty years of shilly-shallying, finally declared his love for Phoenix/Marvel Girl. She actually died! This caused one big commotion in the geek world. (Of course she came back to life a few years later, but that's not important.)

But let's travel forward to the Nineties. The business heads at Marvel had cottoned on to the biggest success story in comic-books since Batman. Now there were about a dozen monthly X-books (*X-Men, X-Man, Uncanny X-Men, Generation X, X-Factor, Mutant X, Excalibur, the New Mutants, Cable, Apocalypse, Untold Tales, The Hellfire Club* to name a few) dealing with the new X-Men, the original X-Men and their hordes of supporting characters. Over half of Marvel's

SOON XAVIER'S SCHOOL FOR GIFTED YOUNGSTERS WILL BE AS OVER-SUBSCRIBED AS THE LATEST DOT COM SHARE ISSUE

output involved mutants in one guise or another. The creative spark couldn't support this many stories. The kids still bought it in droves but the magic, for the old fuckers like me, had truly worn off. The X-Men lived only in fond memories and had been overtaken by the needs of the military-industrial complex.

And now, with the film's release in August, the process seems to be complete. It may actually be a pretty good film, judging by the cast and the trailers. I just wanted to tell you about the time when the X-Men were a secret and select little club that only the weird and alienated were entitled to join. Soon, everyone will be a mutant nouveau and Xavier's School for Gifted Youngsters will be as over-subscribed as the latest stupid dot.com share issue. But I remember the real X-Men, untainted by big business and global media, structuring the pleasures and pain of growing up into the non-mutant world.

The final paragraph of this article is being telepathically projected to you. Please clear your mind and concentrate on the void. Once you have received the message please do not hesitate to act upon it. Professor X is waiting. Thank you. ☻

MAY • 72 •

FACTS OF DEATH

JOHN MOORE hit the top twenty with "The Facts of Life", by his band Black Box Recorder. But a few weeks before its release, his father died

After years of valiant effort, my father has finally succeeded in drinking himself to death. Sixty-seven may not exactly be youth snatched away, but neither is it a ripe old age. Live at a medium pace, die middle aged... not quite a beautiful corpse though, I'm afraid. Still, a corpse should not be beautiful. That's the point. They should look spent. If they've got anything left to offer in the looks and life department, they should still be breathing.

The call comes first thing on a Monday morning. Perhaps dying is like starting a new job. It's been expected for ages, so it's hardly a devastating blow. In fact the timing's quite good. He wasn't expected to see Christmas, the year 2000 or the election of a new London Mayor, so two out of three ain't bad. I had visions of him on a life support machine on New Year's Eve, counting down to midnight. Did the press pay out for the first death of the new century?

I drive over to my sister's through the morning rush hour arriving just before nine. The dog rushes out to greet me and I swear it's wearing funeral plumes. Usually pure white, today her head fur is jet black. My sister comes out. She looks and sounds exhausted – I think she might have been crying. We embrace for several seconds. We're not the most tactile family in the world and it feels a bit odd – in fact, it could be a first. She explains that the dog has been under a car and is not done up in East End style for Ronnie Kray's funeral. It's good to see she's not lost her sense of humor; still, she'll need watching. At times like these, as any family that has experienced "times like these" knows, there is only one thing to do.

I put the kettle on.

A nice strong cuppa, a chat and a ciggie then it's time to decide: do I or don't I go in to see the corpse?

To remember him as a vibrant carefree young man, strolling through Heath Robinson meadows –

A LARGE TUMBLER OF GLENFIDDICH FOR ME AND A FEW SIPS FOR THE OLD MAN... I'VE HAD WORSE DRINKING PARTNERS

as if! Or enter the theatre of death and taste the sickly stench of eternity? It's no contest. "Get out of the way! I can't issue a death certificate until I've seen the dead body." It's a high impact moment seeing him. The duvet is pulled up over his head so he requires unveiling... rather like the launch of a new Rover at the motor show. At the other end of the bed, his toes are sticking out, and, I can confirm, they are turned up. Bracing myself for — I'm not sure what — I lift the quilt. Even though he died in his sleep, his mouth and eyes are open. He has an expression of boredom, as if he's been told a not very interesting fact and answered, "Oh, really, how interesting..." Maybe the Grim Reaper sounded like EL Whisty or tried to sell him a timeshare. Anyway, in my new role as head of the family it is my task to close them. He is still quite warm. The eyes are simple enough, it's just like on the TV cop shows, a gentle flick and it's done. The mouth, on the other hand, refuses to shut. It springs open time and again. No difference there then... I don't want to force it. I lean over his forehead and kiss him goodbye. It occurs to me that he might want a drink. I have to be discreet about this, fearing a family row if I'm caught. It seems to me to be a

reasonable thing to do. A large tumbler of Glenfiddich for me and a few sips for the old man... I've had worse drinking partners.

By mid-morning the house is filling up. Widow number one, my mother, arrives. They had ceased to be "an item" long before today. Her cream trouser suit is hardly what you'd call widow's weeds — if I'd been her I'd have worn a pink tutu. She's got sandwiches. Widow number two arrives. This could be a bit more problematic, she's got donuts... Not quite up to the standards of the late great Roger Vadim, it still has possibilities. Perhaps they'll tear each other's hair out... strangely enough they don't. My mother puts the kettle on. It's all extremely civilised. There is no bad feeling between them, it all happened years ago. I think my mother now regards it as a favour.

Widow number two, although Jewish and from Glasgow, is now a Hindu. The archetypal younger woman from the hippy era seeking spiritual enlightenment. My father bought her home on some pretext in the late Seventies, a meditating vegetarian in a Kaftan coat. Anyway, quite what my father and spiritual enlightenment had in common, God only knows... perhaps she mistook "spirits" for "spiritual". Anyway, this Hinduism... isn't that the one with the funeral pyres and the wife throwing herself on top? I'll go into the garden and start gathering twigs. Fortunately the only thing she burns is incense. I give her a kiss on the cheek as she leaves.

I'm getting good at this.

The doctor arrives and tiptoes around in his suede shoes. Once the death certificate is signed we can set about disposal of the deceased. Satisfied that there are no signs of foul play, we exchange banalities and then he leaves. He does not seem particularly friendly towards me. Maybe he's read in *Time Out* that I am an evil absinthe importer – one of London's premier hedonists. Quite ironic that it came out in the same week. It occurs to me that the father of England's first absinthe importer dying from liver failure could generate negative publicity. Still, no one ever claimed it was good for you. Booze kills! George Best – Booze Kills! Shane McGowan – Booze Kills! But a little drink never hurt anyone.

Next up is the undertaker. Yellow Pages time. You really can get buried by the Co-Op. I always thought that was a joke. We'd discussed this before the big day, he knew what he wanted – the absolute bloody cheapest. "Stick me in a cardboard box. What's the bloody difference"?

"Would Sir allow me to recommemnd a veneer casket? There's hardly any difference in the price and it adds a touch of class to what is after all a final journey."

I know he thinks I'm a cheap bastard and I've made it all up about the final wish. "Cardboard it is then, sir."

The undertakers arrive in a white van just after lunch. They are White Van Men. I wonder if they get into road rage fights while transporting stiffs to the Chapel of Rest. I think they might be father and son. They appear very similar and it's not just the black suit and black tie outfits. The son looks like he might be into death metal in his spare time, and possibly has an unhealthy interest in dead bodies. Maybe he'll go on to create some himself one day. In my wallet I carry a Necro card given to me by Stewart Home. It looks the same as a donor card but gives permission for sexual experimentation to take place on your body after death. The card is not filled in and for a second or two I consider doing so and placing it in dad's pyjama pocket. Perhaps that would be going too far.

The men need five minutes to go about their business. The door is shut. Presumably Father is stripped, lifted and zipped. The door opens and a large parcel is wheeled out on a trolley, through the hall, the front door and into the back of the van. I get the impression they would rather I wasn't watching – in case they drop him. They tell me, "We'll be in touch". Sorted. As the van snakes down the road, I realise that this is really it. It occurs to me that heaven might be like Slough.

Drinking my millionth cup of tea I switch on the radio and tune to Radio One. It's playing "The Facts of Life". ◉

John Moore is one third of Black Box Recorder, whose single, "The Facts of Life", was recently a hit in the British pop charts

NO SHIT, SHERLOCK

NICHOLAS BLINCOE revisits Sherlock Holmes and finds
a hero to freelancers, freeloaders and freebasers.
Illustrations by **LEWIS CHAMBERLAIN**

There is a spectre haunting London — or at least a small part of it. He is lithe, intelligent, often stoned and possibly tone deaf. His name is Sherlock Holmes. From the description, you may be priding yourself that the legendary detective sounds a lot like you. Or Bobby Gillespie from Primal Scream. It certainly sounds like me. But anyone affinity I might have felt for Sherlock Holmes was long ago killed by the experience of living on the real-life Baker Street. I had an apartment there for five years and every day that I chose to leave home, I would run into a man in Sherlock drag outside the Tube Station. He wore his deerstalker like a cold tweed omelette and posed for photographs with tourists. Actually, there were two Holmeses. The regular one looked a little like Jeremy Brett, the actor in the Granada television series. On his day off, he was replaced by a younger stand-in: he looked like an embarrassed teenager in a flaccid deerstalker. Little wonder that the

SHERLOCK HOLMES IS UNDOUBTEDLY LAZY: AN IDLER. AND HIS WORLD IS ONE THAT TOLERATES IDLENESS

Holmes mystique palled for me within a couple of days. But it was replaced by a new mystery: how did a fictional character come to colonise a London Street?

One of the secrets of Sherlock Holmes' longevity has to be the Baker Street connection. Addresses mean something, no one argues with a grid reference. Mickey Mouse is the least engaging cartoon character ever: he could never have survived outside of Disneyland. And think of Hugh Hefner and Donald Trump. Without their mansions and towers, they would just be two sad old men in retro-hairstyles. If their careers teach us anything, it is this: sort out the real estate and the future is assured. The only differences between Sherlock and the Mouse, the Hef or the Trumpster is that Holmes is not backed by a corporation and he does not own Baker Street. He did not colonise Baker street: we did it on his behalf. Or, rather, you did it. I want nothing to do with him.

Baker Street is a wide London trunk road, the last section of the highway that leads from the North into central London. Skinny plane trees fail to make it look anything like a French boulevard and the biggest landowner is Marks and Spencer. 221b Baker Street, if it ever existed, was long ago swallowed up by the half-block large headquarters of the Abbey National. A few doors away there is a restaurant named Hudsons after Holmes's landlady. The restaurant owners have renamed their building 221b: a fairly devious strategy, yet somehow simple-minded. Much like a Sherlock Holmes mystery. On the opposite side of the road is a Sherlock memorabilia shop. Opposite my old apartment is the Sherlock Holmes Hotel, with Sherlock specials on the bar list and reproductions of original Sherlock Holmes artwork from *The Strand* magazine on the toilet walls. Baker Street tube station has specially designed tiles on the Jubilee and Bakerloo line platforms, depicting different Sherlock Holmes adventures.

Everyone, from big business to small, collaborates on the same fantasy: that Baker Street is exactly the kind of place that Sherlock Holmes would have lived in. All their efforts fail, and fail ingloriously. But that hardly seems to matter. They just want to live the dream...

A more perfect version of Sherlock Holmes' Baker Street does exist: in Manchester, my home town. It was once the set for the TV series and is now part of the Granada theme park that includes the Coronation Street set. A couple of years ago, my cousin hired the space for her twenty- first birthday. I took a train from London back to Manchester to eat a meal in a warehouse that was masquerading as my new address. It would have been a freaky and ironic experience except that

Granada's Baker Street looked nothing like the street I knew. It was cobble stoned, lit by fake gas lamps, decorated in tin advertisements for forgotten tobacco products, and had a dance floor in the centre where we did the line dance to the Maccarina. The dance floor aside, this was what the world wanted Baker Street to be like. And the amount of dry ice pumped out by the DJ did make the place look as though it was bathed in a London fog.

Travel to the most remote parts of the world, like the Mekong Delta or rural Kazakhstan, and you find a purified image of Britain, where everything is boiled down to a simple essence. Here you learn what the rest of the world really thinks of you, the touchstone of what is perceived to be British. And it is Manchester United and Sherlock Holmes. I understand this may be vaguely annoying to non-United football supporters. But it was the Sherlock connection that really drove me crazy. In 1997, I gained a reputation as a crime writer when one of my novels won a Silver Dagger for crime fiction. Suddenly I became the crime writer who lived on Baker Street.

Martin Amis once wrote that the public can only hold one adjective about a personality in their mind at any one time. I realised this was true when my address became more important than my books or my opinions or my startling good looks. Whenever I was introduced on radio discussion programmes, my address got star-billing, followed by a question on

Sherlock Holmes. My standard replies were, at first, polite. I said I had read Conan Doyle's stories as a child and quite enjoyed them. Soon I started foaming at the mouth, denouncing the stories as simplistic, saying that they were already outdated when Conan Doyle wrote them, and bewailing the theme park-ing of our culture in general and my neighbourhood in particular. Unfortunately, I came across like a berk. I was missing the point. No one claims that the stories are masterpieces. It is Sherlock Holmes himself that is important. Sherlock and the space that he operates in, underpinning his particular realm in the way that a philosophical principle underpins a conceptual realm.

Sherlock Holmes is undoubtedly lazy: an idler. And his world is one that tolerates idleness. The books teem with examples of men lounging on corners, loafing outside low buildings. Conan Doyle's London often seems like the kind of Third World country where the men on the bottom rung of society apparently do nothing all day. If this is an accurate picture of the end of the Victorian age, then presumably these men are unemployed. It then seems tasteless for Conan Doyle to make a fetish of their idleness in the way he does. But they do make a counterpoint for Holmes and his extraordinary lethargy. Holmes is a man who cannot sit, he has to lie down. He reads curled up on sofas, smokes lying almost prone, his feet always up. In "The Yellow Face" he is described as "a man who seldom took exercise for exercise's sake. Few men were capable

of greater muscular effort, and he was undoubtedly one of the finest boxers of his weight that I have ever seen; but he looked upon aimless bodily exertion as a waste of energy, and he seldom bestirred himself save where there was some professional object to be served. Then he was absolutely untiring and indefatigable."

This is part of the attraction of Sherlock Holmes: the feeling that he has his priorities right. He works when there is interesting work, at other times he relaxes. This has often caused Holmes to be mistaken for an older figure: the idealised "amateur" or gentleman sportsman. Indeed, the *Oxford Companion to English Literature* erroneously describes Holmes as an amateur detective. He is, in fact, a consulting detective: a paid professional. It is worthwhile comparing Sherlock Holmes with the amateur cracksman Raffles, created by Conan Doyle's brother-in-law, EW Hornung. The high-concept behind the Raffles stories is that Raffles only appears to be a languorous gentleman. In order to maintain appearances he has to work like a dog at nights, climbing across the city's roofs. In contrast, Sherlock Holmes is genuinely idle, it is not a pose that he has adopted in order to seem aristocratic. When Holmes goes to work, Conan Doyle details every bead of sweat. He could, so easily, have portrayed him as a man who barely has to try to get the right results.

Where Raffles provides both a commentary and criticism of the ideal of amateurism, Sherlock

HOLMES IS SO FOND OF THE SELF-MADE AND THE SELF-EMPLOYED, THAT HIS BEST FRIEND IS ONE. INDEED, WATSON IS HIS ONLY FRIEND

Holmes has broken with the philosophy entirely. As a professional, Holmes has much in common with his clients. His typical clients are self-made men and women, whether they are rich or simply comfortable or, still, striving to achieve a decent living. They are colonials ("The Yellow Face", "The Gloria Scott"), or barrow-boys made good ("The Stockbroker's Clerk"), or small businessmen ("The Red-Headed League"). He so rarely works for the aristocracy, they could almost be seen as anachronisms who barely belong in this world. In "The Hound of the Baskervilles", Holmes has to travel to the wilds of Broadmoor to find one, they are so far removed from his London.

Holmes is so fond of the self-made and the self-employed, that his best friend is one. Indeed, Watson is his only friend. Holmes is different to these people in two respects — and neither has anything to do with class. The first is that he is idle, while they are often jittery and impatient. The second is that they are startlingly gullible. In "The Stockbroker's Clerk", Holmes's client is told to go to Birmingham on the most ridiculous pretence while an armed robber impersonates him and steals a fortune. The plot of "The Red-Headed League" is, in all

SHERLOCK HOLMES IS A HERO TO SCHEDULE D TAX PAYERS. HE IS A FREELANCE IN CONTROL OF HIS LIFE. HE WORKS WHEN HE IS INTERESTED, AT OTHER TIMES HE CHILLS

important respects, exactly the same. They are even gullible to be taken in by Holmes and his famous detective tricks. In "The Gloria Scott", a man collapses with shock when Holmes suggests that the initials JA mean a lot to him. How did Holmes deduce this? The man has the initials tattooed on his arm.

These people, both men and women, are the new bourgeoisie. Or, more properly, the petit bourgeois. They are rarely the captains of industry, heads of new institutions are industrial empires. They tend to be shop keepers, doctors or merchants. The petit bourgeois have always got a bad press. Marx and Lenin were particularly hostile: although what social class peripatetic freelance philosophers belong to if not the petit bourgeoisie, I do not know. Most writers and all novelists are by definition small-traders, selling one-off products to publishers and living or failing to live by how well these products do in the market place. The unfortunate thing is that novelists are among the least suited people to be small-traders. They rarely have the back-bone for it. Where they need to be level-headed in business and shameless in selling, they are instead neurotic dreamers

driven mad by the anxiety of watching their stock rise and fall. Whether it is self-loathing or self-deception, novelists have always been among the most vociferous enemies of the petit bourgeois. The genre of satire, for instance, seems only to exist to attack the mores of small businessmen.

Conan Doyle, a Scottish doctor turned popular writer, is one of the few novelists sympathetic to the ethos of the petit bourgeois. But he never goes overboard. He always portrays them in the throes of anxiety: essentially decent but uncomfortable in their skin and in their clothes, failing to be articulate and mortified by their limited powers of expression. Beyond the immediate problems that bring them to Holmes' door, the real drama is the story of what it means to move up in the world. Indeed, this is the cause of all their problems. They are gullible because they no longer know how to judge people in their new and alien environment.

It is impossible to read the descriptions of Sherlock Holmes' clients without seeing a portrait of Conan Doyle himself. Despite his success as a writer, he is not much of a stylist. Of all his works, only Sherlock Holmes survives and that is because in Holmes there is a dramatic character that transcends the paucity of the plots and storytelling. Conan Doyle was aware of his short-comings. He turned his unhappiness with being identified solely with Holmes into a public drama: faking Holmes' death in the story "The Final Problem" and then staging a resurrection after what must surely have been a semi-orchestrated campaign. Conan Doyle's bourgeois decency is shown in his care for his family. He did his best to publicly support his sister's husband, EW Hornung, when the younger writer was first starting out. But he was extremely uncomfortable with the idea that Raffles could be a hero. He felt, wrongly, that the public would not stand for a romantic thief. His gullibility is shown by his attachment to spiritualism. He wrote a treatise on the subject and was a soft touch to any clairvoyants and mediums who contacted him. Even when he was proved to have been a victim of simple con tricks, he did not lose his conviction in the possibility of a spirit world.

Sir Arthur Conan Doyle is often compared to Doctor Watson. Watson is, however, rather cooler than Conan Doyle. Watson is a dynamic figure: an ex-army soldier who is a good shot with the pistol that Holmes asks him to bring on dangerous cases. It is important that Watson is his own man, married by the time of the second Holmes anthology and running a successful practice in Paddington. He is less in thrall to Holmes than most biographers are to their subjects. He is always ready to tease Holmes on his execrable violin playing as well as his more anti-social habits, such as his untidiness. Without the occasionally sceptical notes introduced by Watson, Conan Doyle's portrayal of Holmes would be too close to hero worship. The fact is, Sherlock Holmes is exactly the kind of man small-traders dream of being.

Sherlock Holmes is a hero to schedule D tax payers. He is a freelance in control of his life. He works when he is interested, at other times he chills — or occasionally slips into an *ennui* that is relieved through a little casual drug taking. As Conan Doyle says: "Save for the occasional use of cocaine he had no vices, and he only turned to the drug as a protest against the monotony of existence when cases were scanty and the papers uninteresting."

It is his lack of vices that makes Holmes so attractive. He is disciplined in the most relaxed way. He is capable of being bored and flirting with bad habits such as playing with his violin (the Edwardian equivalent of a Sony PlayStation) or drugs, but he does so occasionally. And he does it with style. There is no feverish descent into alcohol abuse, masturbation or housework. Holmes is, in fact, an ascetic: "his diet was usually of the sparest, and his habits were simple to the verge of austerity". But he is an ascetic who idles for months without a flicker of guilt. In short, Holmes is the Über Petit Bourgeois: a concept so impossible that it requires two European languages and an oxymoron even to conceive of it existing. Yet, in his Baker street, it is possible. Believing in Baker Street is believing in a little patch of heaven where the freelance not only has dignity but also behaves with dignity. If you will it, it is no dream, as Theodor Herzl, the father of Zionism once said. Of course, it does mean that some of the original residents have to move out. I am now living the dream in Pimlico. ◉

SWEET VINCENT

Van Gogh is the patron saint of the unpublished, neglected, and insane. Which is why MARK MANNING loves him so

He's always there for us. As we sit in our hovels, banging away. Flat broke, thin, hungry and drunk in our unshaven underwear.

Loving it.

A small picture postcard of the death of Chatterton lurking some-where in our tortured art school souls. Us men of our unfortunate breed, anyway. I think you women carry a small image of Frida Khalo: Frida as a bleeding fawn, the wicked arrows of this oh, so terrible life hanging from her back. A bit like Bambi, sort of. Only more serious.

But we all revere the man. That rugged amelioration of failure, that glorious patron of neglected genius: Sweet Dutch Vincent.

Those intense, burning eyes, star-ing out beneath that flat Arles sun, straight into our souls.

You can almost taste the mistral,

VAN GOGH'S THE NIGHT CAFE ON THE PLACE MARTIN, ARLES (YALE UNIVERSITY ART GALLERY)

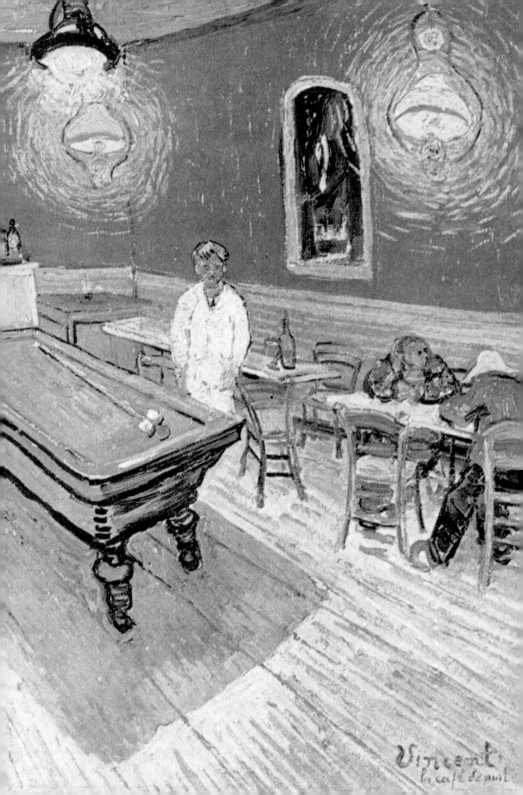

TAKE HIS NIGHT CAFE PAINTING AND COMPARE GAUGIN'S PAINTING OF THE VERY SAME SCENE. THE TWO ARTISTS SAT SIDE BY SIDE AND PAINTED THE SAME SMOKY ROOM

its wild hot breath bending the cypress trees and curling the sky into the writhing shapes of dread that permeate and threaten to engulf our martyr's later paintings.

That visceral, desperate anxiety that has transformed his entire perception of the world around him into a swirling turbulence of juddering insanity.

Take his night café painting and compare Gaugin's painting of the very same scene. The two artists sat side by side and painted the same smoky room. For Gaugin (right), it appears to be a pleasant place, somewhere to spend a few convivial hours of an evening. A smiling waitress looks over her shoulder and flirts saucily with the French artist. But for poor old Vincey baby (see previous page), it's a blood red, skew-angled shithole, stinking of murder, madness and death. A smudge-faced waiter lurks beneath the sickly gas lights, a gun, or maybe a cut throat razor, hidden in his pockets. There's a huddle of absinthe bums, drunk or asleep at the small tables. It's quite obvious from this painting that the poor Dutch bastard would eventually top either himself or some poor innocent French whore that

GAUGUIN'S NIGHT CAFE AT ARLES
(PUSHKIN MUSEUM, MOSCOW)

got in the strapped, razor-toting maniac's way.

Shivering, sweating, headaches, dry mouth, bad wanking, absinthe, fear. Raging and loathing. "Tell me about it Vince," echo his heirs amongst their obscurity and naked light bulbs.

That trembling visionary church at Auvers, yellow against the Prussian blue infinity of the star mad sky. And of course that terrible, terrible Starry Night itself, truly awesome in its wild intensity, those alien suns burning like catherine wheels spinning out of control, an animistic universe teetering way to close to the edge for the over emotional increasingly confused ex church minister.

We've all been in that blood red murder room, played pool on that sickly beige, experienced that scary waiter, last seen hanging around with an equally sinister friend in the background of Edvard Munch's 19th Century masterpiece, The Scream.

Similar to Munch in the fact that both artists painted from something deep inside themselves that lurks just beneath the surface of everything. Even that tragic fucking chair. Especially that tragic fucking chair with Vince's only luxury, his pipe and tobacco. And possibly even sadder is his only friend Gaugin's chair with its candles and books. Gaugin who had just fucked off to Tahiti because he couldn't stand his friend's increasingly demented behaviour, chopping his nob off and everything.

Those overbright sunflowers, painted to brighten up their small rooms. Those coruscating, writhing, insect-like flowers. Their desperate cheerfulness, like a mad woman laughing and scaring children in the street.

And how pathetic is that lonely night, where our dear friend sits alone in his night café feeding his insomnia with Hill's absinthe.

And that other scary area in Vincent's solitary existence, a deeply weird painting of a skeleton smoking a cigar. An odd *memento mori*, reminiscent of Holbein's Dance of Death woodcuts, where Death frolics jestingly with all his eventual victims. A strange painting, it is not often reproduced and is obviously found to be overly unsettling by many critics. I personally find it rather amusing, as if our hero is mocking his own mortality, laughing at death, whistling in the dark maybe, but with a jaunty swagger none the less.

Of course it was not until the end that his muse swung completely sinister, but even in the mid-period paintings the happiness expressed with his cherry blossoms and smiling hoteliers and postmen, there's a desperation about the jollity. Like when you frighten yourself by laughing for too long about what it is you can't remember.

"And now I understand," sings Don Mclean, not understanding at all. This world was never meant for someone as shit scared, manic and completely fucking insane as our ameliorating Saint of hope and inspiration. Our Vincent.

We artists, poets, writers,

whingers, musicians and masturbators. We madmen, sodomites and landscape gardeners. All of us undiscovered geniuses in our misunderstood fields. Suffering, deeply suffering in our blasted chaotic worlds. Feeling sorry for ourselves, yes, but with what style we whinge. How we perform it only for ourselves, desperately demanding attention and telling it to fuck off whenever it appears, making ourselves even more interesting in the private theatres of our twisted and battered egos. One eye permanently on the mirror, the other on ourselves. It is we that understand Mr Don McClean, you bad Bob Dylan with your chevy and your levy, whatever the fuck that is. "I knew you were in love with him when I saw you wanking in the gym?" sings the perverted folk singer in "Bye Bye Miss American Pie". And equally insanely in Starry Starry Night, "This world was never meant for one as beautiful as you." Mr McClean, I'm afraid you're quite mad sir. Vincent was many things, but beautiful? What, like a volcano with its rivers of molten rock is beautiful? I'm sorry, Mr Tambourine Man, but Vincent belongs entirely to us! We unpublished, unpublishable, forgotten, ignored martyrs upon the various altars of our art!

We understand! We alone understand our mad prophet!

Our Vincent Van Gogh!

Like our patron Saint, for us immortality is all!

All or nothing! Death AND Glory!

This life, this shitty insignificant spunk up a venereal whore's suppu-rating cunt of a life is not wasted! A flea's fart in the unknowable massiveness of everything maybe, but some flea farts resonate with the universe and are remembered forever. Bottled and stored in museums and libraries, thousands and millions of resonating flea farts. "It is written!" bawls the mad Jew, head-butting his wailing wall. This angry life, this very ungentle life indeed, stumbling blindly through these dark nights, can not, must not, be squandered. My brother madmen and geniuses, we who vow never to submit, to bend the knee to the unholy Cosmosodomistic trinity of materialism, commerce and commodity. We refuse to drown beneath the electronic black magic of deeply stupid rulers of men, storing up their treasures on earth and dying of colonic cancer of the arse. With their blatantly invisible conspiracies whose only goal is to keep all of us in bondage. Duped into desiring things that we don't need and paying for them with money that we don't have.

Credit? What the fuck is that, if not indentured slavery by stealth?

Master Card and Visa slave. Oh yes master! We cannot live without that turbo, four-wheel drive Adidas, Nike, widescreen surround sound, eight wheel drive, blow job washing machine, with wings! Killing ninety nine percent of all known germs. It is beneath this brain crushing submarine pressure to conform that Vincent gives us comfort.

One fucking painting.

One fucking painting the poor bastard sold.

And even that was to his long suf-

VINCENT WAS AS DELUDED, VAIN, SELFISH, AND AS MUCH OF A COMPLETE FUCKING, WANKER ARSEHOLE AS THE REST OF US

fering brother, Theo. Poor. exasperated, kind hearted Theo who kept all his mad brother's letters. Vincent probably wiped his arse on Theo's letters; none of his brother's correspondence, not one single letter survived, so self-absorbed was our man.

It's in these letters that we learn about the imperfections of our raggy arsed Saint.

In reality, which is why art should never, ever - this is important - be judged by the man who produces it, Vincent was as deluded, vain, selfish, and as much of a complete fucking, wanker arsehole as the rest of us.

This is what truly helps us through our naked lightbulb, Tennants Super, loveless nights. This is when our imperfect Saint gives us much needed succour.

Even arseholes like us, ignored and desperate, can eventually be recognised as great artists. Join the Pantheon of shimmering, flea fart immortals.

There's even hope for a cunt like me.

And how incandescent is Vincent's glowing immortality. Bathed in the light of billionaire imbeciles, flayed on the black altars of the cold cash civil religion in their towering bank cathedrals of Arms deals and Blood Money.

You can see these fools chasing their tails in palaces of ignorance. Making mad hand signals and wearing stupid blazers. And eventually when they are crippled by avarice, shame and the inevitable colonic arse cancers, their ignoble white bones will be tossed on to the piles of all the other forgotten irrelevant millionaires who make their fortunes flogging underwear, Porter, cigarettes, Coca Cola, baked beans, corn flakes, pornography and newspapers full of lies. Silk hat, Bradford millionaires, the lot of them. Small souled tax dodging twin turds living on private islands shivering beneath the black demons of fear and paranoia, unloved and unlovable.

"Better to reign in Hell, than to serve in Heaven," Milton says in *Paradise Lost*, with his sexy Satan as damned hero. You tell 'em, Milt baby.

"The mind is its own place and can make of Heaven a Hell or a heaven from Hell." To achieve a state of grace like Vincent achieved is priceless, and quite free. It is not easy and requires a determination and a will that needs must stray dangerously close to the very antipodes of sanity. But it is possible and there are as many paths towards that palace of wisdom as there are pilgrims willing to risk all for some assurance of the future life.

How else do you think us lowlife, alcoholic, autodidactic, council hovel dwellers are able to ignore the conceits and temptations beamed down upon us from the cosmosodimistic satellites of the rich and powerful? ◉

BAUDELAIRE AND THE QUEST FOR PARADISE

He is one of the world's greatest poets. But, as JOSHUA GLENN reveals, the grumpy 19th century dandy was a counter-counter-cultural, loved by neither the mainstream nor the underground

Je change... le paradis en enfer — Charles Baudelaire, *"Alchimie de la Douleur"*

During his lifetime, Charles Baudelaire was known to the general public as an "Art for Art's Sake"-flogging critic of painting and literature, as an expert on the effects of various drugs, and as the translator who single-handedly established the cult of Edgar Allen Poe in France — but not, except to a small literary élite, as a poet. We're all familiar by now with the cliché of genius unrecognized in its own time, but in the case of Baudelaire this turn of events seems particularly unjust. *Les Fleurs du Mal* was, after all, the last best-selling volume of poetry the Western world has seen. In the 150 years since it was first published, Baudelaire's poems have inspired and influenced the artistic efforts of ecstatic types from Rimbaud and the Symbolists right down to Jim Morrison and Patti Smith. Cultural conservatives, from the French officials who banned the first edition of *Les Fleurs du Mal* to anti-sixties intellectuals like Gertrude Himmelfarb and Daniel Bell, have demonized Baudelaire as a satyr-like corrupter of bourgeois forms and norms. It's largely thanks to Baudelaire, in short, that poetry — a medium dominated by windbags, softies, and shut-ins — ever possessed, for poets of succeeding generations, anything resembling a subversive charge. So what happened?

The answer is simple. The tried and true formula for becoming a successful and famous artist in one's own lifetime (pay attention, now!) is this: one must perfectly embody in one's life and work either the prevailing values of society, or the prevailing values of the self-appointed enemies of the status quo. Thus, although cultural avant-gardists have venerated *Les Fleurs du Mal* because its themes include the derangement of the senses, dandyism, erotic love, wine, blasphemy and death, their idea that Baudelaire celebrated the delights of hell-on-earth is misguided. Baudelaire was indeed possessed by a consuming vision, and it was one which damned him to a life of poverty and suffering. But his wasn't a sexily countercultural vision of hell; it was, if anything, counter-counter-cultural — which would explain why the only people Baudelaire despised more than the bourgeois philistines of post-aristocratic France were the anti-bourgeois aesthetes, republicans, and bohemians with whom he rubbed shoulders every day. Baudelaire's was a vision of paradise... and that is where his troubles began.

Things needn't have turned out the way they did. In 1839, the 18-year-old Baudelaire was launched on what could easily have been an extremely rewarding career as a poster boy for the counterculture when he was expelled from his prestigious Parisian *lycée* — for, it seems, having acquired a scandalously *outré* taste for avant-garde literature and art. To young Baudelaire, the stepson of General Aupick, an ultra-conservative career soldier who'd been entrusted with policing worker strikes throughout France, the progressive sentiments of a writer like Victor Hugo, the populist darling of the July Monarchy, seemed as conservative as those of the government officials Hugo reviled. Baudelaire preferred the amoral sensuousness of novels like Sainte-Beuve's *Volupté* and Théophile Gautier's *Mademoiselle de Maupin*. When Gautier's book was published in 1835, it was prefaced by an aestheticist manifesto which declared that nothing useful can be beautiful, and nothing beautiful useful; Baudelaire, already sick to death of the utilitarian values of the newly triumphant French middle class, agreed completely that art must have no other end than itself. The artist and the poet, then, and not the political progressive, seemed to Baudelaire to be the true heroes of the era. Accordingly, he rejected his stepfather's offer to help him find a respectable calling, and dived into that intoxicating milieu of painters, writers, agitators, prostitutes, and pickpockets which his friend Henri Murger was soon to immortalize in his novel *La Vie de Bohème*.

However, as attractive as he found the sex and the drugs, Baudelaire instinctively rejected the received values of the counterculture. Then, as now, a kind of grungy ersatz proletarianism was the preferred costume of slumming middle class twentysomethings; but the shaggy beards and tattered smocks of the students, republicans, and artistic prodigies of Bohemia left Baudelaire cold. Instead, he aped those *incroyables* of the previous generation — Gautier and his poet/journalist comrades Gérard de Nerval, Roger de Beauvoir, Jules Amédée Barbey d'Aurevilly, and Honoré de Balzac, in particular — who practiced that demanding and esoteric way of life it amused the French (borrowing the term from the English) to call *le dandysme*.

His father having died twelve years earlier, Baudelaire stood to inherit a valuable piece of real estate when he turned 21; he could count, then, on a comfortable monthly stipend for the rest of his life. So he wasted no time running up enormous lines of credit with boot- and glove-makers, with art dealers and bookbinders, and especially with tailors, who cut his trousers and coats to his own exacting specifications. By the time he was twenty, a contemporary could describe Baudelaire as "leading a bohemian life and a dandy to boot, a dandy above all, with the whole theory of elegance at his finger-tips. Every fold in his jacket was the subject of earnest study."

Today, of course, when even the crassest of suburbanites fancies himself a peacock, it's difficult to understand why, in the early part of the 19th century, attending to the most minute details of one's appearance was understood to be anything more than narcissism. In "*Le Peintre de la Vie Moderne*", a sort of retrospective manifesto he wrote in 1859, Baudelaire explained that "dandyism flourishes especially in periods of transition, when democracy is not yet all-powerful and the aristocracy is just beginning to totter and decay. Amidst the turmoil of these times, a small group of men, *déclassés*, at loose ends, fed-up — but all of them rich in determination — will conceive the idea of founding a new sort of aristocracy, stronger than the old, for it shall be based on only the most precious, the most indestructible factors." The Revolution of 1830 was, to aesthetes like Gautier and his colleagues, not so much a triumph of the citizenry over the monarchy as it was a tri-

HE WASTED NO TIME RUNNING UP ENORMOUS LINES OF CREDIT WITH BOOT- AND GLOVE-MAKERS, ART DEALERS, BOOKBINDERS AND TAILORS

umph of the prudent, small-minded bourgeois over the fabulous, high-minded nobleman. Thinking, perhaps, of Louis-Philippe, the "Bourgeois King" who preferred a sturdy felt hat to a crown, Baudelaire sneers in an early poem that the bourgeois wears cheap and ugly clothes because he worships a false (and smug) god: Usefulness (*le dieu de l'Utile, implacable et serein*). To be a dandy, then, during the July Monarchy, was to rebel against the utilitarian values of monarchists and republicans alike. *La mode* was the message, and Baudelaire the most dazzling of messengers.

One needn't have had, as Baudelaire did, the promise of a surplus income to be a dandy, however. As Baudelaire puts it elsewhere in "Le Peintre de la Vie Moderne", *le dandysme* "is not, as many shallow-minded people seem to think, merely an immoderate taste for fine dress and elegant surroundings. These things are for the true dandy only the symbols of the aristocratic superiority of his spirit." Dandyism, inspired as it was by the low-key Beau Brummell, is less a particular style of dress than it is an inward turning-up-of-the-nose at those content to wallow in their own repletion. The no-nonsense clothes worn by the middle class and their rebellious offspring alike may have made Baudelaire wince, but it was only *vulgarity* that could make him vomit. Understanding this, after reading in Baudelaire's journal that "to be a useful man has always seemed to me something very vulgar," one can see why he never stooped so low as to take a job: jobholders are both useful *and* vulgar. One can also understand why the unsentimental Baudelaire wrote so often about his love for cats: admiring that animal's detached, philosophical gaze (*son regard ... profond et froid*, as Baudelaire's early poem "*Le Chat*" puts it), he aspired to be as ironically aloof — from the vulgar getting-and-spending chaos of everyday life — as a cat. This also explains Baudelaire's fascination with prostitutes: to traffic in the pleasures of the flesh without abandoning oneself to anything so sentimental as love is the dandy's ultimate goal.

Alarmed by his stepson's lavish expenditures, General Aupick packed Baudelaire off on a long sea journey, to India. However, having gained a taste for the sweet indolence of life in the tropics ("*Paysage*" and "*Le Soleil*", written around this time, express his desire to live in a paradise where the sun always shines) and for women of African descent ("*A Une Dame Créole*" and "*A Une Malabraise*" date from this period), Baudelaire soon jumped ship and returned to Paris. Once back, he took a luxurious suite of rooms in the Hôtel Pimodan, the haunt of wealthy dandies, artists, and the members of the Club des Haschishins, who experimented with cooking marijuana from India with butter and opium, and drinking it with hot coffee. He filled his room with exotic fabrics and perfumes, and

began spending his days haunting museums, libraries, and art galleries, and his nights exploring the back alleys of Paris; he also began to write poetry in earnest. Around this time Baudelaire met a bisexual, mulatto actress and drug addict named Jeanne Duval. Aware, one suspects, that the ecstasy and misery she'd cause him would inspire the astonishingly bitter, violent, erotic poetry for which he'd become infamous, he took her as his mistress. The stage was set for Baudelaire's triumphant entrance on the literary scene.

"It was thanks partly to leisure (*le loisir*) that I have developed myself," he confided to his journal. "To my great detriment, however, since leisure without an income only increases debts (and the humiliations that follow)." Shortly after he turned 21, Baudelaire's mother and brother contested his father's will. Suddenly, Baudelaire could no longer afford his apartment, his wardrobe, his books, his paintings, or his mistress. Not only were his years of living large permanently at an end, but he was deeply in debt. Humiliated, in 1845 he tried to commit suicide... but failed at that, too.

In "*La Voix*", one of his very last poems, Baudelaire recounts that at an early age he was granted the ability to perceive, behind the veil of occlusion which is our universe (*derrière les décors de l'existence immense*), an unknown sphere of existence — a paradise forever just out of reach. He describes himself as being an ecstatic victim of his own clairvoyance: he's so disoriented by his strange double

A SELF PORTRAIT SHOWING BAUDELAIRE IMAGINING FAME AND FORTUNE THAT LES FLEURS DU MAL WOULD BRING

vision that, in keeping his eyes fixed on that world, he falls down man-holes in this one (*les yeux au ciel, je tombe dans des trous*). How to make sense of this self-description, the poet as visionary clown? At one point Baudelaire intended to publish his poems under the title *Limbo* (*Les Limbes*); I'd like to suggest that we take that not as a metaphor for his gener-ation's interrevolutionary status, but literally: the best way to read *Les Fleurs du Mal* is to imagine that, in 1845, Baudelaire succeeded in killing him-self. The poems in that book, in other words, are so incomparably brilliant precisely because they are the laments of a man living in the world but also dead to it, a man dri-ven mad by his ability to dwell *between* paradise and hell-on-earth.

This notion is supported by one of Baudelaire's favorite metaphors: birds-as-poets. Because *le ciel* in French means both "Heaven" and "sky", in his poems Baudelaire fre-quently uses the sky as a metaphor for paradise. Since he believed that he himself, and poets in general, belonged in Heaven above but were trapped in Hell below, one can easily understand why the plight of birds — who belong in the sky but are forced again and again to the earth — appealed to Baudelaire's imagina-tion. In "*L'Albatros*", for example, he empathizes with an albatross whose huge wings render it unable to take off from the deck of a boat: "This rider of winds, how awkward he is, and weak! How droll he seems, who lately was all grace!" (Richard Wilbur's translation). "*L'Albatros*" was inspired by an incident he'd witnessed on his sea voyage to India, but he didn't write the final quatrain, which explicitly compares the albatross with "the Poet", until two decades later — by which point he'd come to understand what it meant to be "*Exilé sur le sol au milieu des huées*" (Exiled on Earth, surrounded by hooting mockers). In "*Le Cygne*", one of his final poems, Baudelaire describes a swan (*cygne*) frantically thrashing its crippled wings in the dust of the street and lifting its head "*Vers le ciel ironique et cruellement bleu*" (Toward the ironic, cruelly blue sky); the swan is "*Commes les exilés, ridicule et sublime*" (Like all exiles, ridiculous and sublime at once).

The idea that Baudelaire had become an exile, trapped between Heaven and Hell is also supported by his transmogrification — there's no other word for it — from voluptuary to fallen angel in the months immediately following his failed suicide attempt. Baudelaire seems to have taken his friend Barbey d'Aurevilly's recent book *Du Dandysme et de Georges Brummell*, which insisted that Beau Brummell's dandyism was nothing less than a spiritual achievement, to heart. Dandyism is not just an aesthetic but a moral revolt against the vulgarity and utilitarianism of a materialistic age, Barbey d'Aurevilly argued; the dandy is "a man who carries within himself something superior to the urban world," and the modern city is the wilderness through which he wanders in search of inspiration. Shaving off his dashing goatee and cropping his long waving hair as short as a priest's tonsure, Baudelaire abandoned the scarlet waistcoats in which he'd taken such pride and began to wear trousers and jackets in mourning black instead. "*O moine fainéant!*" (O do-nothing monk!) he'd chastise himself in the poem "Le Mauvais Moine" — it was indeed an evil monk, which is to say an ascetic who's renounced the sins of the flesh but remains obsessed with them, that he'd become.

Renounced the sins of the flesh? Baudelaire? Given his reputation as a debauchee and libertine, this certainly seems unlikely, but notice: every single time debauchees and libertines are mentioned in *Les Fleurs du Mal*, they're disparaged. In "*Horreur Sympathique*" the poet demands of a *libertin*, "What thoughts are in your hollow soul?" (*ton âme vide*). In "*Le Crépuscule Du Matin*" Baudelaire ironically describes debauchery as a kind of work: *le crépuscule du matin* is the hour in which "*les débauchés rentraient, brisés par les travaux*" (the debauchees return home, broken by their labours). But what about that intoxicating poem which implores, "*Volupté, sois toujours ma reine!*" ("Voluptuousness, be thou forever my queen!"), you ask? It's called "*La Prière D'un Païen*": Baudelaire is speaking not in his own voice here, for once, but rather in that of a pleasure-worshipping pagan. If one examines only those poems in which the term *volupté* appears, it suddenly becomes apparent that Baudelaire uses it in an idiosyncratic manner, to refer to a kind of engaged-yet-detached sensual pleasure — Jean-Paul Sartre calls Baudelairean *volupté* a "dabbling in Evil when the whole body [hangs] back and [caresses] without embracing" — for which the English language lacks an adequate term.

We get an inkling of Baudelaire's eccentric usage of *volupté* in the escapist poem "*Mœsta et Errabunda*", in which he refers to that innocent paradise (*l'innocent paradis*) where "*dans la volupté pure la cœur se noie!*" (one's heart drowns itself in sinless *volupté*!). This unsullied tropical paradise "*loin des remords, des crimes, des douleurs*" (far from regrets, from crimes, from sorrows), to which Baudelaire begs the boat and the train to carry him is precisely the one, according to "*La Voix*", he sees always before him — the one whose charms cause him to stumble through daily life like a drunkard. Further evidence of this notion can be found in his escapist fantasies "*L'Invitation Au Voyage*" and "*La Vie Antérieure*", in which Baudelaire rapturously describes a tropical land where one may dwell amid "*les voluptés calmes*", and in which there's nothing but order and beauty, "*luxe, calme et volupté.*" I don't translate the terms *luxe* and *calme* here because, as with *volupté*, one gathers that Baudelaire uses them to mean something other than their primary definitions — "luxuriousness" and "calmness" — would suggest. It seems to me that *luxe*, here, doesn't describe costly material comforts but rather a fullness-to-overflowing of the poet's self; and *calme* doesn't refer to an absence of chaos (internal or external) but rather to a Zen-like ability to find peace within chaos. Paradise, for Baudelaire, is a blessed mode of existence in which one is able to forego the physical delights of luxu-riousness, calmness, and voluptuousness for the spiritual fulfillment of *luxe, calme,* and *volupté.*

This vision of paradise is an inspiring one, to be sure, but — as suggested by the tragicomic tone of "*La Voix*", not to mention the bird poems — it seems to have rendered Baudelaire incapable of living anything resembling a normal, productive existence. Then again, "normal" and "productive" are terms which belong to that material dimension in which Baudelaire, according to his own testimony, only half-lived. We can't understand his unhappy life, nor his poetry, nor the reason his genius went unrecognized in his own time and has been misrecog-nized since then unless we think of Baudelaire as a secular saint, with the emphasis on *secular*, walking a razor's edge between worldliness and un- or anti-worldliness. Baudelaire sought *la volupté pure* in its impure reflection: the corporeal voluptuousness of erotic love. Likewise, he sought *la luxe pure* in the tangible luxuriousness of a life given over to the sensual pleasure of chemical intoxication, and *la calme pure* in the somatic calmness of stupor and sleep. The impossible tension between the physical and the meta-physical in Baudelaire's life and work is what makes *Les Fleurs du Mal* so shockingly original and bizarre, and so relevant still today.

Take drugs, for example. In the 1850s Baudelaire, who'd experi-mented with opium and hashish in various forms while in his twenties, discovered that the general public was eager to read about intoxicants. In

1851 he published "*Du Vin et du Haschisch*", which explored the sensations provided by wine and hashish; this was a tremendous success. Later, he discovered the book *Confessions of an English Opium-Eater*, by the British philosopher and bon viveur Thomas De Quincey, and set to work translating it. In 1858 he published two essays, "*Haschisch*" and "*Opium*" (the latter was his translation of and commentary on De Quincey's book) as a series entitled "*L'Idéal Artificiel*". In 1860 these were combined into a single volume, *Les Paradis Artificiels*.

It's ironic, however, that this book should have established Baudelaire's reputation, not just as a connoisseur, but as an advocate of drug use — since *Les Paradis Artificiels* states in no uncertain terms that a prolonged indulgence in drugs can only weaken the will, and destroy a man's dignity and honor. Baudelaire had come to believe that although the pursuit of an artificial paradise through drug use may seem an expression of anti-bourgeois values, nothing could be more bourgeois than to posit happiness as the point of life. (The poem "*Abel Et Caïn*", for example, compares the happy and productive descendants of the Bible's Abel with the hard-pressed and miserable *race de Caïn*, and concludes that it's precisely because Cain's descendants are unhappy that they'll one day revolt against the human condition itself, mounting to the skies to cast down God.) In "*L'Aube Spirituelle*", he explicitly compares *l'Idéal* (Paradise) with *l'Idéal Artificiel*, describing those hungover dawns when "*chez les débauchés l'aube blanche et vermeille/Entre en société de l'Idéal rongeur*" (the white and rosy dawn inflicts upon debauchees a gnawing vision of the Ideal); again the sky is a metaphor for that ideal realm for which he longs: the sunrise is nothing less than a vision of paradise hovering over "*les débris fumeux des stupides orgies*" (the smoking debris of stupid orgies).

On the other hand, Baudelaire would never have produced such intoxicating effects, in synesthetic poems like "*Correspondances*" and "*Tout Entière*", in which "all scents and sounds and colors" are said to "meet as one" (*les parfums, les couleurs et les sons se répondent*) and in which — "*O métamorphose mystique*" — the poet's "senses into one sense flow" (*tous mes sens fondus en un*), were he truly, as he claimed in his notes to a preface to *Les Fleurs du Mal*, "as chaste as paper" and "as sober as water." Judging from the evidence of his letters to friends, although he may indeed have quit using opium as an intoxicant during the early 1850s, by the end of that decade Baudelaire had become addicted to the opiate laudanum, which he used to alleviate the painful secondary symptoms of syphilis, which he'd contracted as a young man. Throughout his entire adult life Baudelaire was probably "clean" for less than six years.

So when Baudelaire described De Quincey, in *Les Paradis Artificiels*, as having been tortured by a drug-exacerbated inability to realize those very same visions which drugs had afforded him, he was speaking from experience. As a dandy Baudelaire had nothing but contempt for those for whom increasing productivity seemed an end in itself; as an artist, however, he was continually frustrated by his own unproductiveness. "Imagine perpetual lethargy punctuated by perpetual debt, combined with a profound hatred of this lethargy and the utter impossibility of escaping from it because of the perpetual lack of money," he whinges in a letter to the lawyer who controlled his inheritance. "Lethargy is rusting me, devouring me, consuming me[!] The totally lethargic life which, superficially, I am leading, at war with the perpetual ferment of my mind, throws me into unspeakable rages." Thanks in part to his near-constant pursuit of *l'Idéal Artificiel* via opium, hashish, and wine, Baudelaire struggled constantly against an affliction which today we'd no doubt medicalize and medicate as "depression," but which he preferred to call — following the Romantic poets, and depending on the circumstances — *spleen* or *ennui*.

The spleen, of course, was once thought to be the seat of melancholy. In Baudelaire's usage, however, the state of mind he calls *spleen* is a despairing conviction that time is racing past while one remains absolutely paralysed, with the inevitable result that one will never live up to one's promise. In "*Un Fantôme*", written around the time he first began to experience *spleen*, Baudelaire chaffs against "*le Temps, injurieux vieillard*" (Time, ruinous old villain), that "*Noir assassin de la Vie et de l'Art*" (Black assassin of Life and of Art) who literally flies by on his "rude wings".

In "*L'Ennemi*", the "flowers" of his

"LETHARGY IS RUSTING ME, DEVOURING ME, CONSUMING ME," BAUDELAIRE WHINGES IN A LETTER TO HIS LAWYER

book's title make an appearance when Baudelaire describes how "*le tonneur et la pluie*" (the "thunder" and the "rain") of his youth have wiped out his "garden", so that now he can barely produce a "flower". He struggles to restore order to the drowned earth of his mind so he can raise "*les fleurs nouvelles*", but Time, the enemy of the title, will — he concludes — surely triumph over his efforts. In "*L'Ame Du Vin*", Baudelaire suggests that wine is the seed of God, which impregnates the poet and breeds "*la poésie/Qui jaillira vers Dieu comme une rare fleur!*" (poetry which will sprout toward God like a rare flower!); but in "*Le Guignon*" and "*La Mort Des Artistes*" he predicts that his "flowers" will bloom only after his death. Sartre puts it best when he insists that Baudelaire's spleen wasn't simply torpor, but "a feverish, sterile agitation which knew that it was in vain and which was poisoned by a merciless lucidity."

If *spleen* is the sensation that time passes too quickly, *ennui* is the sensation that time passes too slowly. In "*Hymne a la Beauté*" the poet asks Beauty herself whether she comes from Heaven or Hell (which he calls, variously, "*l'abîme*", "*gouffre noir*", and "*l'enfer*") — but then asks, rhetorically, "*Qu'importe, si tu rends... /L'Univers moins hideux et les instants moins lourds?*" (Who cares, so long as you render the universe less hideous and the moments less heavy?) Baudelaire's notion that the passing moment is unbearably heavy is repeated again and again throughout *Les Fleurs du Mal*. In *"De Profundis Clamavi"* he cries *"du fond du gouffre où mon cœur est tombé"* (from the depth of a gulf in which my heart is entombed), *"tant l'écheveau du temps lentement se dévide!"* (how slowly is the skein of time unwound!), and in *"La Muse Vénale"* he complains of *"les noirs ennuis des neigeuses soirées"* (the black ennuis of snowy evenings) which keep him from completing his poems.

Ennui is a very fashionable malady among jaded urbanites, even today; the word has passed into English as a chic synonym for "boredom". (One normally doesn't even italicize it.) How, then, to explain *"Au Lecteur"*, the poem which serves as an epigraph to *Les Fleurs du Mal*? After cataloguing the vices of the dandy — *"la sottise, l'erreur, le péché, la lésine"* (infatuation, sadism, lust, avarice [Robert Lowell's translation]) — the poem mourns the fact that for us poor debauchees life is like an old dried-up orange, or *"Le sein martyrisé d'une antique catin"* (the martyrized breast of an ancient whore): the pleasure is gone, yet we continue to squeeze and suck. Of all the vices, then, this epigraph to a book full of vices concludes, the worst of all is *"l'Ennui"*, that *"monstre délicat"* who destroys the earth with his yawn.

With the transvaluation of Baudelaire's dandyism had come a corresponding transvaluation of his *spleen*, and his *ennui*. Previously the former had been nothing more damaging than a passing mood of melancholy,

and the latter no more serious than a passing feeling of boredom with a vulgar urban scene. Now, however, the two had combined into a secular form of *acedia* — that disgust for an irredeemable world with which medieval religious hermits were often afflicted. For Baudelaire, the hours seemed alternately to race and to crawl by; but when the hours raced his mind crawled, and when the hours crawled his mind raced. No wonder he longed for a paradise where, as he puts it in his prose-poem *"L'Invitation au Voyage"*: *"Oui, c'est dans cette atmosphère qu'il ferait bon vivre — là-bas, où les heures plus lentes contiennent plus de pensées"* (Yes, in that atmosphere it would be good to live — over there, where the slower hours contain more thoughts).

In *"Semper Eadem"* Baudelaire pronounces, *"Vivre est un mal. C'est un secret de tous connu"* (Life itself is an affliction. This is a secret which everyone knows). In *"La Destruction"* Baudelaire describes a Demon who, swimming in the air around him at all times, forces him to pursue voluptuous pleasures until, *"Haletant et brisé de fatigue"* (panting and broken with fatigue), he finds himself driven *"au milieu/Des plaines de l'Ennui"* (to the very center of the moors of Ennui). And in those four poems Baudelaire entitled (somewhat confusingly) *"Spleen"*, he fumes that, on rainy or wintry days, "when the low heavy sky weighs like a lid upon a spirit aching for light," and the rain slanting down looks like the bars of a prison cell, *"L'ennui, fruit de la morne incuriosité,/Prend les proportions de l'immortalité"* (indifference expanding to Ennui takes on the feel of Immortality [Anthony Hecht's translation]). *Ennui*, here, has been transformed from a dandy's snobbish incuriosity about the world outside his room into a totalizing force which judges and condemns the world. Even for the king of a world as *ennuyé* as this one, Baudelaire sighs in one of the "*Spleen*" poems, life is not worth living: "*Son lit fleurdelisé se transforme en tombeau,/Et les dames d'atour, pour qui tout prince est beau,/Ne savent plus trouver d'impudique toilette/Pour tirer un souris de ce jeune squelette*" (His bed of fleur-de-lys becomes a tomb; even the ladies of the court, for whom all kings are beautiful, cannot put on shameful enough dresses for this skeleton [Robert Lowell's translation]). The poet, "*l'esprit gémissant en proie aux longs ennuis*" ([his] spirit groaning in the grip of interminable ennuis), is just such a living skeleton.

Women in shameful dresses apparently did nothing for the *ennuyé* Baudelaire. In "*Danse Macabre*", he suggests that the ultimate coquette is Death herself. Imagining Death attending a fancy-dress ball — "*O charme d'un néant follement attiré!*" (Oh what a charm when nullity tricks out! [Roy Campbell's translation]) — he encourages her to tell the "*dandys à face glabre*" (smooth-shaven dandies) present that she mingles among them ironically, because they might as well already be dead. And yet... he's famous for his erotic poetry. This apparent paradox makes sense only once one realizes that what Baudelaire sought in sex was an avenue of escape from the imperfect world in which he was trapped.

Because of her African ancestry

Baudelaire seems to have found in Duval a portal between his squalid surroundings and the tropical paradise about which he dreamed so often. In "*Parfum Exotique*" and "*La Chevelure*", for example, the smell of Duval's hair conjures up for him a vision of "*une île paresseuse*" (a lazy island) overgrown with fantastic trees bearing luscious fruits, under unchangingly blue skies, or "*la langoureuse Asie*" (languorous Asia) and its exotic scents. "*Ô féconde paresse!*" he exclaims. "*Infinis bercements du loisir embaumé!*" (O fruitful laziness! Infinite cradle-rockings of perfumed leisure!). And in "*Sed Non Satiata*", he tells Duval that he prefers her kisses to opium, and that her eyes are "the cistern where [his] ennuis drink."

Although Baudelaire complains constantly in his journals, letters, and poems about Duval's prostitute-like indifference to him — in an untitled poem, he exults that although "*l'ennui rend ton âme cruelle*" (ennui makes [Duval's] spirit cruel), nature moves in mysterious ways, for it has used the Queen of Sins to mold him into a genius — he seems to have found her drugged lethargy exciting. In "*Le Serpent Qui Danse*", for example, he admires the manner in which Duval's head sways, cobra-like, under "*le fardeau de ta paresse*" (the burden of [her] laziness). And in "*Chanson d'Après-Midi*" he rapturously tells her "*tu ravis les coussins/Par tes poses langoureuses*" (you ravish the cushions with your languorous poses). *Luxe, calme et volupté* — in the this-worldly sense of luxuriousness, calm, and voluptuousness — all make an appearance in "*Le Léthé*", in which, after crying, "*Je veux dormir! dormir plutôt que vivre!*" (I want to sleep! I'd rather sleep than live!), Baudelaire finds himself swallowed up by "*l'abîme de ta couche*" (the abyss of [Duval's] couch). Ironically, by seeking paradise in the embrace of his lover, Baudelaire winds up embracing the abyss.

Both paradise and the abyss make an appearance in "*Épigraphe Pour Un Livre Condamné*", a poem written after *Les Fleurs du Mal* had been published and banned — it was intended, as its title suggests, to serve as an epigraph to the now-condemned book. Here, Baudelaire warns those well-adjusted souls among his would-be readers to "*Jette ce livre saturnien,/Orgiaque et mélancolique... tu n'y comprendrais rien*" (Throw away this saturnine, orgiastic, and melancholic book... you won't understand one word of it). *Les Fleurs du Mal* is, to be sure, concerned with saturnine and melancholic states of mind, and orgies are alluded to constantly, but the poem concludes with a plea — to the reader whose eye "*sait plonger dans les gouffres*" (knows how to plunge into abysses) and who "*vas cherchant ton paradis*" (goes seeking [his] paradise) — to pity the author. Pity Baudelaire, indeed! "*Épigraphe*" is an epitaph for that poet whose life swung wildly between paradise and the annihilating abyss, following the hysterical trajectory of his own *livre condamné*.

Baudelaire's book, into which he'd poured his entire soul, was banned — for blasphemy and pornography — upon publication in 1857. Although it was republished in 1861, Baudelaire was by then desperate for recog-

nition. In 1862, sick and in debt, he begged his former hero Sainte-Beuve to nominate him for a seat in the French Academy. That influential critic penned a note to his fellow Academy members describing Baudelaire's poetic achievements as "a strange sort of kiosk, very ornate and artificial but yet elegant and mysterious, where Poe is read, [and] where the intoxicating effects of hashish are sought as the subject of rational analysis, and where opium and a thousand abominable drugs are drunk in precious porcelain cups." At the height of his creative powers, the literary establishment wrote Baudelaire off as a frivolous aesthete whose *livre saturnien,/Orgiaque et mélancolique* was an embarrassment.

Vertigo and the abyss were recurring themes for Baudelaire in the late 1840s and the 1850s. In "*L'Homme et la Mer*", he describes man's spirit as a *gouffre*, and intones, "*Homme, nul sa sondé le fond de tes abîmes*" (Man, none has sounded the depth of your abysses); and in "*L'Idéal*" he describes "*ce cœur profond comme un abîme*" (my heart, as deep as an abyss). "*Le Flacon*" gives notice that "*le Vertige/Saisit l'âme vaincue et la pousse à deux mains/Vers un gouffre obscourci de miasmes humains;/Il la terrasse au bord d'un gouffre séculaire*" (Vertigo seizes the vanquishes spirit and propels it with both hands towards a gulf that is darkened with the foul vapors of mortal decay; It strikes it down on the precipice of a secular Pit). In "*Le Poison*" he describes his lover's kisses as a drug "*Qui plonge dans l'oubli mon âme*" (which plunge my soul into forgetfulness), after which "*le vertige*" washes him to the very shores of Death.

BAUDELAIRE, A SELF-PORTRAIT. CIRCA 1859

BAUDELAIRE'S BOOK, INTO WHICH HE'D POURED HIS ENTIRE SOUL, WAS BANNED — FOR BLASPHEMY AND PORNOGRAPHY — UPON PUBLICATION IN 1857

this final line has been the favourite quotation of *ennuyé* intellectuals ever since.

Although "*La Voix*", as previously noted, describes how he'd been blessed and cursed with the ability to perceive an ideal sphere behind the appearances of this world, and "*Alchimie de la Douleur*" is a self-description of the poet as "the saddest of alchemists," because "*Je change... le paradis en enfer*" (I transform... paradise into Hell), no other mention of paradise appears in Baudelaire's poetry after the publication of *Les Fleurs du Mal*. It is as though that double vision of paradise and the abyss which had tortured him all his life had abandoned him at the very moment his poems finally found an audience. Instead of then being able to see only paradise, however, or only the hell that is life on earth, Baudelaire was stripped of the ability to see anything at all — his final poems are descriptions of the terrifying nothingness over which paradise and Hell alike are constructed.

However, having suffered a minor seizure in 1860, Baudelaire now became afflicted with the sensation that he was falling, surrounded by nothingness. In his journal, he pointed out the irony of this state of affairs: "morally and physically I have always been haunted by the sensation of the abyss [and] I have cultivated hysteria with enjoyment and terror. Now, I am in a constant state of vertigo." Baudelaire's final poems — written from 1860 until 1863, at which point he fled his creditors to Belgium, where he found himself unable to write — express the horrors of vertigo and the poet's longing for death. "*Le Goût du Néant*" expresses the poet's lack of interest in love or politics, groans splenetically that "*le Temps m'engloutit minute par minute*" (Time devours me moment by moment), and wonders, "*Avalanche, veux-tu m'emporter dans ta chute?*" (Avalanche, will you carry me with you in your fall?);

Charles Baudelaire died in Paris, a few months after having suffered a massive stroke, in 1867. He was 46 years old. ◉

IS THERE HONEY STILL FOR TEA?

Thatched cottages, reclining swains, geese in the yard: did this English pastoral idyll really ever exist? JOHN NICHOLSON uses the example of Bedford to explore the identity of the English and how it was created

Between the two world wars hordes of observers: writers, poets, painters and photographers, travelled around Blighty in a quest for the "real" England. Destabilised by the Great War, they were driven by the impulse to save the character of England and to identify it. Their success was the forging of a new kind of Englishness which prevails today.

My project, Emblems, examines one town which may be seen as typical of many — Bedford. As this was the home town of the great allegorist, John Bunyan, the form taken is emblematic. The abstract places — the river, bridge, castle, hotel, meadows — are abstracted to represent Anytown. Thus they enable us to see the essence of the English idea of paradise.

PASTORAL

"Bedford is perhaps the only large town in England that knows how to make the right use of its river,"

wrote the popular travel writer HV Morton of Bedford in *I Saw Two Englands* (1942). "The Ouse is the pride of Bedford, and, instead of flowing through the centre of the town, carrying on its banks a drear assortment of factories and warehouses, it is the town's chief promenade. On Sundays and holidays half the population gathers to sit there as if at the seaside, to walk on grass and under trees in Russell Park, or to embark on the broad bosom of the Ouse itself and exhibit skill, or the reverse, before the assembled town's folk."

HV Morton was the master of a new genre of travel writing: a vicarious pilgrimage. Between the Twenties and Fifties he enjoyed huge commercial success with his formula. Before *Two Englands* Morton had produced *The Call of England*. Published in June 1928 it went into another edition by November and had reached its eighth by 1931. He had also produced five books on London and the first two in the series *In Search of...*: Ireland and Scot-

THE EMBANKMENT PROMENADE, PHOTOGRAPHED BY FERDY RICHARDS C.1906

SPECTATORS ON THE OUSE DURING THE REGATTA, PHOTOGRAPHED BY BLAKE & EDGAR, 25 JULY 1912

land. *In Search of England* was the third in the series and published in 1927. By 1947 it was still in print in its thirty sixth edition.

He would hit gold with another series when he produced *In The Steps Of The Master* in 1934. It went through six reprints in twelve months.

It was not so much social commentary which made Morton's books so popular but a very English mixture. His major ingredients were London, tours of Britain and the Holy Land. This is not accidental for the three merge in the minds of the English. London is England while the Holy Land "is now and here and in England", in the words of the American poet TS Eliot who returned to his roots in Anglicanism. Bunyan and Blake had also conflated the holy lands of Israel and England. Both saw Jerusalem in England's green and pleasant land. This delicate matter belongs to an almost hidden tradition of English mysticism.

Since Morton lived until 1979 when he was 87 the royalties must have been gratifying. But few writers work only for the money, even jobbing journalists. It would have been pleasing for him to know that, as we enter a new millennium, secondhand bookshops rarely have a "library" which lacks a Morton. Morton's ideas have entered our national consciousness. It is appropriately ironic that one whose work had such a deep and lasting influence on the English view of themselves survives only in memory. Despite having been a hugely successful writer, HV Morton has

no entry in the Dictionary of National Biography.

The view of Bedford propagated by Morton as the quintessential English town, indeed a pastoral verging on paradise, clearly entered deep into the national psyche.

THE ENGLISH PARADISE

Morton's visit to Bedford, as everywhere, was a very quick sketch. That is a shame as it would have been interesting to compare his perspective with the elegiac local history by Charles Farrar, *Old Bedford*, published in 1926.

In 1939 Morton went through Huntingdonshire to Northamptonshire headed for Fotheringay castle. He appears to have stayed in Bedford a night at most. He set out in May and travelled through to the end of the year but he had not delivered the book before events overtook him.

His postscript, entitled "And then comes 1940", was added nearly a year later, in that feverish atmosphere of Dunkirk and the start of Churchill's administration. By August 11 1940 the Battle of Britain had begun. What a dramatic gift to heighten the thematic between an England at peace and one fighting for survival, the essential England.

What did Morton find? In the Indian summer of 1939 did Bedford belong to the core of England? Was anything in Bedford worth fighting for, or dying for? Morton recommended Bedford as the town which could teach all others how to benefit from its river. So strong and striking is his praise it is worth quoting the entire passage.

THE SUSPENSION BRIDGE SEEN FROM MILL MEADOWS C.1900

THE SOUTHERN PART OF THE HIGH STREET, DECORATED FOR THE CORONATION OF KING EDWARD VII

"I saw Bedford on a Sunday evening when the sun, appearing in April bursts, lit up a scene of extraordinary animation. Rowing boats, canoes and punts moved here and there on the Ouse, while people on the banks recognised their friends and commented on their handling of the oar, paddle or pole, and also I surmise, on their choice of companion. It is obviously every young man's fancy to take his girl on the river, so that gossip on the embankment misses nothing.

"I thought this scene charming. It would hardly be suitable, even in an unguarded moment, to call Bedford the Venice of England, but wherever there is water on which people pass in pleasure-boats, there is always an air of grace and gaiety. What a pity it is that other towns, whose rivers are now deformed by nineteenth century industrial developments, cannot clear them away and make their streams, like Bedford Ouse, the playground of the people."

ESSENTIAL ENGLAND

Apart from the "promenade" and "playground" the other factor which Morton found worthy of note was Bedford's link with John Bunyan. The mid twentieth century pastoral had merged somehow with the rustic giant of nonconformity. The playground and promenade were for The People. Who would begrudge them their pleasures? Here is the seed of the post-war utopianism which brought in a Labour government.

Bunyan was a man of the soil, the very stuff of England. He expressed the attraction of simplicity versus contrivance, a duality which is the basis of England's natural genius. Bedford's promenade was not natural. The pastoral Morton so admired was a consciously artificial creation. It had been created by sweeping away precisely the unsightly elements he deplored.

Here is what England was, or should be – a pastoral. Morton would abolish factories and warehouses as drear and ugly. Instead, he felt, England should be covered in the exciting animation of pleasure, even if it was gentle to the point of immobility: sitting. The ideal scene comprises drifting on the river or walking on the grass. Hearing music. This is a more tasteful spectacle than the grime of Industry.

In *Old Bedford* Charles Farrar had written of the destruction of the Swan Gardens, which had joined the hotel to the riverside, as a sign of the fall. For the first time in centuries the southern side of the castle became a thoroughfare. A road now passed the hotel running between it and the river to the junction with Newnham Road and Thomas Street. Trees were planted and a balustrade matching the hotel was built to mark the edge of the bank. Beyond the junction, the next stretch of riverside, edging the new Castle Road estate, was transformed by the planting of trees in the 1880s. But Improvers also removed the genuinely ancient and rustic dwellings of Waterloo which, in other circumstances, would have been considered a centrepiece.

By 1890 the area was becoming a

DREAMING ENGLAND
Further reading on the character of Albion

The inter-war writers and painters who would "save" England could only see it as a pastoral. Morton had tapped into a gold mine. Others were not slow to pan for more gold. Here are some of those who found rewards.

Typical were THE CHANGING FACE OF ENGLAND by Arthur Collett, 1926, and ABOUT ENGLAND by MV Hughes, 1927. This last was dedicated to "an exile in Africa" which suggests that the audience included ex-patriots who were nostalgic for Home. ROUGH ISLANDERS OR THE NATIVES OF ENGLAND by Henry Wood Nevinson, 1930, had a different purpose while Major General JEB Seely, aka Lord Mottistone, dedicated his FOR EVER ENGLAND to the boys of England. His aim was to show them "the essential nobility of the English character", an ambition which must have struck chords in school rooms across the land. SPB Mais was another prolific contributor to the genre with THIS UNKNOWN ISLAND, 1932, and ROUND ABOUT ENGLAND, 1935. He continued producing the mixture in the Forties with ENGLAND'S CHARACTER and ENGLAND'S PLEASANCE.

Two examples from 1933 are 'NEATH ENGLISH SKIES: A BOOK FOR WAYFARERS by Fredk I Cowles (illustrations by Doris M Cowles) while a German, H A Piehler, claimed to emulate Baedeker with ENGLAND FOR EVERYONE. Whether this contained a message encouraging social unrest or an appeal to foreigners it would be an ironic precursor of the Baedeker raids by wayfaring German bombers.

Published in March 1934, J B Priestley's ENGLISH JOURNEY: BEING A RAMBLING BUT THOUGHTFUL ACCOUNT OF WHAT ONE MAN SAW AND HEARD AND FELT AND THOUGHT DURING A JOURNEY THROUGH ENGLAND DURING THE AUTUMN OF THE YEAR 1933, was full of social comment and enjoyed a lasting reputation, to be surpassed only by Orwell's ROAD TO WIGAN PIER, 1937. That was a similar attempt to isolate the core of an English character.

THE ENGLAND I LOVE by James Turle and ENGLISH VILLAGES AND HAMLETS by Humphrey Pakington both appeared in 1934, the latter steering attention even more to so-called natural, ancient and quintessential communities. In 1935, the Batsford publishing house released an anthology called THE LEGACY OF ENGLAND: an illustrated survey of the works of man in the English countryside. The foreword tells us it was intended as "a companion volume to THE BEAUTY OF BRITAIN, published last Spring in the same series, The Pilgrims' Library." Batsford made an industry out of such material, usually illustrating the books with watercolour landscapes which were interchangeable with those in railway carriages.

The Council for the Preservation of Rural England had its Aims and Objects included in a weighty tome called THE SCENERY OF ENGLAND: A STUDY OF HARMONIOUS COMMUNITY IN TOWN AND COUNTRY, 1937. The same year came an offering called The Right Book Club, which aimed to counteract Victor Gollancz's Left Book Club. It published WS Shears' THIS ENGLAND: A BOOK OF THE SHIRES AND COUNTIES.

Also in 1937 an American novelist, Mary Ellen Chase, who spent two years living in England offered IN ENGLAND NOW which was less unquestioning and even lightly quizzical of English social habits. The transatlantic alliance starting to emerge was, naturally, far from accepting the official English line.

Not that all the English travellers were blindly obedient. THE GOOD COMPANIONS, Priestley's 1929 hit novel, described the travels of clapped-out acts searching for an audience. The metaphor of England as a desperately shabby show haunting decayed Empire theatres would be developed thirty years later by John Osborne in THE ENTERTAINER. In his factual exploration Priestley had given a twist to the genre with his three Englands. Morton had offered only two. ◉

civic attraction and, every summer, a steam launch called the Lady Lee, plied from a landing platform at the foot of the bridge catering for those who wished to commune more closely with the river.

GENUINE ANTIQUITY VERSUS FAKE

The demolition of the riverside houses and businesses began the process of municipalisation brought to a peak by Norman Greenshields, who was Borough Surveyor from 1901 to 1932. He is responsible for the Embankment Gardens with its floral flans. Russell Park was both a Victorian public benefit and the bounty of the Duke of Bedford to the town, opened in 1894.

The southern side of the river was also a construct. Even the ability to walk across to it was a recent innovation with the introduction of the Suspension Bridge. This link from the Embankment to Mill Meadows was opened on 11 July 1888.

The river had the habit, like the Thames, of freezing over. In London this occasioned winter fairs on the ice. In Bedford it also gave the chance to skate, an activity catered for also by an indoor roller skating rink, built in 1912 next to the Swan hotel. By 1920 the craze ended and the building was divided and used for other purposes. Less energetic pursuits might be enjoyed at the Embankment Hotel. Apart from the Swan it was the only pub allowed on the genteel promenade, a grand affair with a fashionable Elizabethan high half-timbered gable. Whilst the select Swan Gardens had given way to the general Embankment Gardens

NATURE, SUCH AS A RIVER, WAS PART OF THE MORAL ORDER OF GOD'S CREATION AND THEREFORE SHOULD SERVE A PURPOSE

Bedford was not eager to encourage lax behaviour.

To the east the next crossing remained the footbridge by Newnham Mill. It was not until the Sixties that a road crossed the river here. This would have been too much of an exertion for walkers who could now accomplish a generous circulatory promenade between the town and suspension bridges on firm hard footpaths. By 1906 a bandstand adorned the south bank where weekly concerts were a successful interlude on the promenade. On 25 July 1912 a Regatta was held in the cultivated stretch so bringing a new use to the municipal river area.

So Bedford now had its Embankment to echo London. The river was turning from a working commercial inland port into the ornamental paradise admired by Morton. The town was making the "right use" of its river as the centrepiece of its playground.

This ambition climaxed in the Fifties plan which envisioned a complex of civic showpieces stretching from the bridge to the Rink Islands. The area around the Duck Mill, for centuries used for trade, was to be replaced. The boat sheds and modest cinema would be replaced by an

AN EDWARDIAN POSTCARD VIEW OF BEDFORD'S PROMENADE C.1910

THE PRIORY STREET BOWLING GREEN C.1920

THE TIN LID

An extract from the introduction to English Cottages and Small Farmhouses, an exhibition catalogue, 1975, by Paul Oliver.

"There are probably more cottages displayed on calendars in homes in England than there are standing on the ground. The cottage features on birthday greetings and Christmas cards; it is the subject of jigsaw puzzles and wall plaques; it is fashioned into teacosies and firescreens, distorted into teapots and marmalade jars. The cottage, in fact, is so much a part of the popular romantic picture of Britain that it is now difficult to consider it without the associations of a thousand images of leaded lights, garden walls, hollyhocks, fluffy clouds and pink skies above golden thatch."

ornamental boat-house and grand cinema, theatre, restaurant and indoor swimming pool. Bedford would have its rival to London's South Bank. In the Eighties the closure of the rambling shop in St Mary's dealing in plumbing with its large factory behind caused a big vacancy at its rear. It is currently used as a car park.

SANCTIFIED

So the promenade admired by Morton as a pastoral was unnatural, an invented landscape. But it was also aspiring to an invented tradition, a false antiquity. Bunyan would have had no idea of either this landscape or understood such an attitude to the river. Nature, such as a river, was part of the moral order of God's Creation and therefore should serve a purpose.

Any hint that walking back and forth along the Embankment had a deeper purpose than pleasure, that it somehow offered a form of a spiritual progression was as false as the genre of travel writing epitomised by Morton. Everything should be experienced by proxy. Travel, patriotism even religious feelings were second-

hand in your armchair. England existed as a paradise in the mind's eye. Readers went on toy pilgrimages, taking the spiritual journey as a jaunt.

Promenading was the opposite of Bunyan's call. Making a spectacle of oneself and envying or admiring others who showed off was more an echo of *Vanity Fair*. It was an expression of self-satisfaction, of the sort of pride which in 1902 had made Bedford display itself to the Saviour of Empire, General John French, fresh from his triumph over the Boers, as the triumphant, essential England. ◉

The EMBLEMS PROJECT envisages the creation of a series of national studies of the English heritage and character. Please contact the EMBLEMS Project at History Today magazine's website: www.historytoday.com

Sources: We are grateful to The Pictorial Archivist, County Hall, for permission to reproduce the Bedford scenes. More appear in Richard Wildman's five books of photographs of the town including Bedford, published by Alan Sutton, £4.99

EARTHLY DELIGHTS

Ever since the garden of Eden was depicted as a sensual paradise in the Koran, says TIM RICHARDSON, gardens and sex have been inseparable

Pictures from Visions of Arcadia by May Woods (Aurum, £25)

At the top of the turgid, swollen stem, the sexually mature bisexual opens itself up and awaits the moment its trembling pistil will receive fertilisation. Here comes the hairy vehicle for this moment of creation, buzzing as he comes. There! A speck of rich male dust from some distant stamen hits the towering stigma, travels down its stalk and finds the ovary of its dreams. Union is complete. A seed will follow. The hairy vehicle, satisfied, moves on and forgets his conquest in an instant.

The garden in summer is a botanical orgy, where plants can be male or female, or male

NYMPHS AND NUDITY IN A DESIGN BY ISAAC DE CAUS FOR
THE GROTTO OF NEPTUNE AT HEIDELBERG, 1615

GARDENS HAVE LONG MADE RICH AND VARIED VENUES FOR EROTIC TRYSTS, ILLICIT OR OTHERWISE

and female at the same time. If they get desperate they can even have sex with themselves.

But gardens have this goody-goody reputation. Percy Thrower, vicars, respectable ladies in sensible shoes: the media's approach to gardens this century hardly quickens the pulse. But it hasn't always been this way. Gardens have long made rich and varied venues for erotic trysts, illicit or otherwise.

The Garden of Eden is supposed to be where we began. Enough said. In the Koran, Paradise is mentioned many times, always as "gardens watered by running streams... where the righteous have all they desire" and a few times quite specifically:

"But for those that fear the majesty of their Lord there are two gardens (which of your Lord's blessings would you deny?) planted with shady trees. Which of your Lord's blessings would you deny?

"Each is watered by a flowing spring. Which of your Lord's blessings would you deny?

"Each bears every kind of fruit in pairs. Which of your Lord's blessings would you deny?

"They shall recline on couches lined with thick brocade, and within reach will hang the fruits of both gardens. Which of your Lord's blessings would you deny?

"Therein are bashful virgins whom neither man nor jinnee will have

touched before. Which of your Lord's blessings would you deny?

"Virgins as fair as corals and rubies. Which of your Lord's blessings would you deny?"

This bit of scripture was honoured by Islamic architects throughout Asia and southern Europe in the "cross garden", in which a courtyard space is bisected by two straight low rills, as at the Alhambra in Granada. But the architects also made sure that they created discreetly screened areas just off the courtyard, where earthly "dark-eyed houris" and "wives of perfect chastity" could minister sherbet and other pleasures.

Among the earliest depictions of gardens in the West are the views of the medieval *hortus conclusus*, or enclosed garden. Here, a lady is willingly trapped behind high walls, with a locked door visible. Often she is conversing with a gentleman in a bower of flowers, representing purity. It may just be me, but there does seem to be a delicious sense of potential transgression in many of these chaste scenes.

Early Baroque gardens of the late 16th century are peopled with statues of scantily clad denizens, elegant ladies and gentlemen, or innocent swains and swainesses. They help to create a sense of a holiday from reality. But it was the 17th and 18th centuries that saw gardens become universes of sexual fantasy, parallel worlds where proscribed activities suddenly seemed possible.

In 1561 the influential designer Du Cerceau published elaborate

THE GENERALIFE AT THE ALHAMBRA IN SPAIN, SUMMER PALACE OF THE SEXY SULTANS OF GRANADA

fountain plans, including one with mermaids spouting water from their nipples. This sort of semi-sexual statement was common. Nymphaeums — semi-circular theatres adorned with sportive, nubile nymphs — were de rigeur in gardens at this period. There is a good one in the Boboli Gardens in Florence. The figures may be made of stone, but they lighten the mood and ease the passage of flirtation.

Water tricks were another way of creating infectious delight and gaiety among visitors. All over Europe throughout the 17th and 18th centuries, aristocrats were squeaking with delight at being soaked to the skin by strong jets of water bursting upon them from statues, model ships, bushes and even the ground.

The royal summer palace at Aranjuez in Spain was famed for the variety and number of its water tricks, and the holes for up-the-trouser-leg water fun can still be seen in the paths in the gardens of the royal palace in Seville. Isaac de Caus was supremo of Europe's water tricks industry. He perfected incredible feats such as artificial rainbows in grottoes or metal balls suspended on jets of water.

The advantages of having lots of over-excited, soaking wet women on the premises were not lost on royals and aristos. During a visit to the Villa Arvedi near Verona last summer, Comte Arvedi told me about one of his ancestors who would deliberately get female guests wet,

LADIES GALORE IN THIS PAINTING BY J. COTELLE OF LA MONTAGNE D'EAU, ONE OF THE MANY INTIMATE FOUNTAINS AT VERSAILLES, 1693

THE ADVANTAGES OF HAVING LOTS OF OVER-EXCITED, SOAKING WET WOMEN ON THE PREMISES WERE NOT LOST ON ROYALS AND ARISTOS

and then suggest they might like to dry off inside.

Another way of creating a frisson of excitement among guests was to create what we would recognise today as fairground rides. Swings and carousels were popular, but the apogee was the rollercoaster. There was a celebrated early one made at Marly, next door to Versailles, to which the Duchesse de Bourgogne apparently became addicted. Catherine the Great had a more ambitious contraption at Tsarskoye Selo called "The Flying Mountains".

Versailles was in a way an exercise in flirtation on a massive scale. Louis XIV's fêtes, to which hundreds were invited, were much more than fancy-dress parties, with gauzily costumed female aristos performing plays in the thirty or so bosquets, or wooded glades, on either side of the main allée. On one occasion a fleet of gondolas loaded with toga-clad girls attempted to woo the king on the shore.

The atmosphere at such night-time parties was described some seventy years later by the English voluptuary William Beckford, who accidentally gatecrashed a racy event organised by the Portuguese Infanta at the Palace of Queluz near Lisbon. "Amongst the thickets, some of which received a tender light from tapers placed low on the ground

LOUIS XIV CONSTRUCTED THE CHINOISERIE TRIANON DE PORCELAINE AT VERSAILLES FOR HIS MISTRESS, MADAME DE MONTESPAN

under frosted glasses, the Infanta's nymph-like attendants, all thinly-clad after the example of her royal and nimble self, were glancing to and fro, visible one instant, invisible the next, laughing and talking all the while with very musical silvertoned voices."

Gardens have also proved ideal for secreting away mistresses. Louis XIV constructed the chinoiserie Trianon de Porcelaine at Versailles for his mistress, Madame de Montespan. This was a pavilion and enclosure devoted to escapist pleasure, its exterior walls adorned with cupids.

The idea that *risqué* decoration suited garden buildings quickly gained popularity. The dwarfish, gap-toothed but witty and notorious Duchesse du Maine held meetings of her Order of the Beehive in her Menagerie Pavilion at Sceaux, her palace outside Paris. As Queen Bee, she held a series of all-night ban-

quets famed for their licence. Voltaire attended.

The Comte d'Artois was a rakish young fellow who dressed like an Englishman and liked horseracing. The interiors of his little pavilion at Bagatelle, in the Bois de Boulogne in Paris, were decorated to the highest standard with variations on the theme of sensuality, featuring Venus, Cupid, Mars and a figure called the Amorous Turk. The bedroom was "wittily" themed on a military model, as a play on the idea of the bedroom as a battleground. The gardens were filled with little getaways such as Druids' Cabins, an Egyptian obelisk, the Tomb of the King of Hearts and the Philosopher's Pavilion.

At this time Marie-Antoinette was planning her Petit Hameau at Versailles, the model village where she could dress as a dairymaid. This is a little bit kinky, clearly. The potency of the dairymaid fantasy for many men is advertised by the sheer number of model dairies created in the 18th century (there are good ones at Rambouillet and Temple Newsam near Leeds) and also in the not inconsiderable number of dukes who

actually married dairymaids.

The most emphatic sexual garden statement at this time is the Temple of Venus at West Wycombe Park, Buckinghamshire, made for Sir Francis Dashwood. The architectural design is based on "the female anatomy" and the pavilion was the venue for parties for Dashwood's notorious Hell Fire Club.

Architects in the 18th century could let down their hair with their designs for garden buildings, and the most outlandish edifices in Britain can be found in our landscape parks. William Chambers, designer of Kew, summarised the variety among his Chinese-style buildings: "some of them contrived for banquets, balls, concerts, learned disputations, plays, rope-dancing and feats of activity; others again for bathing, swimming, reading, hot nookie, sleeping or meditation." Hot nookie was admittedly my addition but these buildings were certainly used for liaisons.

To see proof of this, pay a visit to Wrest Park in Bedfordshire, which is now a rather serious-minded place owned by English Heritage. At the end of a long central canal stands a magnificent pepperpot pavilion designed by Thomas Archer. This was used as a banqueting house in the early 18th century, but behind concealed doors you can find secret passages which lead upstairs to several small rooms lit by single windows. These little cells are nothing to do with the servants, and are just big enough for a bed...

Even our original idler Dr Johnson equated gardens with sensuous delight, claiming that the greatest pleasure available to man was the experience of riding downhill in a carriage over smooth sward in the company of a beautiful and intelligent woman.

In the 20th century the link between sex and gardens has diminished. Now we have Charlie Dimmock and her hyped-up breasts. Charlie has done more than anyone since Mellors to add sex to the herbaceous border. But her appeal is essentially *Carry On*. It's time for the re-injection of some really witty flirtatiousness into the rather earnest contemporary garden scene. ◉

THE FLYING MOUNTAINS, AN 18TH CENTURY ROLLER-COASTER, AT CATHERINE THE GREAT'S GARDEN

GET YOUR LOVELY BACK ISSUES HERE

Go to idler.co.uk, or make a cheque out to "The Idler" and send to: The Idler, Studio 20, 24-28A Hatton Wall, London EC1N 8JH. P&P is free

1: August '93
SOLD OUT
Dr Johnson

2: Nov~Dec '93
SOLD OUT
Homer & Will Self

3: Jan~Feb '94
£5.00
Bertrand Russell

4: April~May '94
SOLD OUT
Kurt & Matt Black

5: July~Aug '94
SOLD OUT
Douglas Coupland

6: Sept~Oct '94
SOLD OUT
Easy Listening

7: Dec~Jan '95
SOLD OUT
Sleep

8: Feb~Mar '95
SOLD OUT
Jeffrey Bernard

9: May~June '95
SOLD OUT
Suzanne Moore

10: July~Aug '95
SOLD OUT
Damien Hirst

11: Sept~Oct '95
£4.00
Keith Allen

12: Nov~Dec '95
£4.00
Bruce Robinson

13: Jan~Feb '96
SOLD OUT
Stan Lee

14: Mar~Apr '96
£4.00
Bruce Reynolds

15: May~Jun '96
SOLD OUT
Hashish Killers

16: Aug~Sept '96
SOLD OUT
John Michel

17: Nov~Dec '96
£4.00
John Cooper Clarke

18: Spring '97
£4.00
Thomas Pynchon

19: Summer '97
£3.00
Psychogeography

20: Winter '97
£3.00
Howard Marks

21: Feb~March '98
£3.00
The Gambler

22: April~May '98
SOLD OUT
Alan Moore

23: June~July '98
SOLD OUT
Summer Special

24: Aug~Sep '98
SOLD OUT
Krazy Golf

25: August '99
£10.00
Man's Ruin
320 page book-format

SHORT STORIES

A VISIT FROM VAL KORAN

A short story by JEREMY DYSON.
Illustrations by EDWIN MARNEY

....

Feddy, not for the first time, was thinking abut the star in Miranda's bedroom. They had both noticed it in the morning, quite early, high up on the whitewashed wall behind her bed, almost touching the ceiling. A strange, luminous star, looking as if it had been stencilled on to the woodchip. It seemed at first to be caused by a shaft of light coming through a gap in the heavy curtains. However, Feddy realised this couldn't be. The rest of the room was still too dark — the curtains so thick they excluded the presence of the bright April morning.

Miranda was perturbed. She stood up, naked, trying to ascertain the star's cause. Feddy, more attuned to what was around him, had guessed that the light was coming from behind the wall, through some kind of ventilation grille. Miranda would have none of this. She leapt off the bed and threw open the curtains, expecting the star to disappear. It didn't. It remained shining stubbornly, despite the sunlight now filling the room. Those mornings, thought Feddy. Those mornings were beautiful. Just him and her. They made love in the mornings. He preferred the mornings to the nights. Naturally aroused it seemed the simplest thing in the world for him to slide into her and fuck them both awake. I miss doing it, thought Feddy, even after all this time; I miss her long heavy substantial body and her pungent femaleness next to me at night and upon waking. Her scent was always strong, but never unpleasant. Like him she enjoyed slipping into bed without preparation, not teeth cleaning or face washing. Sneaking up on sleep. Maybe that's why they slept together as well as they did. Some nights the sleep was so deep Feddy thought he could have been anaesthetised.

I miss her peculiarly bright diamond eyes. I miss the fulness of her mouth. It was rare that Feddy stared directly into her face. She was never comfortable under his gaze. But he knew her beauty well. He observed it in brief glances, or when she slept. I can stay here, he thought. I can settle here quite happily. He suspected they could have been something very good indeed. He didn't have time to find out. It hadn't surprised him to wake and see a star shining on her wall.

He sat outside his bar, gazing down the hill into the town. Mdina could still look quite lovely to him despite twenty years of mornings such as these with the sun rising slowly, turning the old white stone orange and then yellow. The rest of the island, or at least the rest of its major towns, was quite charmless and even unpleasant (Valetta aside — though that was far too busy for Feddy's tastes). But Mdina was Malta's concealed jewel, five kilometres inland, away from the cheaply built hotels and the English tourists. The tourists came, of course, but somehow they were absorbed by the antiquated buildings — their irritating presence neutralised. Besides, they rarely strayed up to this part of the town. Feddy's patrons were the locals, the native Maltese who ran the surrounding businesses — the barber shop, the tannery, the bakery. He'd never relied on the tourist trade to sustain his income. When he'd bought the place in the mid-seventies the vendor had encouraged him to rename it. You should call it Feddy's, sir, or Jason's if you don't mind me saying, he had suggested. But that was a time when Feddy had been reluctant to announce his presence to the world. Instead the bar remained Stetson's. It also retained its red leather sofa seats and malfunctioning juke-box along with its heavy aroma of cigar smoke and stale beer. Feddy had never seen any reason to renovate or refurbish. In fact sometimes he liked to sit at the back on quiet evenings and imagine it in earlier times, before he had arrived, forty, fifty, even a hundred years ago. He pictured the customers coming in and out. The details of their lives not so different from their descendents. Their loves, their needs, their fears, their pleasures. The past was there in the scuffed wooden floor, in the depressions in the stone steps that led to the lavatories, in the tobacco-stained alcoves that filled the wall opposite the bar. And Feddy took comfort from its presence. Thinking of Miranda, as he did most days, he reminded himself that she would not have liked it here. But then he would never have found himself here had it not been for her.

"Mr Feddy. Mr Feddy." Here was the baseball-capped figure of Aldi hurrying up the hill. That in itself was an unusual sight. Not just the hurrying, but at this time of day. It was rare to see his barman lit by a sunrise.

"What on earth brings you out at this time?" Feddy looked at his watch theatrically. "Don't tell me. I leave you in charge for one night and you were robbed."

"Mr Feddy. We not take enough to be robbed." The little man wiped the sweat from his upper lip, blackened by a day's growth of beard. He must have been five years older than Feddy but he had all the authority of a paper boy. "I come with an important message."

Feddy laughed. "Now what could be so important to get you scurrying out here at this time?"

Aldi paused whilst he caught his breath.

FEDDY FELT HIS LEGS GIVE WAY. HE REACHED OUT FOR THE EDGE OF THE BAR TO PREVENT HIMSELF FALLING

"I just get some water, Mr Feddy. Would you like some?" Feddy shook his head. Aldi lifted the shutter so as not to have to bend to get under it. Feddy looked down the road then went inside after his assistant. He didn't like the fact he looked so scared.

"Who brought us a message? O'Donnelly hasn't been at you again with his gangland stories, has he?" Aldi, always the barman, was fussing with lemons and ice cubes. "They're all made up. The only criminals he knows are some dodgy builders in Buggeba." Feddy was aware he was babbling. He sensed something difficult was coming.

"Someone come for you. A man." Aldi sipped at his water.

"What man? Did you know him?"

Aldi shook his head. He was holding his glass with both hands like a child. "No. But he say you know him. He say he was your friend." Feddy tried not to let the expression on his face change. "He ask me to give you this." The little man put his glass down then reached inside the pocket of his suede jacket. He pulled out a small piece of white card.

Feddy turned it over. It was a photograph. An old one from about thirty years ago. About five inches square, glossy with a white border. It was of Miranda. Feddy felt his legs give way. He reached out for the edge of the bar to prevent himself falling. His heart was racing so he sat down.

"There was something funny about this man, Mr Feddy. I'm not sure he was your friend. I not like how he said I had to give this to you."

"What?" Feddy's throat was tight. He found it hard to get the word out.

"He did not shout at me. He said it soft and he smiled. But it made me feel bad inside. Like if I not get it to you something bad would happen to me." Feddy found a stool and sat down. "Are you all right, Mr Feddy?" He nodded. "Do you know this man?"

"What did he look like?"

Aldi looked down, his forehead furrowed. "He wore a white suit and a hat. A little straw hat." Feddy was surprised to find himself smiling. "He said he come back tonight. Or if you not here tonight he come back the night after." Feddy nodded again. "Is he trouble, Mr Feddy? Is it bad news?"

Feddy poured himself some water from the jug Aldi had prepared. "He's my executioner." He looked out at the oblong of light beneath the shutter. It was going to be a beautiful day.

Feddy sent Aldi back home and locked up the bar. He walked the half-mile to his apartment smoking a cigar all the way. He rarely smoked in the mornings. His head was crowded with even more memories. Naturally he thought of Miranda. Of the time that photograph had been taken. She had been in the second year of her degree. He had just started his third year teaching.

Koran had been there only a year more than he, although his natural authority suggested otherwise. It was Koran who had introduced Feddy to Miranda. It was Koran who had first been her lover. Miranda had been a student in his department. He taught a course in Metaphor and Meaning, although his real interests were far more esoteric. But when Feddy had been introduced to her — at one of Koran's Friday night "services" — he had fallen instantly in love with her. She was truly beautiful. He was surprised to see her there; Koran had a strict rule about not allowing students to sabbats, even those who had expressed a genuine interest in matters of his "reputation". Miranda's pale skin shone, burnished by the candle flames, glowing with an inner light. When she turned and smiled at Feddy, she cast her long-lashed eyes down slightly. He knew at that moment that he had to have her. When he found out later that evening that she was Koran's, he trembled inside. Trembled because it made no difference. Something had happened and he had to have her, regardless of consequence.

Feddy kicked at the heavy oak door at the front of his apartment block. It always stuck at the bottom corner. The wood was scuffed and scarred from the ten thousand strikes it had received over the years. He ground the cigar butt against the side of the doorpost and entered, the clack of his feet hollow on the tiled floor of the entrance lobby. He wondered if Koran would be waiting for him here. Of course he would know where Feddy lived — the apartment was no harder to track down than the bar. The locks would hardly have kept him out. Feddy would talk to him, reason with him. They were nearly old men now. The past was gone. It was time to let go. As he walked up the banisterless steps, past the doorways lined with terracotta pots, Feddy even allowed himself the possibility that this was why Koran had finally come. Surely time and age would have softened him. That possibility was not enough to prevent Feddy entering his flat with supreme caution. The thing was not to allow Koran to kiss him. That was the thing.

As far as he could tell, the apartment was empty. He scanned the three rooms, even the tiny bathroom — as if Koran would have allowed himself the indignity of hiding behind a shower-curtain. Eventually Feddy sat down on the edge of the bed, his heart pounding. There must be something he could do.

Feddy had never thought it serious. Feddy had considered it nonsense. Well, not nonsense exactly, but affectation; theatre. He'd liked the buzz and the thrill of the ceremonies. And the sex, of course. But it just went with the times. The age of Aquarius. Their Satanic Majesties Request and all that. Sure Koran was a charismatic man. A charmer. An entertainer. But when he spoke of magic and power and rivers of fate, Feddy had assumed they were just more metaphors. He hadn't thought ... If he'd thought for a moment that any of it were true ...

M iranda wasn't just another conquest. Miranda was unique. "Do whales have faces?" were the first words she'd ever spoken to him. She wasn't one of his students but she'd sat in on one of his Moby Dick classes after they'd met at Koran's. She'd invited him to her flat, which she shared with two other girls — one a music post-graduate and the other a mathematician. Even this, thought Feddy, had been charming. He remembered that first visit clearly. The imposing entrance hall of the old Victorian building. It was ochre yellow, with a mosaic floor. On one wall was a faded cut-out from the Yorkshire Evening Post telling you about the house. Some minor poet used to live there. Feddy couldn't remember which one. Novels were his thing. He avoided anything that wasn't prose. Miranda loved poetry though. She would send him poems, neatly typed on plain white paper. Jacques Prévert, Allen Ginsberg. It charmed him, impressed him even. One poem he'd assumed was by someone else, someone famous although there was no name at the end. It turned out to have been written by her. Feddy even admitted to himself that he was vaguely threatened by what she called her "attempts". Who knows how far she might have travelled in her life had Koran not cut it so short?

Feddy stared at his reflection and sighed. Not a day went by without him thinking of her. Of her beauty, of her talent, of the life that should have been theirs. After she had died and he had fled, first to California and then — when his attempts to legitimise his presence had failed — to Malta, Feddy had tried to involve himself with other women but with no success. Miranda's perfect memory always interrupted. Miranda had been the one he had waited for all his life. Then Koran had taken her. And now Koran was here to take him. Feddy thought of fleeing. Of packing his brown leather suitcase and leaving the island, maybe to Africa or the Middle East. But if he was honest he knew he didn't have the energy. In truth he had been waiting for this moment since he had arrived. He was too weary to wait any more. He went to the bathroom, turned on the shower and began to undress.

"Ah, Mr Feddy. A pleasant surprise." Shiloh the barber put down his broom and went to shake Feddy's hand. "A drink for you, sir." He reached behind a pile of pomade jars and brilliantine tins, producing a labelless bottle of what was presumably whisky.

"I won't if you don't mind."

"Oh yes you will." He was already filling a teacup. "I hear you have had a visitor." Feddy found himself tightening. He refrained from saying anything. "There are no secrets in this town, sir, you must know that." He handed the cup to Feddy. "But do not worry. I will not ask any unnecessary questions."

"I want to look neat, Shiloh. I want to look ... together. In charge. You understand?"

"Of course I understand. I always understand. We will shave you. We will trim your hair and I will press your trousers. You will look a picture for your visitor." The barber's foot depressed the pedal at the base of the chair and

Feddy lurched backwards. "Let us begin." He slapped a hot towel on Feddy's already sweat-sheened face.

The last days. Feddy still remembered the last days. It had begun with the inevitable visit from Koran. At the time neither of them had been that concerned. Miranda had a T-shirt which read "Love Conquers All" and that was very much their attitude. It had been a wonderful time. Feddy knew that Miranda was "the one". He had been waiting for her since the early days of his adolescence. This perfect creature whom he desired infinitely, who engaged him completely. Those days after they had decided they were going to be together were a joyful anticipation of their life to come. There was no need to talk of marriage, there was enough certainty in their togetherness to dispense with the artificial bonds of ceremony. Feddy imagined — for some reason — a small house by a river, autumn afternoons, a range in the kitchen, overhanging trees. He had never felt so complete. A visit from Val Koran was hardly going to disrupt things. Let him come. He would see the truth — maybe even give them his blessing once he apprehended the strength of their feelings for one another.

And so he did come. One Thursday afternoon as Miranda and Feddy were discussing their move to London. Feddy had made inquiries about a teaching post at London University and Miranda had made a decision to give up her studies completely. She was going to pursue her poetry (and work part-time for her friend Fiona who had a hat shop in Chelsea). The doorbell had rung and Madelaine the mathematician had run down to answer it. Feddy and Miranda were sitting in the kitchen. Feddy was both surprised and not surprised to see Koran standing in the doorway. He had heard they were leaving. He wanted to see them both before they went. There was a long silence. Feddy contemplated beginning an apology, or at least an explanation. This was the first time all three of them had been in a room together since he and Miranda had become lovers. He started to speak. Koran cut him off. He had only come to say goodbye. Feddy had stood up and put his coffee cup down. He extended his hand but the gesture was ignored. Instead Koran moved to Miranda and brushed back her thick black hair exposing the pale skin on the side of her face. Feddy wondered if he should defend her in some way: she suddenly seemed very vulnerable. But Koran was only going to kiss her. He leant forward and gently kissed her just below her ear where her jaw-bone began.

"Goodbye, my love," he said softly. Then he left without looking at Feddy.

Feddy would have been lying if he had said he wasn't unnerved by the visit. He and Koran had been good friends, at least on a professional level. Even given the circumstances of the visit he had hoped for a farewell of some kind. Something that might have hinted at some future reconciliation. The complete stonewalling he received he found considerably unsettling. Miranda was quiet too for a couple of days afterwards. Doubtless she felt guilty about the way things had happened. Feddy even put the rash that had begun to spread across her face down to being a psychosomatic expression of her feelings. Funny how its epicentre seemed to be the exact spot on her jaw-line that Koran had kissed her. On the

BUT NOW, AS HE SAT WAITING FOR HIS NEMESIS, HE THOUGHT THERE WAS SOME SINCERITY IN STOICISM

third or fourth day the inflammation seemed to cover her whole body. She said it was painful to the touch. Madelaine was concerned about Miranda's rising temperature. By the weekend she had been admitted to hospital. The following week they had moved her to the infectious diseases unit at Seacroft. It was a virus of some kind. At least that's what the doctors kept repeating, though Feddy knew they had as much idea as he did about its actual nature. She passed into a coma after her fever had refused to respond to any of the steroids they gave her. Before the month ended she had died. Feddy had been so distraught he became ill himself, although he recovered. He thought about contacting Koran but all his instincts told him to run away, to get as far away as he could from the man and his power. Was it senseless to think he could escape? Whether it was or not he knew he could not remain.

Feddy sat himself outside the bar. It was approaching five o'clock and once again the white walls that stretched away from him were washed in orange. Perhaps finally it was time for courage. He'd always thought it an overrated and precocious virtue – almost a neurosis. At least cowardice was an honest state. But now, as he sat waiting for his nemesis, he thought there was some sincerity in stoicism – at least in these circumstances. He was too tired to run. Let it end now. Aldi brought him out another *citron pressé* – he wouldn't drink alcohol until his visitor arrived. He took small sips and watched the gentle incline of the road.

About seven o'clock, half an hour after it got truly dark, a shadow appeared at the foot of the hill about a quarter of a mile away. It walked slowly but lightly up the road, becoming more defined in shape as it approached. A Panama hat was clear in outline against the moonlit buildings. Eventually the figure reached the bar.

"Jason Feddy." The hair was grey, but the face was undoubtedly Koran's, the green eyes still bright, even in the flickering fairy lights and lanterns that illuminated the front of the bar. Feddy was taken by surprise for his first emotion was one of delight – the delight of seeing an old friend for the first time in many years. It seemed that Koran shared the emotion. He broke into a broad grin and held out his hand. "I always knew you'd end up in some disreputable establishment." He squeezed Feddy's hand with enthusiastic vigour. "May I join you?"

"Of course. Aldi!" Feddy called back to his barman. "What would you like to drink?"

"Some brandy would be nice."

Feddy looked at his old mentor. A melée of emotions filled his belly. He remembered being in awe of the man's intellect. Being honoured at being invited into his inner circle. The thrill whenever Koran spoke to him like a friend. How likeable he could be. How frightening too, particularly when he spoke so intensely about his esoteric studies.

"Would you like a cigar?"

Koran shook his head. He studied Feddy's face. "I was visiting Malta. I hope you'll forgive my calling."

Feddy searched his pockets for a match. He knew Koran was playing a game, but maybe everything was going to be all right. The wisest course of action was to co-operate. "Are you still teaching?"

Koran looked at him as if he were surprised that Feddy had spoken. "I'm no longer attached to any single institution. I have a number of students I've been instructing privately — though in subjects few universities would recognise."

"Have you been writing?"

"Indeed, but, again, no conventional publisher would have an interest in the texts." Aldi came out with a bottle of brandy, two large glasses and a small porcelain jug of water. He stole a quick glance at Koran before scurrying back inside. "And how do you find the victualler's trade?"

"I make a living."

"Do you still teach?" Koran poured himself a drink.

"God, no."

"A pity." He slooshed the liquid in the glass. "You were a good teacher." Feddy felt pride spreading in his belly that Koran held him in some esteem. It warmed him like the brandy. "Well, you have chosen a beautiful place to live. There are few of the inane distractions of the modern world here. Tell me, are we in Rabat or is this street still part of Mdina?"

"Technically it's in Rabat although I think of the whole place as being Mdina. Do you know Malta?"

"There are two sets of catacombs here, one of which has occult connections. It lies in the crypt of St Paul's church. I have often wished to visit. Have you been?" Feddy shook his head and sipped the brandy. Maybe that was the reason Koran was here. Maybe he was more interested in the arcane history of the area than Feddy"s long-forgotten misdemeanours. "How do you fill your days, Jason?" Feddy instantly revised his opinion. There was ice in the question, although Koran was still smiling. Abruptly he changed tack. "Did you ever read Alisdair Macintyre?"

"Hmm?" Feddy was thrown. The charm had returned to Koran's voice.

"Alisdair Macintyre. 'After Virtue'. I used to teach it. 'In his thought and his actions, man is a narrative animal.' "

"I don't remember." It had been a long time since Feddy had talked philosophy to anybody.

"Come now. You must remember the concept. We used to speak of it."

Feddy reached for the matches. His cigar had gone out. "Remind me."

"Macintyre asserted that narrative lies at the heart of who we are. That stories are vital to us because that's how we understand the world and our place in it. Stories are a model of how our minds make sense of things. We like beginnings, middles and ends. A man comes home to his wife. She asks him how his day has been. He makes a story of the events. I did this, I did that, then he said this etc, etc."

"Seems like a reasonable idea."

"But the downside is the stories – their shape, their structure – can be more important than the truth. Because accuracy matters less than things making sense."

"You know I never went in for any of that stuff."

"What 'stuff' is that?"

"Things not being as they are. 'Rose is a rose is a rose is a rose' always made more sense to me."

"Even when things happen that don't make sense?"

"'It is only a shallow person who doesn't judge by appearances', as Wilde said." Feddy was beginning to enjoy this parrying. It reminded him of better times.

"But appearances can be so treacherous. Particularly the appearances of things that are not here."

"But they're all we have."

"All some of us have," Koran corrected him and grinned. "Now does your establishment serve food?"

"It does, but I wouldn't eat it. There's a Moroccan restaurant two streets away that's very good."

"I shall try it." Koran drained his glass then stood. Feddy stood also.

"Let me pay. It will be my treat."

"No. Thank you. I shall eat alone." There was a firmness in Koran's voice that made it clear he wasn't open to persuasion. "Perhaps you would be good enough however to accompany me on a tour of the catacomb of St Paul's tomorrow morning. Shall we meet here? About ten thirty?"

"If you like."

Koran nodded and was off down the street into the darkness with a surprising speed. Feddy stared after him. He thought about running after Koran but he knew he didn't dare. He poured himself some more brandy. When he returned the bottle to the tray he noticed that his hand was shaking.

That night Koran came to him in his dreams. Things were as they were. As they had been thirty years earlier. Koran wore a suit of purple velvet and presided over one of the monthly ceremonies – the one that coincided with a new moon. The room was lit with candles whose reflections flickered in the silver cloths draped over the furniture. He turned his eyes on Feddy who felt himself disappear. He reappeared in Miranda's bedroom. She was in bed — naked, waiting for him, but Feddy was unaroused, not wanting to sleep with her. Then they were lying on silver sheets. Koran and the rest of the coven surrounded them — fully clothed, scrutinising them with their gaze. Feddy tried to cover himself but he now had the body of a child. He looked down at his hairless penis and was ashamed. He awoke sweating and nauseous. He went into the bathroom. There he perched on the toilet, the seat cold on the back of his thighs, waiting for it to get light.

Feddy made sure he arrived promptly for his meeting. It was warm for late September. He didn't bother to open the bar. A light wind gathered leaves half-way down the hill and rattled the shutters behind him. Once again Koran appeared — hat first — marching with purpose up the road. He carried a small canvas bag over his shoulder. Feddy felt none of the unexpected delight of the previous day. There was now merely a sense of foreboding — like a long-postponed dental appointment.

"Good morning, Feddy."

"Morning."

"Have you taken breakfast?"

"I wasn't hungry."

"A pity."

"Why a pity?"

"No matter. Do you have anything planned for this afternoon?" Koran was at his side now. He wore a large pair of sunglasses with tortoiseshell frames. They gave him a faintly comic, matronly air.

"Nothing in particular."

"That's a good thing." He removed his sunglasses and polished them with a silk handkerchief. "You may want to lie down after our business is completed this morning. You may feel a little ill."

"What business?" Feddy's legs went weak again. His heart was racing. Koran regarded him with his unearthly eyes before covering them once more with the opaque lenses.

"Come. Let's see what lies under that church."

It was about fifteen minutes on foot to St Paul's. The shops, bars and houses gave way to large scrubby patches of empty ground. The wind picked up in the exposed areas, lifting small clouds of dust from the dry earth. Koran paused occasionally and looked back down over the town. There was no small talk. After a journey that felt as if it had taken hours rather than minutes they arrived at the small whitewashed church. A faded, crudely painted sign directed them to the catacomb, which had a separate entrance about ten metres from the chapel. A shrunken white box of a building stood at the side of the road like a bus shelter. There was an iron gate across its entrance.

"It looks like it's closed," said Feddy hopefully.

"Surely not. We've come all this way." Koran smiled. He approached the gate and it seemed to swing open. "It's merely pulled to." He beckoned for

Feddy to follow him and dropped some coins into the honesty box at his side.

A very steep staircase led down into the dark. Koran gestured for Feddy to go first. As they descended the gate clanged firmly shut. Feddy was certain he heard a bolt being drawn and a lock click although there was no one there to have performed such an action.

The steps went down much further than it felt they should. The air became chilly as they reached the bottom and rounded a corner into the catacomb. The flickering light — an unsettling combination of electric bulb and wax candle — revealed an architecture that was anything but church-like. The place seemed to have been carved out of the rock although no geometry governed its shape. It was more a random collection of alcoves and recesses with oblong holes hewn out of their dividing walls. Hidden in these spaces were black letterboxes full of bones. Feddy was shocked that these remains had been strewn in such a casual manner.

"It is ironic that this catacomb is connected to the church above," said Koran in tutorial manner. "It is far older and has little to do with Christianity. Come. Let's see a little more." Feddy was uncomfortable walking away from the stairs but Koran was keen to walk among the narrow walls. They turned a corner, then another, before walking down a long, narrow passage. There were more stone bays at regular intervals, each one piled high with random bones. "The Knights Templar are responsible for some sections — others were established by older, even more secret societies."

"I never even knew it was here."

"And it's so close to you." Koran had removed his sunglasses and placed them in his pocket. "It's funny. When we were talking about Macintyre last night — I never mentioned his key insight: Only in fantasy do we live what story we please. In life, as both Aristotle and Engels noted, we are always under certain constraints. Yet fantasy can be so tempting, can't it." Koran had opened his canvas bag and removed a small bottle of mineral water. He placed this on the brown stone at his side and produced a small bag of dark powder from one of the bag's pockets. Feddy was thrown by his action and the sudden change of subject. He watched as Koran twisted open the bottle of water and tipped the black powder into it. The water fizzed and sparkled slightly in the iridescent light. "I thought long and hard about what to do, Jason. I wasn't going to kill you. I knew when I took her I wasn't going to kill you. I wanted something that would satisfy more completely. So I waited. And waited." Koran shook the bottle. The black powder which had appeared as heavy as iron filings had now dissolved completely. The water was clear.

"Val, I —"

"Shut up, Feddy." Koran's eyes flashed. "You desired her certainly. And you could have her. So you took her." For a moment the natural authority seemed to vanish from Koran's voice. He sounded like a lovelorn teenager. "We each have our areas of weakness," he continued. "No man can perfect himself entirely. I never seemed able to penetrate or work with a particular area of my self-esteem relating to women. That is why Miranda was a gift to me. Until you came with your charm and your looks and enchanted her. You took her from me. But you never really wanted her."

HE WATCHED AS KORAN TWISTED OPEN THE BOTTLE OF WATER AND TIPPED THE BLACK POWDER INTO IT

"Now that simply isn't true. I loved her. She was the woman I'd waited all my life to meet," said Feddy.

Koran started laughing. "Oh Feddy. If you could hear yourself."

"Damn it, Val, it's the truth. Not a day goes by without me thinking about her."

"I know. I know." He ceased laughing but he grinned broadly. His teeth were white in the candlelight. "But you mistake your thoughts for the truth. I know you so well, Feddy. Far better than you know yourself. Even though we haven't seen each other for thirty years. You don't know how pleased I am to find you unchanged." He unscrewed the top of the Evian bottle. "Now I want you to drink all this down for me." Feddy looked at him helplessly. He felt sick and small. "I don't know if I can do that."

"Oh you can. It's a very simple thing." Koran handed him the plastic bottle. "Surely you don't want me to make you drink it. I can do that, you know."

Feddy took it. He couldn't help but sniff the contents. "What ... what will happen?" he asked fearfully.

"Just gulp it down." Very slowly Feddy raised the bottle to his lips. "That's it – swallow." The water hardly tasted of anything. There was a slightly bitter feeling at the back of Feddy's throat. That was all. The smile had dropped from Koran's face. "Really it's a good old-fashioned curse. Administered orally – like medicine."

"What do you mean, a curse?" Feddy felt himself tensing up.

"Were you a younger man you might consider it a gift. There are people who meditate for years in order to attain the insight I have just bestowed upon you. However you can be sure you will not thank me when I am gone. You will find something has happened to your mind."

"What has happened? What have you done to me, Val?"

"From now on – whenever you turn to your memory – you will find it has been replaced with the truth. Not a past that you have constructed for your pleasure out of the dots and lines of what occurred – but a cold and actual record of things as they happened. You will never again have the experience that is labelled 'nostalgia'". For you, Feddy – dreamer that you always were and still are, I have no doubt – this will be a forbidding place. I am afraid this state will continue until you die." Koran took the now empty plastic bottle from him and placed it back in his canvas bag. He then took Feddy's arm and led him back towards the daylight.

"I suggest that you spend the afternoon at home. I think you are liable to feel a little ill." Koran had returned him to the shuttered bar. "You will not see me again. Goodbye, Jason Feddy." He walked back down the dusty slope. Eventually his distinctive hat disappeared beneath the brow of the hill. Feddy stood there for some time watching the empty road. Eventually a car went past, disturbing his reverie.

By the time Feddy got home he was beginning to wonder if he'd dreamed the whole morning. There was something insubstantial about his recollection of the events, something feverish. He was about to dismiss the whole thing as a fantasy when he was gripped by the most intense stomach pain. He went into a sudden spasm – as if all his limbs were joined by strings like a wooden puppet's that emerged from a hole in the base of his spine and someone had abruptly pulled those strings taut. He fell to the floor with his knees drawn to his chest and his elbows tight against his belly. The pain hit his head like a rockdrill. Somehow he managed to manoeuvre himself on to the bed. Then the nausea began – a terrible sensation – an imperative to empty out everything from within. He tried to fight it but was unable to. He opened his mouth and vomited.

Time disappeared. All there was for Feddy was the desire for the pain and sickness to stop. It went dark outside. Someone knocked on the door but he couldn't speak. It became light again.

He must have slept although he couldn't remember closing his eyes. There was puke and fluid around him on the bed. When he tried to move he felt raw and brittle – as if he had been remade, or had shed a skin like an old spider. Somehow he managed to swivel his legs off the bed. They trembled beneath him as he found his way to the shower.

At first Feddy thought Koran's curse an elaborate joke, but he didn't dare call on any memory to test it. The first inkling he had that something might have happened was on the Saturday night. He was in bed trying to sleep but the events of the day before were far too vivid in his mind. He remembered how much change he had given for every transaction. He did drop off but woke again about a quarter to four in the morning. A look at the clock brought to mind a limerick he once uttered trying to make his class laugh at the start of a new academic year in 1967. A girl had asked the time. It was three forty-five and he had told her so before quoting:

"My back aches, my penis is sore,
"I simply can't fuck any more,
"I'm covered in sweat,
"You haven't come yet,
"Christ! It's a quarter to four."

But he had misjudged their mood and temperament. There were a few nervous giggles but mainly embarrassment and disaproval. He felt, once again, the agony of his own shame at trying to be amusing and failing in such a crass and coarse way. Then another memory came to his mind. It was about the poem that Miranda had sent him — the one he had thought had been authored by someone famous, which in fact she had written. Except the memory was different now. It had all the unwelcome brightness of camcorder footage. It was the other way around. It had been authored by someone famous. It was by Thom Gunn. Feddy had mistakenly assumed it was hers. He had been ashamed at his own lack of knowledge in front of Miranda. But worse were his memories of a poem she sent him after that. A poem about their relationship. She had once again left a name off the bottom — although he knew it was hers. It was childish and adolescent. It had made him wince. He could even remember that at one point she had spelt "their" as "there". That led to another memory of lying in bed one night and not wanting her because she felt young and foolish. He recalled the excruciating feeling of her touching his flaccid cock trying to arouse it. He remembered driving down Otley Road one day and seeing her walking into college. She didn't see him. She had her hair tied back. Her face looked odd and unattractive. He didn't want to be with her.

The following day Feddy sat outside the bar, cradling a glass of brandy. He stared down the dusty hill at the distant white roofs shimmering in the noon haze. Many other memories were coming unwelcome into his mind. Most upsetting, of course, was the revised version of their first week together — formerly the most precious recollection of all. It was no longer the soaring peak experience he had savoured all these years. He now saw the fantasy in it. Miranda was just a girl. He was just a young man. There was little more to it. Then there was the morning with the star on the wall. The star was still there. But it was joined by his disinterest in it, by the fact that he was more concerned with being late for a lecture, by the smell of Miranda's fart in the bed. He remembered walking to work that day, wondering if he should end it with her and if Koran would have her back. It had been sunny yes, but he was not particularly happy. Things had been OK but that was all.

He knew these memories were the truth. He knew he had constructed something else around them, a structure he had built and built over many years. That structure had now had its foundations removed. It had collapsed silently around Feddy leaving him exposed and cold. He drained the glass and called for Aldi to fill it once more. Perhaps later he would go for a walk. Perhaps he would visit the catacombs and stare at the bones. It was going to be a long afternoon and an even longer night. ✆

Taken from Never Trust a Rabbit *by Jeremy Dyson, to be published in June 2000 by Duck Editions. Jeremy Dyson was born in Leeds. He is one of the award-winning comedy team The League of Gentlemen. He now lives in North London.*

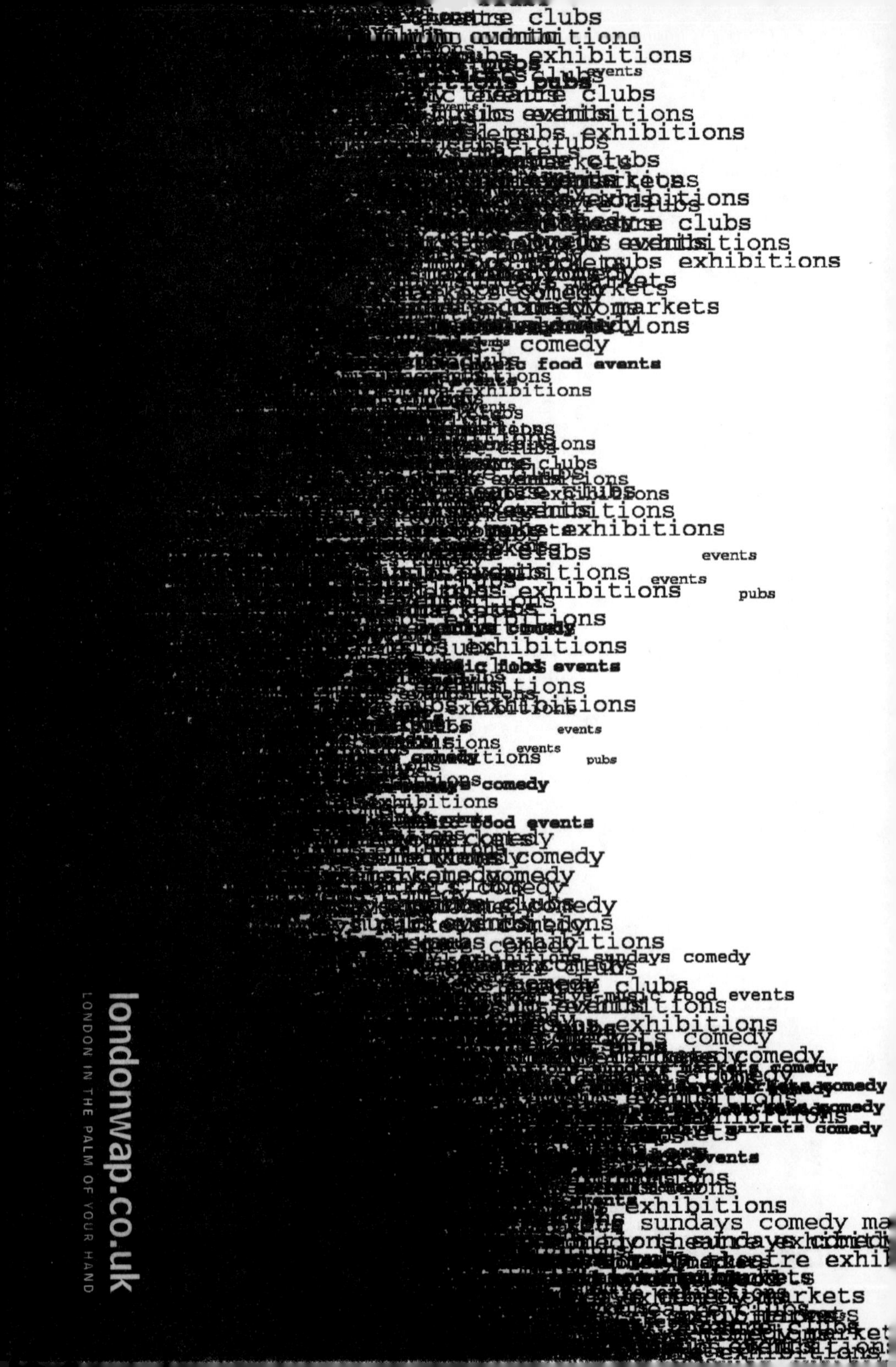
londonwap.co.uk
LONDON IN THE PALM OF YOUR HAND

A WASTE OF PARADISE

The true story of the Bounty Bar Hunters. By JOE CORNISH

In May 1977 the world famous Bounty Hunters first appeared on British television screens. Many still believe them to be the concoction of advertising executives, but startling new theories, revealed here for the first time, suggest a more sinister reality.

Sources suggest that it was 1975 when Mars Confectionery executives first heard rumours of a mythical "Bounty Bar", believed to be the actual "taste of paradise". According to legend, the bar was produced by a tribe of natives on an undiscovered South Sea Island. It formed their sole diet, held powerful aphrodisiac properties, and took centre stage in the tribe's mysterious fertility rituals. Excited executives immediately despatched a team of sexy explorers to search for the bar, together with a camera crew, to capture their adventures and turn them into television commercials.

The resulting campaign was to become one of the most famous and enduring in the history of confectionery advertising. But many believe that behind the images of beautific tropical islands lies a true story of obsession and sexual peversity. The evidence is there for all to see in the original adverts.

...

ADVERT ONE: THE BOUNTY HUNTERS (1977)

ACTION: Three scuba divers, one man and two women, emerge from the shallow waters of a paradisical desert island. They undress and head up the beach to discover two Bounty Bars behind a palm tree. They settle down and bite into the bars, then proceed to eye each other up accompanied by the famous Bounty Song: "The Bounty Hunters are here, they're searching for a paradise..."

ANALYSIS: From the moment we first see these so-called Bounty Hunters, it's clear they're after something moist and tender that isn't coconut. In a telling early shot, one of the

ADVERT ONE: THE BOUNTY HUNTERS (1977)

ADVERT TWO: VILLAGE OF THE BOUNTY HUNTERS (1983)

women unzips her wetsuit to release her captive breasts, which swell forth eagerly in big close up to sparkle in the sunlight. The Bounty Hunting component of their expedition is derisory. They find the bars too easily, laid out on a palm leaf beside an artfully split coconut. One of the women then lies back on the sand and bites the top off a bar. The way she guides the top between her lips with the tip of her tongue suggests she may well have a background in porno. The way the man watches her with an evil look in his eye suggests he might have a serious criminal record. And the way the second woman watches them both suggests that she swings both ways and that any second now they might all start to "party". The final post-coital shot of all three watching the sun set behind their yacht suggests that they did, it was fantastic, and they've decided to live there together forever. Many believe that this is what actually happened, and the second advert, filmed six years later, supports this theory.

...

ADVERT TWO:
VILLAGE OF THE BOUNTY HUNTERS (1983)

ACTION: A blonde woman wearing a skimpy bikini clambers through a tropical jungle. She arrives in a small clearing where five other beautiful scantily clad young models of both sexes have established a small Bounty Hunting commune. She's

THE MALNUTRITION THAT RESULTS FROM CONSTANT BOUNTY EATING KEEPS THEM SLIM AND PHOTOGENIC

immediately offered a refreshing Bounty Bar from a large carved wooden bowl. She sits next to a blonde man and laughs at whatever he's saying while she eats her Bounty seductively. Soon they're all munching on Bounties and eyeing each other up suggestively. The accompanying voiceover explains that "the Bounty Hunters have made their home in paradise, for here they have found the Bounty Bar, the taste of paradise."

ANALYSIS: On close observation, the people in this second commercial are recognisable as the original Bounty Hunters. They have clearly settled on the island and built bamboo huts to live in, with the Bounty Bar as their sole diet. The powerful aphrodisiac property of the bar has led them to create a Charles Mansonesque sex-based commune. The constant sunshine keeps their complexions free from zits, and the malnutrition that results from constant Bounty eating keeps them slim and photogenic. Their beautiful new companions are either the original camera crew, or friends who have dropped out of society and travelled to the island guided by a secret Alex Garland-style map. They now spend their lives gathering Bounty Bars,

ADVERT THREE: CHILDREN OF THE BOUNTY HUNTERS (1993)

ADVERT FOUR: CENTRAL PARK (1997)

lounging around eating them, then engaging in prolonged group sex sessions. One can only imagine the number of small children who must be sheltering inside the huts. It's highly possible that this scenario actually existed, masterminded by Mars Executives, who dispatched a camera crew every few years to capture their superficially idyllic but actually deeply disturbing lifestyle.

...

ADVERT THREE:
CHILDREN OF THE BOUNTY HUNTERS (1993)

ACTION: It's midnight on Bounty Island, and a perfect quarter moon hangs in the starry sky. A dark skinned girl lies on a branch over a silvery rock pool, stuffing her face with a Bounty. A muscled man with flowing black hair comes running through the surf towards her. Soon they are holding hands beneath a palm tree, and leaning in to kiss one another. A coconut falls from a high palm tree, then smashes and spilts perfectly on the rocks below, gushing moonlit coconut juice, a clear symbol for sexual intercourse. Back on the beach, the girl reclines on the man's chest, chewing on a post coital bar. They look bored, depressed and gorgeous.

ANALYSIS: Ten years have passed since the Bounty Hunting commune was established. However, there is no longer any sign of their bamboo huts

or any of the original founder members. Instead, what we could be seeing here are their last surviving children, who have lived their entire lives on the island. Their skin-tone suggests possible inter-breeding with the island's native tribe. There is a mix of sadness, insanity and animal arousal in their eyes as they perform the perpetual ritual of Bounty Hunting, Bounty eating and Bounty stimulated sex. Deviod of education and ignorant of the outside world; this is the only life they know. Inbreeding has meant that their siblings have long since perished. Now the two last Bounty Children live on the island like lab rats, visited only by the occasional camera crew, who capture their sad empty lives for the sake of selling Bounty Bars in the Western world.

...

POSTSCRIPT

It's no coincidence that in 1997 Mars changed the Bounty adverts entirely. The Bounty Hunters and their paradise island were never to be seen again. They were replaced by a new concept featuring a girl lying in Central Park eating a Bounty, the grass around her coming alive with miniature jungle animals. Perhaps the rumours and the risk of exposure were too much for the company to take. Rumours that the current adverts use genetically bred mini-animals rather than digital effects, are unsubstantiated. ◉

GREEN AND PLEASANT BRAND

HILL'S ABSINTH

··········

WWW.EABSINTHE.COM
CREDIT CARD HOTLINE: 01992 511445

ADAM & JOE'S
WORLD OF THE FOOCHOR

Now that the hysteria about the millennium is more or less behind us, we can look with a fresh sense of perspective at what the foochor holds. Using a powerful Sinclair ZX Spectrum and an old Pokémon we have been able to predict with 96% accuracy what we can expect, like it or not...

MUSIC

In around 2010 music as we know it will run out completely and we will start listening to albums filled with exciting sound effects only. Classical fans will purchase albums filled with the natural sounds of birds, babbling brooks and champagne flutes clinking, while pop and rock aficionados will go for noises made by cars, cash registers and the tinny beats that used to leak out of people's Walkman headphones. The punk and indie fans of the new millennium will favour the sound of puking, glass shattering and de-tuned radios, while clubbers will go for jack hammers operating at various speeds. After about ten more years these groups will fracture, and in the case of clubbers your credibility will be rated by what brand of jack hammer you enjoy and whether it features samples of classic American jack hammers or just regular Lambeth council pneumatic drills. These too will eventually have their day.

FASHION

In years that end with an even number, flares, leg warmers, lime green man-T-hose (tights for men) and stonewashed jeans with loads of rips in the arse will be in, unless more than 65 people find out in which case khaki socks, groin gloves and knitted cycling helmets will be the choice of the fashion élite. If it's an odd year everyone will be forced to wear wetsuits and "Frankie says Relax" T shirts. No exceptions. It may sound harsh, but that's fashion.

FILM

The unprecedented success of last year's The Blair Witch Project will completely transform the world of film within five years. Studios, salivating at the prospect of making mega bucks for films that cost nothing to produce, greenlight a slew of similar projects covering various genres. The Scary Room features a grainy black and white polaroid of a darkened room. Nothing happens at all. Oooh the suspense! Speculation on the internet is rife. Is there someone in the room? Could it be a real room? Another successful project is Cat in which a cat lies curled up by the fire for an hour and a half. This is a big hit with older audiences who are sick of being shocked all the time. Then after a few years of this, audiences demand a return to the innocence of Hollywood's big budget golden age. Star Wars: The Phantom Menace is re-released with all the computer generated scenes lovingly removed and recreated with real actors and models. Five years later these new scenes are themselves lovingly removed and replaced with black & white polaroids of darkened rooms.

TELEVISION

In the year 2002 the government will implement plans to conscript everyone into national television service for at least five years of their lives to keep up with the demand for real life docu-dramas, dramadies, soapumentaries, cockumentaries, and lavvydocs. Soon every man and woman in the country will have their own digital, cable or satellite channel showing rolling repeats of Friends between shots of them talking about their sex lives. Inexplicably, Lenny Henry will still be working a great deal.

TRANSPORT

Matter transporters of the sort made popular by Star Trek will become a reality by 2030. Tubes and buses will be replaced by public transporters beaming people directly to their places of work. They will be cheap and prone to faults, causing people to appear in the wrong jobs at random often with their DNA fused with others so that a race of worker mutants will be created and forced to find employment at large record stores or fast food outlets. The streets will be a mess of teenagers and business men appearing and dissappearing irritatingly as they make costly and unnecessary transports for the sake of it. 🌀

Controversial "in-your-face" maverick film maker, pop svengali and renaissance man **KEN KORDA** reflects on what we might find in his personal paradise

GUCCI AFTERSHAVE

Whenever I'm going anywhere special, like Stringfellows or the Hippodrome, I always wear Gucci aftershave. When I say "wear it" I am of course talking about my testicles. I tend to empty the aftershave into a stainless steel bowl and then carefully dip the balls until they are fully suffused with Gucci. I feel that even if no-one meets the balls that night, the sweet sexy smell of them will invest my entire body with Guccicity and make me magnetic to the various female *Eastenders* cast members I might bump into.

THE FULL MONTY

It's hilarious! I voted it the funniest film of all time last year although I think this year I'll vote it my best film of all time. I like the bit when they're doing the auditions and the big bloke comes in and he can't dance or anything and Hamish

McBeth says "What can you do then?" and he gets his wink out and everyone goes "Wow!" and Hamish says "The lunchbox has landed!" which is very good. I think it would have been a little better if you had actually seen his willoi like in *Boogie Nights*, but no matter, it's still marvellous stuff.

LEE EVANS

Lee Evans makes me laugh so hard! He's a genius. You know, when I think about it, I'd say he combines the funniest aspects of Jerry Lewis and Norman Wisdom with his own crazy energy! In fact you could even say he's like Jerry Lewis and Norman Wisdom... ON ACID! Can you imagine that? Yes, that's exactly what he's like. He sweats rather too much though, it's revolting. Why doesn't he wear darker suits or some kind of underarm tampon? Ten minutes and he's sopping wet. Come to think of it, he's just a revolting sweaty man.

LEE EVANS: A REVOLTING, SWEATY MAN

makes me feel great! It's amazing like that, music. My favourite kind of music is CD but I think MP3s are great! No moving parts, and all on the internet which has changed our lives completely!

FORKS

Forks are a godsend! I'd really be lost without mine. The only bad thing about forks is that you can't really eat Sugar Puffs or other cereal with them because of the long holes. I've been working on a utensil that combines the handy watertight bowl of a spoon with the indespensible precision prong of a fork that would solve this problem beautifully. I call it the Spork. Actually, maybe I call it the Foon. Or the Fachunka.

THE SPORK, THE FOON OR THE FANCHUNKA

MUSIC

Music's great. I think it was Joe Pesci from *Lethal Weapon III*, who said "If music is like food you love, play more, play more!" which is absolutely spot on. Whenever I'm feeling in the mood I'll put some on and it

GIRLFRIENDS

I don't approve of girlfriends. They don't understand me and I haven't got time to understand them. ◉

THE DUALITY OF ALL THINGS

By JAMES JARVIS

Night has fallen in the far northern ranges.

In the deep valleys that lurk beneath the titanic peaks, the people of that far-flung region are communing with the spirits.

Outside their geometrically harmonious mud huts they gather. Tonight their high priest will select one to be specially blessed.

The still-beating heart is held aloft.

The crowd go wild around the fire.

O Most Ancient One, please accept this token of our esteem!

The priest hurls the organ into the flames.

From the far horizon comes a great rumbling.

From amongst the clouds a miraculous apparition materialises.

It is the Old One. He salutes this kind gesture from these most innocent of his subjects.

Many leagues to the south a wave of weird feeling washes over the city.

At the state-controlled sports shoe factory, Keith is suddenly distracted from his stacking.

For an instant his mind is awash with sensation...

And then just as abruptly the vision leaves him.

Despite the transience of this revelation, the feelings of beatific calm and security instilled by it persist.

Returning home that night he notes from the faces of strangers that others have been similarly blessed.

And far away again, the elves in the mountains raise their spears in salute.

They, best of all, understand the Old One's mastery of the World.

BEFORE YOU KNOW IT

A short story by MATTHEW DE ABAITUA.
Photography by MARC ATKINS

....

I told him about Lee, right there on the porch, as he was leaving for a meeting in San Francisco. He'd heard some stories about me and asked if they were true. I said yes. When he asked me if I could guarantee it wouldn't happen again, I was honest and said no, I couldn't. It was brutal of me. I let him know what had been going on since January and I made sure he realised it was going to carry on, and that I felt no shame or guilt about it. Behind him, the taxi idled on the meter, the cabby doing the crossword and pretending not to listen. He said: "Why did you sit on this all week and only tell me now? You know I have to go."

I told him that I didn't use a condom with any of them. That crushed him, he staggered into the cab and waved weakly in the direction of Heathrow. He doesn't like flying at the best of times. A long haul chewing over that little bombshell would have him back on the booze in no time. Especially considering what we'd done the night before. What I'd insisted upon. Up the arse. Serves him right.

I wanted him to hit me. Lee said that if he hit me, we'd be able to take him for everything. Unfortunately, he calculated instantly what that brief satisfaction would cost him further down the line.

He suffers from anxiety. It runs through his family. Bad hangovers bring it on. The only way for him to outrun the fear is to keep drinking. I've heard all about it at great length. The palpitations come suddenly, he feels a catch in his chest then the plunging sensation of falling asleep that jerks him awake. Phantom heart attacks, claustrophobic panics. On the Underground, he hallucinated that the platform was the size of our living room. It cost us a fortune in cabs before he could go down there again.

I've woken up to how tame he has made me, how over the years I have been coerced into being polite and controlled when deep down, my spirit is wild. He lives in fear of life, he's always trying to hold it together. I told his mother, I said "he collects life, he doesn't live it. I intend to live it to the full now and I want my son to feel he can do the same." "You can't bring these strange men back," as ever she had sought out the worst possible outcome for an awfully ordinary situation, "you don't know who they are, what they're capable of. At least think of your son." But that is precisely what I am doing. "I want Greg to feel he can be like me, and not scared of life like his father."

I go to Chester races with Lee. We drive down together in my Golf. A Saturday in early July. In the member's enclosure, he has to wear a tie, which he never has to normally, and his thick neck wriggles against it. It's so hot his sweat stains the yellow collar of his shirt orange. I am drinking gin and tonic with an eighty quid hairdo, a stone and a half lighter since I kicked my husband out. "I've worked hard to look like this. Now nothing solid passes my lips unless it's attached to a man." It was the funniest thing said all day, and I said it.

I see his pack of mates, in amongst the bookies. I watch him tell them about me, and they leer over at me as one.

I love it in the North. When we first moved down South, I was so intimidated by their houses and their dinner parties, I became too humble. I fitted in, only at the cost of my true hell-raising self. But this is my real home, it's where I made my legend as a teenager. The wildest girl in town, up for a fight, tearing off the brittle lacquered fringes of my rivals in furious cat-fights in the bearpits of nightclubs.

When the horses start running, I push my way through to the front of the barrier and urge mine on. Three winners. We get a cab to First Avenue in the Wirral for the over 25s night. There's a fat man dancing so I pinch his arse. I get up on the podium and scream out "I'm a fucking winner" while Lee laughs and his mates clap me on. The DJ plays "Criticize" by Alexander O'Neal and I sing along to it as if I'm spitting it in the face of my husband and my fucking in-laws.

On the backseat, the cabby watches Lee delve into my blouse. When Lee touches my nipple, I let the cabby see how much I like it.

When I get home, I ring him on his mobile and across the continents I tell him everything I have been doing, and more, just to hear him lose it. Then I fuck Lee.

YOU KNOW SHE'D RATHER BE ON HER HANDS AND KNEES TAKING IT FROM SOME FACELESS BLACK STUD THAN ON HER BACK GRIMACING AT THE INCOMPETENT EFFORTS OF SOME CHINLESS SAP WITH AN ISA

It's better for my son that we are apart. Greg is nearly twelve years old, and very susceptible to influence. I don't want him to be raised with his father and so take on those characteristics I despise. His father would always bring him back model police cars from whichever country he'd been working in that week. It looked like Gregory was going to be a real man's man — and nothing scared me more than the thought of him growing up into his father and grandfather, taking his place in a long line of sexually repressed authoritarian men who mate for life with women that will pick up after them. I've read enough psychology to know why they act like they do. Their repression comes from their anxiety: they have to control everyone around them in case one wilful element gets out of hand and brings down disaster on them all. That's why the whole family hates me now, I'm like a force of nature that can sweep aside their safe little world.

Lee stayed again. I come gritting my teeth, his hand clamped over my mouth. Initially, I insisted we keep the noise down so as not to disturb Gregory. But now it helps Lee get off, which is annoying because I really like to express myself during orgasm.

As it's a Saturday, we sleep in. Bright daylight lurks outside, punishment for the night before. I try not to look at myself first thing. The morning face is not my face, the morning hair is not my hair.

Rather than let Lee see me like this, I push him out of bed. Grumbling, he pads out to the toilet, naked. I hear his piss slosh and stop, slosh and stop, slosh and stop.

"I saw your son, he was on the landing," says Lee, when he returns. "He really stared at me."

"What do you mean?"

"I don't know. He just stared at me."

"You didn't cover yourself?"

"Yes, of course, once I realised he was there."

I panic that Gregory might tell his father what he's seen, and they might be able to get an exclusion order to stop Lee sleeping here.

"Don't worry," says Lee, "an exclusion order requires proof of actual harm." Lee knows plenty about divorce law. He lives with his mother, who was divorced when Lee was a teenager. Throughout the whole negotiation, he's been a godsend. It was Lee who pointed out how meagre the settlement was, how I was entitled to so much more. It was Lee who made me realise how well I could do out of the whole thing. How much I deserve for all the years of suffering I have endured.

Lee wanted to stay all week but in the end he was gone by Wednesday. He caught me wiping stray dead hair from my face as I spooned Pedigree Chum into the dog's bowl. I clutched my dressing gown to me and fled to the lounge, sobbing. He went back to his mother's.

I am watching Tricia. The programme is about the New Sex Rules. A woman captioned as "feisty feminist" comes on and says that in the future, the few men capable of holding down jobs will have their masculinity crushed beneath the heel of a tyrannical female boss. Just like my ex. The majority of them, however, will be too thick and begrudging to work in the new service economy and so will divide their time between Internet porn, junk food and football. Just like Lee. To think I have already had sex with the future of mankind.

Girls prefer living alone, she says, now they can earn so much there is no need for them to have some man under their feet. Then, some bloke from a men's mag drones on about masculinity. "Real men take responsibility," agrees Tricia, but you know she doesn't believe it. You know she'd rather be on her hands and knees taking it from some faceless black stud than on her back grimacing at the tireless incompetent efforts of some chinless sap with an ISA. Responsibilities are just habits men gather to protect themselves against the unexpected: she knows it, I know it, the men know it.

Realising that they are losing the audience, the two journalists pretend to argue. He responds to her insinuations about his cock with insinuations about her dalliance with lesbianism.

"I see women's sexuality becoming more ruthless, the men they pick up will become like fuel for the blaze of their glorious new individuality."

"And the men just get burnt?"

"The lucky ones," she says. Very sassy.

The last sunny day of autumn. I decide to book a course on the sunbeds to keep up my tan through the winter. While I'm booking the dates with the receptionist, I see a poster for Thorpe Park. Fairgrounds used to be my favourite, all the girls would go on the waltzers but I was always the one who dared them to spin us faster and faster. No-one screamed louder than me. Greg's father always takes him out somewhere when he's in the country, whereas most of my son's time spent with me is divided between moping at school and sulking at home. Why shouldn't I treat him for a change? I don't want him to know me only as a drudge. I want to be his best friend as well as his mother.

It turns out his best friend is called Tim, who I've never met before. I am surprised how tall he is — a good head taller than Lee even. He can't be more

than two years away from his sexual peak. Sixteen or seventeen. They lurk around together while Lee and I pack the boot of the Golf.

On the drive down, I put on Gabrielle's Rise. I'm really getting into music again, now I'm going out more. "Do you like this Tim?" I say. "Or is it a bit old for you. Do you like Rewind Bo Selector?"

"I'm not really into clubs," says Tim, with a voice already weathered by cigarettes and alcohol. Tim's acne is in retreat, he's coming out of pubescence just as Gregory is going into it. It's healthy that my son is mature enough to have friend of Tim's age.

I put on the Moby album, and turn it up for that one off the advert.

The boys took some bullying before they'd go onto the rollercoaster. The track twists and plunges underground, I scream just to enjoy screaming. My mouth open to the pitch black. Then I drag them all over to the log flume. I lift my jumper just as we go over the crest. Sure enough, on the photograph of us all, you can see my bra. It appears on a TV screen as we leave the ride. I buy four copies of the picture, one for each of us. "Here you go Tim," I can't resist winking, just to make him blush, "something to keep under your pillow."

Outside, I catch Greg gripping his wrist, secretly checking his pulse, a concentration technique his father uses to hold off an anxiety attack.

"Greg, are you alright?"

"My head is busy," he walks away from me, rests his hand on a bear-shaped bin outside the ghost train. Lee lights a fag, passes one to me.

"What's up with him?"

"He must be coming down with something." I can't be bothered telling Lee about the anxiety. He is too thick to understand. I go to Greg. The cackle of the ghost train's ghouls startle him — we pick our way clear of the crowd until we are in a lawn. Scale models of the world's largest buildings surround us. I had no idea the pyramids were so big.

"It feels like I have bees in my head," he says. A frown has him in its grip. He actually shakes his head to try and dislodge it. I know enough not to try to cheer him up with some vacuous gesture. This is not a mood swing. Slowly and carefully, I must lead him from under the shadow of this anxiety.

"Everything is going to be alright. There's nothing wrong with you. It's all in your head. Let go of it, let yourself relax. Me and Lee are here to look after you."

I clutch him to me and hold him, my head turned away, so he doesn't get a blast of the gin.

Once against my breasts, I expected him to sob but he doesn't. We walk on through the garden, wandering through the minaturised wonders of the world. We stop at the Statue of Liberty, the only wonder he has seen in real life, on a family trip that was so long ago it might as well be another life.

"Do you remember when we climbed up into her head? It was busy up there too, full of people?" I don't know why I said that. I said it just to say something. It doesn't reach him, he's folded in on himself now for the rest of the day.

The rollercoaster rumbles past us, everyone gripping onto the arm rests, the women loving their fear, the men trying to kick their's under the seat. They don't know how to embrace danger anymore.

I insist we all go on it again and this time, hold our arms up in the air. I hope Greg will learn to be brave.

I KNOW WHAT THEY'RE SAYING BECAUSE I SAID IT MYSELF, WHEN I WAS MARRIED. SHE'S GONE TOO FAR. SHE'S JEOPARDISING THE SAFETY OF HER CHILD BY TAKING IN THOSE MEN. SHE'LL GET WHAT'S COMING TO HER

The old crowd at the school gates have cut me out. I don't hear any of the gossip now, because it's all about me. Carol with the fat ankles even tried to lecture me. She has a toddler, I have forgotten his name. "Some of the things he says," she says, "are so uncanny, I think 'how could he know that'. It's like they have an angel near them, an older spirit who lets them see things we can't. I've decided to get him baptised, and I'm going to get confirmed at the same ceremony."

"What kind of things has he said?"

"When he was playing, I heard him talking and I just thought 'well, he's got an imaginary friend' but when I said to him 'Billy, who are you talking to,' he said 'I'm talking to the old woman' and of course, that old Mrs Marks used to live in our house."

"I don't remember her," I say, rummaging through my bag for my fags. Did I leave them in the Golf?

"Mrs Marks died long before you moved here," she wrinkles her face quizzically. "You've seemed very distracted these last few weeks. How is everything at home?"

"Fine, fine." I light one, her hand tuts at the smoke.

"Oh, you're smoking again."

"It keeps the weight off," I flick ash. "You should try it."

She is wearing a turquoise anorak with a pink trim, the kind of thing a woman should only stoop to when her arse has gone. Her face withers as she gathers the indignation to take me on. Me!

"Are you still with that builder?"

"No, I'm with the bouncer now."

"And what does Gregory think about that?"

"He doesn't mind. I don't see how me being fulfilled sexually could be bad for my son. Maybe you should try it."

"You know, you run around acting like you've been liberated from this terrible prison, like you've become something free and wonderful. But you haven't, you know. Someone should give you a piece of their mind."

"Like you? Are you sure you can spare it?" It was the funniest thing ever said at those school gates and I said it. Funnier, even, than that time I pretended to punch Mr Evans behind his back.

Carol sneers, and walks to the other side of the gate.

She turns back to me when she's out of range and mouths "whore".

My face feels raw in the cold. I have to breathe deeply, exhale my anger and inhale the calm.

I know Greg doesn't really want me to pick him up anymore, but when I don't, I know the other mothers turn their heads to one another and gossip about me. I know what they're saying because I said it myself, when I was married. She's gone too far. She's jeopardising the safety of her child by taking in those men. She'll get what's coming to her. I've stood at these gates and put down those who've strayed. I understand the psychology of it. It's the only way you can feel secure in your decision to turn your back on all the new experiences you could be enjoying. It's the only way of justifying not having had a decent fuck since Changing Rooms started.

The kids pile out through the gates, in their gangs and their couples, talking a language I can barely understand anymore. Eventually, Tim and Greg appear, dawdling together apart from the rest. Greg is growing his hair out into an unruly blonde tangle, he's experimenting with character. It's not a sexual thing, but I think all mothers admire the bodies of their sons. Almost professionally. So much care has gone into raising his body, carefully cultivating it with the right foods, protecting it from damage, washing it until he learnt to wash it himself. School and their friends take control of their minds, but their bodies bear a mother's expertise.

I smile and wave but when he sees me, Greg winces.

I knock on the bedroom door before easing it ajar. Greg is lying on his bed holding a comic. The room smells like his father left out in the rain.

"Have you any plans for your birthday? I was wondering, you know, if you want a party, that's fine. You can have it here."

"I hadn't thought about it."

"You can have all your friends over."

I watch him calculate, he doesn't leap up with enthusiasm but by the end of his deliberations the balance is tipped in favour of the party.

" I'll warn the neighbours. I could even get Lloyd to do security, that'd be cool wouldn't it?"

"Does that mean Dad can't come?"

"He can come, we've moved beyond that now. I told Lloyd that your father didn't mean some of the things he said about me. Lloyd won't do anything to him. He understands that your father was just being over-emotional."

"He mightn't be in the country anyway."

"Exactly. You should see him on the day but maybe it's best if he doesn't come to the party. He's drinking a lot at the moment, I don't want anything to spoil it for you."

I call Lloyd on his mobile to see if he's available for Greg's party. I know his phone flashes up my name when I call. Sometimes he picks up and sometimes he doesn't, which infuriates me. I know he's standing there in his puffa and earpiece, laughing with the others. I can

THERE'S NOTHING MORE EROTIC THAN THE KNOWING SMILE THAT PASSES BETWEEN TWO PEOPLE WHO ARE USING EACH OTHER FOR SEX

imagine him, his phone goes and he squints at the display and his thumb considers whether I'm worth it.

He picks up. "It's slow tonight, why don't you come down and liven the place up?"

The club is out of town, so I have time to put my face on in the back of the cab. I assemble it piece by piece in my compact, adjust my hair in the rearview mirror. Close my eyes and give it a blast of hairspray. It's a rush job but then it's only a Monday night. Annabelle's is not what you'd call sophisticated, sandwiched between B&Q and PC World. Girls get in free before nine. Drink four pints of Fosters and get the fifth free. DJ Choones and Dave T in residence. It's the kind of place I'd have turned my nose up at when I was married, the tack and the grot didn't fit with who I thought I was then. Now it reminds me of being young.

It's uncanny how little these places have changed. All night feeling the itch of threadbare velveteen upholstery against sheer dernier. The Ladies still smell of fags and feet that have danced all night in heels. The boys still wear hairgel and still get fall down drunk. The same glitterball twists silently over us all. The music isn't even that different, not really.

Lloyd comes over to me. I am sitting at the bar, drinking gin and tonic. Doubles only one pound seventy. "My son's having a birthday party tomorrow. I thought it'd be cool to have you do the door. Do you fancy it?" He keeps his diary on a Psion - his thick black fingers tap daintily at its mini keys. Turns out he's busy, he'd love to do me the favour but he has prior commitments. Then he puts his hand on my thigh and says why don't I sit tight for an hour? "We can go out back about eleven." There's nothing more erotic than the knowing, sleazy smile that passes between two people who know they are only using each other for sex.

"Please Lloyd, it would mean so much to me if you'd do Greg's party. It would be so fantastic, I can't bear the idea of you not coming. Having you there would make the whole thing look so cool. Please Lloyd. You don't have to worry about, you know, seeing my son. It doesn't mean anything. I'm not asking for a relationship, it's just you doing me a favour." I watch him consider it. It's the ruthless calculation that turns me on: the weighing up how little of himself he can give to get back all that fucking in return.

"Just do it for a couple of hours. I'll make it worth your while."

He smiles like my nasty talk is a funky beat. Double gin and tonic for the lady. After getting me my drink, he says "laters" and I just sit there and smoke for a while, moving my head to the music, catching the reflected gleam of my earrings in the corner of my eye. When I run out of fags, I go to the machine but they only have Superkings left. I don't like smoking them, they make me look like an estate mum. Still.

I hold the black and gold pack up and show it to the barmaid: "They should make Superqueens too, don't you think?"

When I get home, Tim is standing in the middle of the lounge, wearing only his boxer shorts and a T-shirt, a duvet rucked up in his arms. "Is it all right if I stay on the sofa? It's too late for me to go back now." He speaks in a burst, as if to leap in before I can tell him off. They are so self conscious at that age, it's sweet. He's about the same age as my ex was when I started going out with him.

When I return from the kitchen with a drink, Tim is lying on his back on the sofa, his arms by his sides, the duvet rather primly drawn up just over his nipples. I pick the ashtray off the mantlepiece. He accepts a cigarette.

"I don't normally smoke Superkings but it was all they had at the club. They just reek of poverty. I mean, aren't normal cigarettes long enough for these people? Do they really need that extra half inch just to make their grim lives that little bit better? It's mainly men who smoke them and believe me, they are not superkings. They should make some for woman and call them superqueens, don't you think?"

"I like Embassy Filters, the little ones."

"Oh, old man's fags."

"Yeah, but that's what's cool about them. You wrinkle your face up like Steptoe and do the whole thing in one drag." He takes his arm out from the duvet and mimes it.

"Be honest with me Tim. Does Greg smoke?"

"No, he can't. Honestly, it makes him anxious."

I finish my drink, stub my fag out even though it's barely lit. In the ashtray, the superking is bent like a broken leg.

"That sofa used to belong to my mother-in-law. She passed it onto me when she got a new three-piece suite." I reach out and pull at its cushion, we look at how shabby it is. "It's older than Greg. In fact, me and Greg's Dad used to roll around on it when we weren't much older than you."

That embarrasses him, I can sense his body shrink inside the duvet.

"Thing was, we'd be in the lounge doing it, and his granny - who used to live in this little room off the lounge - would be lying in bed watching telly. She was a bit deaf. But not that deaf! In fact, to be honest, I use to make as much noise as possible just to see if the old bat would dare to tell me off."

That wasn't true, but I want to see his face as he imagines me groaning and panting on the sofa. I want him to lie awake running his fingers over the seat covers, imagining my sweat and sex engrained in them.

"She'd get her own back on us, though. She was too old to be bothered going upstairs to the toilet everytime she wanted a piss so they had this orange potty for her, and when we'd be passionate in one another's arms I'd hear this splashing as she pissed next door. Spoil my whole night. Young men don't like to think about older women do they?"

"I don't know," he says. Like all boys, he is incapable of making the first move, but unable to resist someone who can. I'm flirting on autopilot.

"Do you think of me as old? I mean, I know I'm older than you. But do you think of me as really old?" It's a clumsy line, but it doesn't matter.

It's not that I desire him. I really just want to know what he thinks of me, and fucking him is the easiest way to find out.

"I don't think of you as old. I mean, I know you're Greg's mum, but you're nothing like other parents."

"In what way?"

"You go out. You don't hassle us all the time."

I've never seen Tim on his own before. He's always had Greg in tow, and so I've bundled them both together as boys. But seeing Tim undressed, with a fair rug on his chest, changes that. Suddenly, he is much closer to being a man. I notice his ears have been pierced, even though I've never seen him wear an earring. It's the smallest hint of a past, of something adult he tried but cast aside.

"Tim, would you like to have sex with me? Just for fun. It doesn't have to mean anything." Now, I've shocked him. He forgets to exhale. Smokes tumbles from between his lips. I get up and lean over him, letting my cleavage become his world, while I smooth my hand under the duvet and straight into his shorts. His cock is sticky, still wet. For a moment I wonder if it's because he's come just from talking to me, just from the sight of me, and I close my eyes, almost ready to cry at the joy of that thought. But when I open them, I see Greg standing at the end of the sofa, naked. His face and chest are flush with rage, and when he flies into me, hitting me, I notice his face is wet with tears.

I must have interrupted them. He must have been hiding there, all along.

He smells like his father and I push him off me and before I know it I'm screaming too, my mouth open and there's no stopping it. When Tim struggles away from me, I rake him and grab his hair and he doesn't put up a fight. Greg comes back at me, defending his friend, his fucking lover for chrissake. I can smell it on both of them.

I'm out on the porch throwing anything I can get hands on at Tim. "This man abused my boy," I am pointing him out to the neighbours, who have given up pretending not to notice. Greg is crying on the lawn, he's still naked. It's like he wants everyone to see him. Not a word from Tim, he ducks the plates and paperweights while he struggles into the leg of his trousers. "I'm sending the police around after you," I stride out to the edge of the lawn. "I'll see you in jail for this you fucking pervert!" Some of the neighbours have come out of their homes, mainly the wives, pushed forward by embarrassed husbands. Some of them are wearing nighties, they hover at their front doors like ghosts. I've lived here for ages and I still don't know their names.

HE STUMBLES AWAY FROM ME, SPRAWLED OUT ON THE GRASS. FINALLY, I GRAB HIM HARD BY THE FOREARM, SHAKE HIM AND THROW HIM FORWARD. THIS TIME HE FALLS INTO THE GUTTER

Greg is rolling on the lawn, beating it out of anger and frustration. "You ruin everything, I hate you. I hate you." He flashes me a look of complete and utter loathing. The passion in it is all-consuming, he is completely within the emotion. "Go to Tim, then if you hate me so much." I walk back into the porch. "You don't have to stay here with your mother, go off with your friend. Go on then." I wave him away. He looks from me, to Tim, who is frozen at the sight of this drama. Right there, I know I am ready to let him leave. I don't want him to stay if he is prepared to put the needs of another over me.

Greg lets his head loll back, like he's going to faint. It's an act, pretending to be too weak to get up and go with Tim, it's an excuse to avoid making a decision. I run up to him and yank him up by the forearm, he shouts like he's scolded. "Go on then." I heave him forward but he just falls onto his knees. I pick him up again, and again thrust him after Tim. "Go to him, leave me." He stumbles away from me, sprawled out on the grass. Finally, I grab him hard by the forearm, shake him and throw him forward. This time he falls into the gutter, flopping down in one exaggerated, agonised motion.

He is crying so much, he is gagging. He keeps taking these big, whooping gasps. It takes him a while to say it, but in the end he does. "I don't want to go, Mum."

I kneel next to him, and gently pull him over to me until we are hugging. We rock together, and I take a tissue out and wipe all the grime and tears and snot from his face, smooth his hair back out of his eyes, take a good look at him. Close up, I can see there is so much more of me in him than his father. That means trouble, I tell him as much. "You're going to be like me. A real handful. You'll let no-one stop you from doing what you want to do, and that's just the way you should be." I take him back inside. I see one of the neighbours is still out on her lawn. She looks concerned, I can see it from here. Silently, from behind the double glazing, I mouth to her. "It's all over now. Everything is going to be alright."

I sit by his bed for the rest of the night, waiting for him to fall asleep, then smoking quietly as the dawn comes up. It takes me a while for the adrenalin to leave my system. Then I drift in and out of sleep. Five dreamless minutes of sleep. Switched off, switched on again. ❧

STEWART ENQUIRY

In 1998, the mysterious Stewart Enquiry was appointed
Idler Racing correspondent. Two years later,
he is hoping to attend his first significant race meeting,
in Punchestown, Ireland. We join Enquiry after a drink-fuelled
ferry trip. As related by JOCK SCOT.
Illustration by CHRIS WATSON

....

O n docking at Dun Laoghaire, the trio of Shane McGowan, Junior and
Stewart Enquiry brace themselves for the forthcoming battle, nay, war!
For war it would be, a bitter and perhaps bloody war, with a constant
and unforgiving foe: the Bookmaker. Untroubled by his heavy losses at
Cheltenham, Stewart was "Up For It". In fact, Liam-style, he was "Mad For
It". He drains his final pint of champagne in one eye-popping flourish and
declares loudly that he intends to "Blow the Bookmakers out of the Water".
And that as soon as possible he must "Engage the enemy more closely". This
Nelsonian quotation may have been brought on by his time spent on deck
during the voyage, staring at the wake as the UK receded and Eire drew ever
nearer. This was to be a "Cutting-out expedition" unparalleled in Stewart's
chequered gambling career and he fully intended to rise to the occasion.
Shane was merely delighted to be back in the Republic and looking forward
to the Craic. He needed no pep talk and grunted and guzzled supportively,

as Stewart's Nelson impersonation carried him away with its insane enthusiasm. Soon, he too was "Mad For It", and Junior would get them there safely.

Driving into Dublin, Shane announced that "Base Camp #1" and "Jumping Off Point" would be the Shelbourne Hotel, the finest the city had to offer and an establishment which had always extended a warm and uncritical welcome. It would be his pleasure to pick up the tab until they got "organizised". This suggestion was heartily welcomed by Stewart who was no stranger to the Shelbourne's hallowed portals. Junior had no idea what he was in for, but set the mood by slotting Thin Lizzy's "The Boys are Back in Town" on the car stereo, a ferry purchase that they all heartily sang along to. On arrival at the Shelbourne, the doorman helped carry Stewart into reception while Shane collected the keys to his usual suite before heading to the Horseshoe bar for a livener. The bar was empty save for a human crow with a stunning blonde on his lap. It was none other than rock legend, tax exile, and racegoer, Rolling Stone Ronnie Wood! He greeted Shane like a long-lost brother. Intro's were made and drinks arrived. The gorgeous blonde flashed her millennium push-up bra while Ronnie explained his presence. He was having a few days off from recording basic tracks for the new Stones LP and kindly suggested that they should team up for Punchestown, extending an invitation to the three to stay at his renovated castle, Coolmore, for the duration of the meeting. They gratefully accepted. Having arranged to begin the night's celebrations at Lilly's Bordello they retired to the suite for a power nap. Stewart got on the phone. Bookies, trainers, punters, press men, TV and radio presenters began arriving — room service was hard-pressed to keep up with their constant and eccentric demands. A card game took shape in a smaller room. Shane slept, Stewart held court, Junior rolled spliffs and DJ'd. Stewart was starting to get hunches and retired to his room just as Shane woke up. Ronnie said goodbye to repair and await their arrival.

We'll draw a veil over events at Lilly's Bordello, but on the following morning, heavily hung over, they felt a great need to chill out. They re-convened in the Horseshoe bar for a summit meeting. MacGowan was incoherent but Stewart more than made up for his silence with unbounded enthusiasm.

After one more drink for the road they left the Shelbourne for the drive to Coolmore. The journey was uneventful, Shane and Stewart napped in the back, Junior smoked endless reefers and attempted to teach Rabbi — their luminous green teddy mascot — Gaelic. On arrival at Coolmore they were overtaken by a saddled giraffe as they negotiated the drive (Ron has it in training and it has thrown him into the rhodedendron bushes which line the drive). Their Ford Capri splattered gravel on to the front door, Stewart and Shane fell out of the motor only to witness an eight-year-old digging a hole in the croquet lawn. When asked by Shane what he was doing, the child replied, "I'm looking for the devil, man." They were cracking up as they

RONNIE AND KEITH LEFT AFTER MORE DRINKS ON THE CROQUET LAWN, WHERE THE YOUNG CHILD WAS STILL DIGGING

transferred their bags and deposited them in the hall where friendly Irish Wolfhounds unthinkingly pissed all over them. Having noticed a gipsy caravan parked by the stable yard they were not altogether suprised when top model Iris Palmer appeared. She ushered them through to the main reception room where a barrel of Guinness was warming by the log fire. Coolmore is a mixture of crumbling towers, corrugated iron out-houses and a high-tech interior. There are many rooms with people littered on sofas and easy chairs blending into their surrounds. Ronnie appeared in muddy racing silks, all bruised bonhomie. A noise from upstairs was irritating Shane. He asked: "Is someone hoovering?" Ronnie explained: "It's Keith rocking out." They threw him up some fags and a bottle of Jack Daniels and returned to Iris's overflowing glasses. The wrinkled retainer, Shaun Shenanigans, an eighth son of an eighth son, asked if they would like any more to drink. Deeply in love with jockey Charlie Swan, he is Ireland's leading tipster. He suggested they back Helen's Nest, Cornelius Cohort and Snowdrop at the forthcoming meeting. MacGowan surfaced in a tartan dressing gown obviously having taken more drugs and hallucinating wildly, just as well-known editor James Brown crashed his Mercedes convertible close to the front door. He was dressed as Rommel on an MC5 kick, and strutted into the cosy fireside enclave, "Heil Hitlering!" as he went, and immediately the company devised a plan to depart for the races in a "Flying Column" using Ronnie's vintage cars as the conveying vehicles. James was to lead the column, Junior would follow driving a vintage Bentley with Shane and Stewart, both unconscious. Ronnie and Keith left after more drinks on the croquet lawn, where the young child was still digging. At the crossroads they threw fistfuls of two pound coins to starving beggars, remnants of the Irish Potato Famine, such was their joy, confidence and general high spirits. They arrived at the races in triumph. James Brown (Rommel) is detained on arrival. After an initial skirmish with the Garda he is told to wear an overcoat. He complied and adopted a smart, full-length leather trenchcoat, adding to his cool look.

Everyone was studying form: lots of side-mouth whispering, priests and jockeys in the changing rooms. They availed themselves of the generous hospitality which Ronnie had laid on in his private box. Stewart went serious as he considered his first bet. ⊚

Commit the Oldest Sins ...

... The newest kind of ways

The Canongate Prize for New Writing

Britain's biggest and most democratic award for new writing.

£30,000 of prize money will be divided between 15 winners.

The competition is open to all writers, professional or amateur.

Submissions must be unpublished prose of between 2,000 and 5,000 words and must address this year's theme of Sin. The closing date for entries is 31st August, 2000.

All new writing is welcome. Journalistic investigation, open essay, dramatic dialogue, travel writing, political polemic, short story...

Entries may be sent to:
The Canongate Prize, Canongate Books, 14 High Street, Edinburgh EH1 1TE.
Visit the website **www.canongateprize.com**

The HERALD   sundayherald
WATERSTONE'S

THE RAKE

Life's a beach for Clive D'Arcy,
dashing young blade about town.
By ANDREW COPEMAN. Illustrations by RAYMOND WEEKES

....

I t's a beach.
A sheet of sand, golden and untrammeled.
It's a beach.
A single sun beams on the amber shore and gently simmers the sea.
It's a beach.
And the dream always ends there.
The kerb feels like sandpaper against my cheek, shirt collar soaking up gritty water, back of my head bearing a drain's imprint.
It's a gutter.
A single street light washes my face spectral white.
There's blood on my socks.
Whilst I've been lying here, someone has taken the opportunity to crawl inside my nervous system. There's a drilling sensation behind my eyelids, yet the pain's buzzing hot through my fingers. A monogrammed sheaf of matches waltz down the pavement caught in the backdraft of a speeding mini-cab. Then silence.
Darkness encoded, I scrape together what's left of my senses and contemplate how I'm going to get home.
If guardian angels are paid on commission, mine must have qualified for a holiday in Disneyland by now. The eventual arrival at my unmade bed, undeniable proof of another outstanding target successfully reached. Minor explosions of dread detonate across my bruised carcass as I sift through scraps of memory: an invitation; pristine midnight-blue Paul Smith suit; expensive eau de toilette expansively applied; three double shots of Bombay Sapphire gin — neat; the prowl through the park; the party; faces colliding as the night wears on and the inhibitors wear off; a strawberry-blonde in soiled cocktail dress; taking the air on the balcony; parting her pubic hair on the bog; her smell on my fingertips; chauffeured elopement with retired Admiral to private members club; his hand on my thigh all the time in the Daimler; entry; melding in the catacombs; scarlet lips on my belly; pleasure

blackout; wrong pair of lips on my bell-end; strangled terror; pre-cum spots moustache bristles; knee to chest; escape; tripping upstairs; blackout; chauffeur's leather fist; blackout; worked on/over; blackout; the street; blackout; home.

Blackout.

It's a beach.

A gentle breeze skims the surface sprinkling sand over my face.

It's a beach.

Heat fuses me to the sinking ground as waves hiss in the distance.

It's a beach.

Maybe two days have elapsed before I awake. The dole cheque hasn't arrived which means my pile of dry cleaning now resembles a small festering pyramid. At its base, as inscrutable as the Sphinx, a phone; its receiver off the hook. Groaning, I scoop up a weeping bottle of Cognac and hobble to the bathroom.

Outside everything's a negative print; shapes and their parameters bleached white/ grey. There's damaged goods on the corner. I'm waiting for the lights to change. "Clive D'Arcy: Dashing Young Blade About Town!" how pathetic that soubriquet sounds now as I push change so loose it's unwound around my trouser pocket. My teeth hurt. I have no solid idea of where I'm going; I only know I'm gone. I cross on a red-man. Wheel squeals and "Wake up you stupid cunt!" bounce around my shoes.

Attention: phantom passing.

Steering a course between light and shadow, I feel drawn to the sleaze 'n' sauna parlours on the cracked edge of town. A cluster of roads crouch and turn like a badly soldered circuit-board. I follow the gusts of litter, a tatty paperchase, past shuttered shop fronts and twisted residents. Then, without thinking, I stop. It's found me. Thrumming in between a Turf Accountants and padlocked lock-up; "The Shangri-La Escort Agency". Three windows tinted in descending shades of brown; beige, hazelnut, dark chocolate, trip-licate my reflection. I step to the door.

No one seems bothered that I'm in the building. At least that's how I read the situation as there's no one around. This desertion is not in the least bit disturbing: in a strange way, I expected it. A corridor runs before me; fluo-rescents in the ceiling shade the carpet dull amber. I wade forward. To the left and right, dug into the walls, there's a succession of heavy black doors. On each, stencilled in white, a title. "Hospital." I don't trust doctors, "Yacht." St. Tropez; too blasé. "Gymnasium." I despise exercise. "Bus-stop." I'm not in the suburbs —

Stop.

The word I've been searching for, as plain as this door.

"Beach..."

Taking a deep breath I push down the handle and slip inside.

Two tatty deckchairs sit in the centre of the room, running around the walls there's a bile-yellow band; badly smudged streaks of paint masquerading as sandcastles. A scratchy tape loop of breaking waves and gull choruses programme the air. I take a chair and wait. I'm not entirely sure for what. Gazing at the floor, I notice a hole in my left Burlington

STANDING OVER ME IS URSULA ANDRESS; THE DISQUIETING THING IS, IT APPEARS SHE'S BEEN FORCE FED BLACK FOREST GATEAU LACED WITH STEROIDS

sock. Hunching over I prod the tear. Footsteps. "Looking for something?" Standing over me is Ursula Andress; the disquieting thing is, it appears she's been force fed Black Forest Gateau laced with steroids. "Lost your balls, sweetie?" Sweat shines in bursts on her pectoral slabs. "Is that thing real?" I point at a diver's knife strapped to a bulging thigh. She giggles.

"Want to find out?" she yanks out a black dildo and hits the vibro switch.

Whatever survival instinct I still carry, trips into life. Yanking the deckchair next to me, I kick mine away and brandish striped canvas and varnished wood. Mutant Ursula squeals with delight. Scanning one hundred and eighty degrees for an escape route, I notice the door's vanished. "Oh, you tease!" the temptress lunges. Parrying the angry phallus, I manage to get in a sharp dig with the chair's wooden strut; head shot, opening up a gash in the pumped Amazon's forehead. "Fuckery!" she yells, dropping the dildo and slamming a rubbery hand to the wound. The situation has now transgressed the laws of desperation. With no visible means of exit I appear to be trapped. "Maybe we can come to some understanding." Squinting through a stringy red veil of plasma, the contorted Valkyrie advances. "I don't think so," she snarls. Panic infects my motor neurones. I start patting the wall, frantically searching for an opening. "I'm going to work you till you scream!" Ursula spits blood 'n' hate.

My hands are beating out a spastic tattoo on the brickwork but the portal still remains elusive. Somewhere above, there's the tiny clatter of a fairground organ. If I close my eyes, maybe all this will change. Maybe I'll be able to will my way out. Ursula's trunk looms behind me. Slowly I sink to my knees. A motorized buzz gnaws at my ear, chunky digits curl into my hair, warm liquid spatters my neck. "Play time..."

It's a beach.

The unfiltered sky is unforgiving.

It's a beach.

The tide is coming in.

It's a beach.

I'm washed up and left for dead.

And the dream always ends. ◉

THE SHORT HAPPY LIFE OF AUGUSTUS MAPPIN

The story of a beautiful boy. By JAMES PARKER.
Illustration by HANNAH DYSON

....

Yes, I remember Gus Mappin. Augustus, as he was christened. Who could forget, who knew the man? He was our Batman and our morning star. His beauty was a byword. Oh Mappin, Mappin, return! Still I see you, refulgent at schoolboy sports, ball in hand, racing. With such a sweet certainty of flesh do you fill the seat of your cricket whites, the black-gowned dons are haggard with lust. See, an entire pack of them haunting the boundary like electrified crows — arseless, correct, shuddering in their wool trousers. And I see you in the classroom, most gorgeous of my oppressors. You teased me cruelly for my speech defect, and yet I was not angry at you. I was angry at Pendleton, your fat little adjutant, because he — his jellied chins a-jiggle — was not beautiful. (What right had he to mock me?) But never at you, though you mocked and danced and raised from Pendleton those peals of porcine enjoyment. My stammering tongue could not speak my love for you, or my hatred for him. Intensities clawed for air within me. Hope or rage, rage or hope? A small boy who was also a huge and blocked combustion, I closed my eyes and saw trees bent like used matches over a flayed landscape. But though I destroyed the world in my head you were ever outside it — dancing, endlessly mocking, your white hair flying.

Oh I remember Mappin. He holidayed in Jamaica, sand between his toes, with executives from Island Records. When he was in England I would see him at the enormous charity balls which it was the curse of my class to attend. The White Knight, the Banana Ball... Nightmares of celebration, mere rutting-grounds for drunken teenagers, with flushed tuxedo'ed rugby-players hoofing along to The Jam's "Eton Rifles" and shivering the marquee with their bellows. Mappin always had a girl on his arm — some deb double-barrelled in body and name, the summer of fourteen shires in her hair and a sozzled adoring grin on her face. His narcissism was a pure flame and needed no foreign fuel, but he would lump these big girls around as a sort of courtesy. Perhaps out of kindness, at these functions he would pretend not to recognise me.

After school I lost touch with Gus Mappin. He was a familiar sight in the society pages, photographed here and there, leering vampirically over some glossy shoulder, and like thousands of others I experienced the exaltations of his entrepreneurial fire — the vast illegal raves he organised. Our mage, our impresario: truly the sky itself was his big top. The great raves! Dawn and the waning laser, the sweated-through clothes suddenly clinging like unwanted new friends. Concentric circles of awareness — in the middle the seal-like ravers, plashing idiotically with invisible beach-balls on their noses. Around them, less innocent, the watchers and puffers and hawkish dealers. And then at the rim, wariest of all, the bouncers — small eyes looking outward, headsets tuned to the unforgiving frequency of bouncer alertness. And Mappin up in his counting-house, rolling in receipts. There was Rapsis of course, and then I believe Plasmation and finally (and most notoriously) Fluology, where whole squads of police Alsatians were rendered senseless by trays of ketamine-dosed dogfood. In that myth-hungry time Mappin put on the lineaments of legend. It was rumoured, for instance, that at the Criminal Justice Bill riot in Hyde Park he had unseated a mounted policeman by muttering an incantation to the horse, a thing taught to him in his boyhood by an octogenarian stablehand at his father's estate in Ireland. Later that same day (and to this I can testify) he delighted rioters by declaiming from Shelley's "The Mask Of Anarchy" during a cavalry charge. A Jaggeresque moment. He was wearing, I recall, a flapping green parka and a dreadlock wig — it seemed less the disguise he claimed it to be than a fit of inverted dandyism.

Pharmaceutically cured (it seemed to me) of acute class consciousness, I immersed myself in all this. As a direct consequence I saw imaginary spiders

AND THERE WAS FLUOLOGY, WHERE WHOLE SQUADS OF POLICE ALSATIANS WHERE RENDERED SENSELESS BY TRAYS OF KETAMINE-DOSED DOGFOOD

out of the corner of my eye for two years afterward. Nor could I ride the London Underground. Mappin, however, was made of sterner stuff. He had something silvery, elven, inviolate – we felt sure no chemical could dent him. When his rave organisation was forcibly co-opted by a Maltese security firm he departed upon a fresh adventure: an interior one, this time. In a large blank house in Enfield he gathered around himself a cadre of penniless extreme sportsmen. Skydivers and snowboarders. By day they drove vans and made deliveries, by night they bounced uselessly at the end of bungee cords. And now, led by Mappin, they hurled their psyches into the abyss. Stockpiling the latest psychedelic technologies, they tripped like buccaneers. They made discoveries: just beneath reality they found a fizzing, insectival layer of information, a molecular data war in which they scried the birthagonies of an entirely new system. Plans were laid. Men from the future introduced themselves, in a cloud of numbers. It was all very exciting. Mappin communicated with fellow investigators on the West Coast of America, and thought he might write a book. Then suddenly, unaccountably, it was all off. The sportsmen dispersed, and we heard no more of the Enfield project. As if starved of air or light Mappin flung himself outdoors – pilgrimage, safari. He visited distant monasteries, shot big game. His mountain-climbing expeditions – the Andes, the Himalayas – grew ever more ambitious. He claimed to love the harsh novelties of altitude sickness, saying that the ringing in one's ears at 8,000 metres was like a wire being drawn through raw meat. He called this vein of his character "a relish for the hellish".

A year or two later I ran into him in Central London, and was surprised to find that my stammer, long since ironed over by several expensive courses of speech therapy, returned immediately. He smiled at my difficulty as I re-introduced myself, and invited me to visit his lapdancing club in Soho, still in its maiden week. There was, I thought, a slightly megalomaniacal bounce to his step as he led me down the stairs. I declined the offer of a dance on the house, but lingered a good while nonetheless. The girls, of course, were unforgettable. Muscled and sunbed-tawny, their faces blankly energised, they reared and rippled over their terrified clients like snakes swallowing rats. But equally unforgettable to me was the sight of Gus Mappin in his dimmed control room, his eye divided between seven small video screens, his face lean and saintlike in the secondhand light. On each

**HE TALKED UNTIL THE CLUB
CLOSED, AND AS NEON
FLICKERED BRUTALLY OVERHEAD
I SAW HIS FACE TWIST IN
PANIC. THE HALF-DARK, IT
SEEMED, WAS NOW HIS HOME**

screen a dance was in progress, and he drawled his assessments to me (or to himself – I could never be sure which): "Good form, yup, she's showing good form... Nice articulation... That's what I'm paying her for... Hold on, she's not allowed to do *that*. Christ! Now that's the charlie, you see. The snow. They all need a couple of lines to get moving, I've got that arranged, but this girl's having some sort of alpine emergency. She's going to put somebody's eye out. I'll have to talk to Fabrice about her..." and so on. These images remain.

A fortnight before his death I saw him by chance in a club, propped against a dark wall and seeming oppressed by the music. His face was pale and had an odd impersonal lumpiness to it, is if some alien presence pouched beneath the skin was dimly seeking release. I could hardly see his eyes. He talked moodily of the past, forgetting my name frequently. He expressed his disillusionment with the Enfield project, abandoned – he told me – in circumstances of considerable squalor. Various minds (not his) had apparently crumbled like gingerbread; there had been a dank rising of ghosts, screams in the dawn and so on. He referred to the experience as "his one good chance" and disparaged his erstwhile comrades as "lightweights". He talked until the club closed, and as neon flickered brutally overhead I saw his face twist in panic. The half-dark, it seemed, was now his home.

He was killed more or less by accident. Which is not to say that he was not murdered – only that his death had a clumsy, uncertain quality. He was half-smothered, half-bludgeoned, and probably died laughing. His killers – a pair of washed-up gangland torturers with whom he had been planning to write a book – only did it, I think, because they weren't sure what else to do with him. Were any of us? He crossed our vision like a fever-trail, a bright slur upon perception. Do I see double? Do I see triple? I am not myself. I am Gus Mappin in the hammered instants of his demise, fading beneath the blows, the soul dragged blinking from its nest of nerves and rushed up shafts of starlight, to a cold and angry throne. Behind a pub in Dalston these men became the instruments of his will, the rough tools of his final transformation. It is said they urinated on his body – a strange and sacramental gesture which (I'm certain) he appreciated. ◉

www.idler.co.uk

stop working start living

PIGS, NOT GRAVEL

A story of genteel protest and a celebrity-studded drinks party.
By FRANK SKELTON
Illustrations by MARCUS OAKLEY

....

"*L*isten to us. We want pigs. Not gravel... Listen to us. We want pigs. Not gravel.*" It was strange experience seeing my wife on television. At last, here was a single issue which had really caught her imagination, and which she felt was worth doing something about. There was a tense, angry look on her face. It was a face which registered that an injustice was taking place, and that it was her duty to confront it.

"*Listen to us,*" she was shouting, along with a group of slightly older Conservative Party activists outside a local authority building. "*We want pigs. Not gravel.*"

My wife was holding a placard, on which I could make out the words "Leave Oving Land Alone".

I suppose it was quite ironic seeing my wife, a lifelong and fiercely committed conservative, engaged in street protest activity. Looking at the scene, you might have thought the protestors were a rabble of hard left union activists camped outside a loss-making nationalised industry, not a well-heeled group of Sussex conservatives. How the country had turned upside down.

But perhaps it was complacent of me to make such an observation. The Government's acceptance of the DETR Inspector's targets for aggregate extraction, based as they were on the largely discredited predictions of demand made in Mineral Planning Guidance Note 6, posed a serious environmental threat to the countryside, and, my wife would argue, for no real purpose.

In other words, Oving would shortly become a building site.

For my wife, the protest represented more than some local objection. It went right to the heart of her ideological position, which was a robust defence of the doctrine of the market, and the rights of local people to make decisions about the way they lived.

"*Listen to us,*" I could hear her shouting. "LISTEN TO US."

The *South Today* newscaster concluded her commentary on the protest, and we went back to the studio. I turned the television off and went into the kitchen to finish the washing up. My wife would be back in London in an hour. There was time to make myself some form of sandwich. We were not due at Mark and Brigitte's for over two hours. It wouldn't do to get hungry before that.

In the kitchen, I turned the radio on. It was Radio 4. Clive Anderson, a rather self-indulgent television entertainer who had previously been a barrister, was discussing civil liberties and the challenges faced by public authorities as a result of the Government's decision to incorporate the European Convention of Human Rights into domestic law. No wonder Clive's guests were feeling pleased with themselves. From what he was saying, the new Human Rights Act would inspire a mass of rights-based litigation, with, from what I could understand, the only people really benefiting at the end of the day were the lawyers and their bank balances.

Mark had telephoned earlier in the week.

"We're having a few people round for drinks and a bite to eat. Helen will be there. Nikos and Alison, and one or two others. We've also invited Baroness Ruth Rendell, the celebrated detective author and the inspiration behind the successful *Inspector Wexford* series on Meridian television. But don't worry. We're keeping things quite low key."

"Wexford," I mused. "Isn't he the one played by George Barker?" Once my wife Becca had returned, we made the necessary preparations and left. Since Mark and Brigitte lived nearby, we decided to drive. We would leave the car there and walk back. I could then wander to the house the following morning and pick the car up. We'd been round to Mark and Brigitte's several times. It was a tested formula. It worked.

Mark greeted us at the door, and warmly welcomed us into his quite substantial kitchen. There were some quite exquisite cooking smells. I turned to

ON THE OTHER SIDE OF THE KITCHEN TABLE, BRIGITTE WAS TALKING TO A VERY TALL, BEARDED MAN, WHOM I IMMEDIATELY RECOGNISED AS THE FORMER CELEBRITY HOSTAGE, TERRY WAITE

Rebecca and said:

"I believe that Brigitte has prepared a gratin."

On the other side of the kitchen table, Brigitte was talking to a very tall, bearded man, whom I immediately recognised as the former celebrity hostage, Terry Waite. Waite, who had been some sort of envoy for the Archbishop of Canterbury in the eighties, had been on a mission to negotiate the release of Westerners held hostage by Hizbollah militia in South Lebanon.

I turned to Helen, a friend of my wife.

"The Department of Environment, Transport and the Regions have got it totally wrong haven't they?" I said to her.

"What do you mean?" she replied.

"Well, in terms of mineral planning, they have set ludicrous quotas, and are basing their policies on 'predict and provide', which goes against all common sense. What's needed is more 'monitor and manage'."

I sensed that a number of people were moving towards us to listen to the conversation.

"What we're seeing," I continued, "is large swathes of British countryside going under the bulldozer. The place where Becca and I married," I added, fighting back the tears, "all that farmland has now been sold off to the mineral companies."

"But the construction companies," said Terry Waite, "need aggregates, and they need to get them from somewhere. Surely it is absolutely right for the Department of the Environment, Transport and the Regions to centrally plan for provision, particularly when, as in the case of aggregate extraction, there is an environmental and social impact?"

"With respect, Terry," I replied, turning to Waite, "if the Government must plan centrally, and that is not a premise I necessarily accept, then at least they should base their planning on reliable figures, not on statistics which have been rubbished by the British Cement Association, the Council for the Protection of Rural England, and the British Geological Society.

"The Government," I continued, manouevring for the knock-down blow, "is basing its figures on an assumption that aggregate demand bears a direct relationship with economic growth. Independent statistical analysis clearly demonstrates that this assumption is totally wrong. Demand in real terms is falling. That is the point. And yet Government inspectors are riding roughshod over local authorities and imposing quotas, accusing local protestors of nothing more than NIMBYism."

Terry filled his glass and moved to the sitting room.

"I'm sorry," I said to Brigitte. "It's just that this is an issue that Rebecca and I feel passionately about."

That moment, there was a frisson of excitement which passed through the assembled guests like a current of electricity. A rather small elderly woman had walked in. Mark greeted her and motioned her to a chair by the fire. The woman, whom I clearly recognised from a photograph as Ruth Rendell, the inspiration behind the hugely successful "Inspector Wexford" series on television, whispered something to Mark. Mark left the room and returned with a travel blanket which he placed over Ruth Rendell's knees.

Having observed all this, I moved back to the kitchen, where I started talking to Limahl, the former lead singer of the eighties Pop Group, Kajagoogoo. I had never met Limahl before, and I have to say that, while evidently not a terribly intelligent man, he was quite charming. There was no trace of the ludicrous hair style with which he had found fame. Limahl was talking about his bicycle, with which he seemed to having some problems.

"It seems to creak everytime I push down the left pedal. It doesn't happen with the right."

"I think," I replied, "that the kind of creaking which you are describing is caused by the interface between the crank arm and the bottom bracket easel."

"Oh yes?"

"Is your chainset alloy and axel steel?"

"I'm not sure."

"You see, if it's not the pedal it's probably the crank arm. You'll need to take off the dust cap, removing the nut and using an extraction tool to pull the crank off. After that, you'll need to clean the crank and axel and make doubly sure you've done the mating surfaces. It should be all right then."

Suddenly, I was aware that Terry Waite was at my shoulder.

"You'll need" Waite said, in his booming voice, "to put WD40 on it"

"Forgive me Terry," I said, slightly displeased with his interjection. "That will only make matters worse."

I made my way over towards Dave Allen, the Irish stand-up comedian who had been popular in the seventies.

"Why is there this gap," asked Dave, after I was introduced, "between the enactment of the Human Rights Act and its coming into force?"

"Ah," I replied, happy to help out where required. "The incorporation of Convention rights into domestic legislation will require the judiciary to undergo quite extensive training, because it's expected that the impact of the act will be substantially far-reaching. What you mustn't forget," I continued, "is that those public authorities which will be vulnerable to the legislation

I HAD NEVER MET LIMAHL BEFORE, AND I HAVE TO SAY THAT, WHILE EVIDENTLY NOT A TERRIBLY INTELLIGENT MAN, HE WAS QUITE CHARMING

will need a considerable amount of time to ensure that their activities are compatible with Convention rights."

"But does that mean," said Limahl, who had moved over to where Dave Allen, and I, and now Terry Waite once again, were standing, "that public authorities at the moment are by implication infringing human rights. Because if that is what you are implying, it is a matter of grave concern."

"No, Limahl," I replied. "The European Convention on Human Rights accepts that in certain circumstances the Convention rights will need to be restricted. But what the Convention emphasises is that these restrictions must be in accordance with the law. Some public authorities infringe rights at the moment in ways that do not have a legislative framework. They may have guidelines and a thorough system of internal checks and balances, but the Convention clearly states that this will not be good enough."

"What about this issue of proportionality?" asked Roy Hattersley.

"This is the real issue, Roy," I replied. "If public authorities are going to infringe rights, they are going to have to establish explicitly that the action is proportionate to the end expected. And there's going to have to be an explicit internal system whereby this question can be addressed right up the management chain. Independent external oversight is another factor."

"Well, the impact on the judiciary, and also on public authorities, will be not inconsiderable," concluded Sting, as I withdrew from this particular group, and made my way towards my wife, who appeared to be engaged in conversation with the celebrity author, Ruth Rendell.

"Baroness Rendell," I said, interrupting Rebecca and the author. "It is delightful to see you looking so well. Can I say how much I have enjoyed your Inspector Wexford books? They seem to be such rewarding explorations of the minds of people who commit murder either through — how shall I say — obsessive love, or perhaps social inadequacy."

The old lady looked slightly confused, and Rebecca looked embarrassed. Nevertheless, having committed myself, I continued.

"I think that in the television series of the same name George Barker captures the genial, Trilby-wearing Chief Inspector perfectly."

"Frank," my wife said. "Mark's grandmother is telling me how she always has a Yorkshire Pudding when she does Brisket of Beef." ☻

BOOKS

A VIRGIN'S PARADISE

What is the strange allure of The Wicker Man?
MATTHEW DE ABAITUA investigates

What goes around, comes around, as the Buddhists are fond of saying. At the tail-end of 1973, THE WICKER MAN snuck into British cinemas. There was no West End première, its release was desultory - as if someone, somewhere, didn't want it to be seen.

Twenty-seven years later, the cult of THE WICKER MAN has finally spilt over into mainstream consciousness. FilmFour recently tracked down and broadcast a rare extended edit of the film, and now there is a long overdue book that gathers together the intriguing story behind this extraordinary and unique piece of British film history.

INSIDE THE WICKER MAN: THE MORBID INGENUITIES by Allan Brown, (Sidgwick & Jackson £14.99) diligently assembles interviews with all involved, digs out contemporary reviews, and painstakingly tracks the growth of the cult around the film as it gradually unwound in the British and American cultural psyche. It is indispensable for anyone who has ever tasted the strange magic of THE WICKER MAN, and left wanting more. It fills in the blanks to both the film's chequered history, and to the film itself − Christopher Lee insists over two and half hours of scripted scenes were shot, yet the longest surviving cut is only a hundred and two minutes long.

As Allan Brown rightly notes in his introduction, THE WICKER MAN gestated in the unconscious of Britain and America after its release, seeping into the culture through drive-in screenings, late night TV broadcasts, and word of mouth. Despite the destruction of much of its original footage − and despite it being loathed by the studio that made it − the film has an otherworldly quality that puts down roots in the minds of everyone who sees it, roots that have slowly erupted to the surface. For example, the American countercultural event, The Burning Man Festival, is a mutated trace memory of THE WICKER MAN: a libidinous bacchanal in which the consumerweary recreate the excitement of the old gods for a weekend. Like the film, it climaxes in the burning of a giant effigy. Like the film, it suspends propriety: revellers enjoy the brief license to get their kit off, paint their knobs blue, and wave them at all and sundry.

The plot of THE WICKER MAN follows the trip of Sergeant Neil Howie (Edward Woodward) as he travels to the remote Scottish island of Summerisle in search of a missing girl, Rowan Morrison. When he arrives at the island, he questions the local fishermen, showing them a photograph of Rowan. They deny all knowledge of her, which strikes him as strange for such a small community. As his search continues, he realises that the islanders are not Christians. They worship the old gods, the pantheistic pre-Christian Celtic mythos of sympathetic magic, rebirth, and sun gods − a belief system encouraged by the ruler of the island, Lord Summerisle, played by Christopher Lee. The theological arguments between the strict Christian lay-preacher, Sergeant Howie, and the wry, heathen Lord Summerisle form the thematic core of the film: monotheism versus pantheism, Christian individualism versus the libidinous community.

There is no-one more libidinous on the island than Willow MacGregor. Daughter of the landlord of the Green Man pub, Willow −

played by Britt Ekland – is a rite of passage for the male islanders. In one of the recently restored scenes, we see Lord Summerisle bring an adolescent boy to her to be inducted into sex. While we listen to Willow deflower the boy in her room, the patrons of the pub sing the slow, sensual folk song Gentle Johnny, while Sergeant Howie writhes with repressed lust in the adjacent bedroom. It's a lust he cannot express. Although Howie is engaged, his strict Christianity forbids him sex before marriage. Sergeant Howie is a virgin copper.

His virginity is key to the film. What Sergeant Howie doesn't realise is that he has been tricked into coming to the island. There is no missing girl. She is a ruse to lure the perfect sacrificial victim to Summerisle. The previous year, the Summerisle crops failed and now, in accordance with their beliefs, they need to appease their gods. Nothing less than the sacrifice of a man who is a virgin, a Fool, who has come of his own free will, will do.

To test the sergeant's virginity, Willow tries to seduce him. In a legendary scene, a naked Britt Ekland dances around her bedroom, calling to Howie with another one of the film's peculiarly alluring folk songs while lustily slapping the walls and her buttocks. As Allan Brown's book reveals, they are not in fact Britt's buttocks. A body double was used for these shots. Nor is it her voice. Ekland was overdubbed for the entire film. So the character of Willow is essentially an amalgam of the advantages of three different women, which is rather appropriate for the goddess of love.

Willow's song lures him out of bed. Slowly, Howie lays himself against the wall that separates them, the sweat of his inner conflict running down his face. But he resists.

It was this scene that first enthralled me as an adolescent, one who was still as regrettably pure as Howie himself, and one who would have gladly sacrificed body parts for a woman like Willow to call to him in the night.

After the film, I realised I wanted to live in Summerisle. It was a virgin's paradise.

It isn't just the charms of Willow that make Summerisle such an enticing place for a virgin male. When Sergeant Howie wanders outside The Green Man at night, he comes across numerous couples having sex in the moonlight. Everyone is at it. Young and old, as Lord Summerisle makes clear when he shows Howie naked teenage girls leaping over a flame in the hope they may be impregnated by the fire god. Wait, there's more. Howie's search for the missing girl takes him to a local school, where the legendary Hammer actress, Ingrid Pitt, is teaching her female pupils on the meaning of the Maypole. Outside, the boys are singing about the cycle of life while performing a ribbon dance. At the climax of their dance, the boys lay their hands against the maypole, while Pitt enunciates in her distinctive Polish accent – "it is the phallic symbol". Summerisle is steeped in sex. Sex is in the soil. In this, the island reflects the male virgin's perspective of society, in which everyone seems to be sitting on a secret he desperately wants to be in on. Howie's search for the missing girl, the way he is wryly rebuffed by the islanders, and faintly patronised by Lord Summerisle, reminds me of a virgin's quest for the secret of what goes on during sex, whose ignorance amuses the adults.

In Summerisle, writer Anthony Shaffer and director Robert Hardy created a world where sexuality was stripped of its Christian complications, and restored to its natural state. It is telling that, when Howie stumbles across the couples rutting in the fields, the woman are all on top. Here sex is not the climax of arduous seduction, in which the man imposes his will on a reluctant woman. The men of Summerisle are sexually passive – the woman lustily grab at them in the Green Man, or they call them to their bedrooms. What could be more alluring to a passive male sexuality than a society in

BRITT EKLAND DANCES AROUND HER BEDROOM, CALLING TO HOWIE WITH ANOTHER ONE OF THE FILM'S PECULIARLY ALLURING FOLK SONGS WHILE LUSTILY SLAPPING THE WALLS AND HER BUTTOCKS

which boys are ritually deflowered?

Summerisle is a virgin's paradise. If you stay pure there, you are liable to be sacrificed, so the social structure and religious beliefs are dedicated to getting you laid as soon as is physically possible. That Summerisle was intended to be a form of paradise is clear from Anthony Shaffer's original script: "no terrain since Arcadia was ever so fecund," he writes, describing Howie's view of the island from his seaplane. The island fuses the charming bric-a-brac of Seventies village life – the Post Office, the Chemist, pubs – with the ancient rituals and beliefs of the pre-Christian age. You get the sheer excitement of having your gods all about you, and you get electrici-

ty. The appeal of the Summerisle community is not solely a sexual one - their religion is appealing too. There is an allure to pantheism, the way it energises the natural world and renders mysterious all that which seems obvious and banal to the rationalist. No doubt it has its downfalls: the film itself cocks an eyebrow at some of the villagers' odder beliefs, like keeping a frog in your mouth to cure a cough, or indeed, burning a policeman alive to make your apples grow. But even this irrationality is strangely appealing, if only because it wrestles reality free from the deadening hand of science. The truth only spoils your fun.

When I think back to the works of Seventies sci-fi and fantasy that enthralled me when I was younger, the virgin's paradise repeatedly crops up. In ZARDOZ, Sean Connery is a savage in a red nappy who sneaks into a community of epicene immortals. Jaded by their eternal existence, the immortals find the virile Connery intriguing. They show him pornographic films, and titter when he turns away from them and gets an erection at the sight of one of the female immortals. You'd think they hadn't seen a hard-on for a thousand years. A similar scenario is played out in A BOY AND HIS DOG, in which a young and horny Don Johnson prowls a post-apocalyptic landscape with his telepathic dog, who sniffs out women for him. Johnson ends up in a subterranean society, a

twisted take on Fifties America where the men are infertile. For a moment, he presumes this means they want him to individually impregnate every woman down there. No such luck. Instead they strap him to a milking machine and pump the semen out of him. In John Wyndham's DAY OF THE TRIFFIDS, the hero ends up in a remote Scottish community where it is his duty to take on more than one wife and impregnate them.

The virgin's paradise, then, is somewhere where sex seeks you out, where you're obliged to do the deed, as opposed to real life, where you have to put in a fair amount of legwork. Whether it is a futuristic mechanised sexuality, or a recreation of an nymph-filled lost world, the Virgin's Paradise is a place without repression, without inhibition, and full of willing women who will take the initiative, and not mind too much if you spread it about a bit. As John Donne wrote in his seventeenth Elegy, "How happy were our Syres in ancient times who held plurality of loves no crime." Or, as Lord Summerisle puts it, "I trust the sight of the youngsters refreshes you." ꙮ

INSIDE THE WICKER MAN:
THE MORBID INGENUITIES,
by Allan Brown
(Sidgewick & Jackson £14.99)

IDLE CLASSIC

TONY WHITE celebrates Flaubert's satire of middle class mores

An extended hymn to the futility of effort, and a satire of bourgeois intellectual dilletantism Flaubert's last, comic, novel follows the efforts of two hapless office workers to understand – and live their lives by – the total sum of human knowledge. After being named the sole beneficiary of some hitherto unknown relative's will, Messrs Bouvard and Pécuchet decide to give up their jobs and decamp to the country. But that's where things start to go wrong. Unable – through a mixture of sheer stupidity and a desire for betterment – to take advantage of this opportunity for idleness, these proto-Laurel and Hardys decide that the rustic way of life could benefit from the application of theory, and so set themselves the sorry task of learning everything there is to learn about, well, everything. Their reasoning – always logical – leads them from the Classics through Politics to Literature and every other sphere of human endeavour – each of which, they think, will provide the answers they're looking for, but which, if they stopped and looked, they'd find under their own noses. B&P retreat further and further into their academic meanderings until, ruined, they realise that their friendship must stand above all else, and that their greatest love is for the life they had before – that of the copy clerk. Thus they will spend the rest of their lives assembling a users' manual for civilised living. Unable to finish "their" encyclopaedia before he died in 1880, Flaubert's notes – entitled "A Dictionary of Received Ideas" – are published in its place at the end of this novel. Intended as a satire of reactionary common sense, the dictionary is a primer of bourgeois platitude and cliché. First published in 1881, it could have been written yesterday.

ABSINTHE: Extra violent poison: one glass and you're a deadman. Newspapermen drink it while writing their copy. Has killed more soldiers than the Bedouins.

CELEBRITIES: Find out the smallest details of their private lives, so that you can run them down.

EARLY RISING: A sign of morality. If one goes to bed at four in the morning and rises at eight, one is lazy; but if one goes to bed at nine in the evening and gets up the next day at five, one is an active type.

HASHEESH: Not to be confused with hash, which produces no voluptuous sensations whatsoever.

IDLERS: All Parisians are idlers, although nine out of ten Parisians come from the provinces. In Paris nobody works.

LITERATURE: Occupation of idlers.

BOUVARD AND PÉCUCHET (WITH THE DICTIONARY OF RECEIVED IDEAS) by Gustave Flaubert is published by Penguin Classics (£8.99)

UNDER THE INFLUENCE

STEPHEN THOMPSON, author of Toy Soldiers, discusses the books which inspired his first novel

Well, it's actually two books – one that inspired me to write full stop, and another that gave me the structure for TOY SOLDIERS. The first one was a novel called FIRE-FLIES by Shiva Naipaul. In many ways it's a very conventional, almost old fashioned,novel. But the simple style lends itself well to the story, which is about a family of Trinidadian Indians which implodes due to a series of long-running feuds. It's a really short book, can easily be read in one sitting. But it's fantastically written, really moving, funny too, and it lingers long in the memory. Naipaul manages to capture the flavour of the Caribbean – which is a place I know a little bit about – in so few words. I was just amazed that he managed to cram the experience of a whole generation into such a short book. And I just

thought: "Man! I'd love to be able to write something like that." Structure-wise, I read this book by Rupert Thomson called THE INSULT, which is divided into two halves; the first one urban, the second rural. Briefly, it's the story of a guy who has an accident and loses his sight. Most of the first half takes place in hospital and is about this guy's relationship with his sinister doctor. You're never quite sure what's going on, Thomson keeps you guessing till the end. It's a superb psychological thriller, paranoia being its chief theme. The novel then shifts from an urban into a rural setting. What's remarkable is that Thomson manages the change with what appears to be little or no effort. I read the book and thought: "Shit! I wish I could do that." I decided to try.

BOG STANDARDS

There are few things in life more enjoyable than dipping in to a book while on the bog. Tony White sifts through the pile on his cistern

CHEAP DATE: ANTIDOTAL ANTI-FASHION Edited by Kira Joliffe (Slab-O-Concrete £7.50)

Cheap Date features highlights from the previous six issues of the eponymously titled magazine, plus "a load of new stuff". Well, it's technically true to call it "new stuff", but more in-keeping with the spirit of Cheap Date to call it "nearly new" – not that Joliffe and co need to employ any euphemisms for the second-hand: they positively celebrate it. If you haven't seen the ultimate "anti-fashion, anti-lifestyle and alternative consumer" magazine before, then pick up this primer from the excellent Slab-O-Concrete, and you'll never be able to walk past charity

Stephen Thompson's excellent first novel, TOY SOLDIERS, is published by Sceptre (published 2000, £10.00)
Shiva Naipaul's FIREFLIES was published by Penguin in 1971 but seems to be out of print. Check out second-hand book shops .
Rupert Thomson's THE INSULT is published by Bloomsbury (pbk 1996, £6.99)

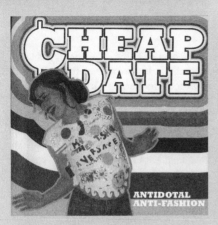

Eighties cartoon Wicked Willie (well, WW's inventor, Gray Joliffe, is Kira's dad); Andrew "The Rake" Copeman's tips on "Budget Suave"; Harmony Korine making up stories about the previous owners of junk-shop clothes; interviews with Christopher Biggins, Gene Simmons, and Loot-founder David Landau; not to mention salvaged pin-ups of Chloe Sevigny, Sophie Dahl and Jerry Hall. All of this makes Cheap Date perfect dip[material. You'll be tempted to piss sitting down if you don't already. Should a copy turn up in your local Oxfam I suggest you snap it up – though this might be one book that reviewers hang on to, so don't hold your breath.

shops in the same way again. Highspots include the welcome res'erection' of popular

MOB RULE

Rabble-rousing readings
reviewed by TONY WHITE

The audio-book market has hitherto been dominated by Martin Jarvis reading Richmal Crompton's JUST WILLIAM stories. Excellent though they are, this has left a huge, contemporary fiction-shaped gap in the audio market. But not any more – at least if King Mob have anything to do with it.

As well as nobly calling for the Shipping Forecast to replace the National Anthem, King Mob have released a selection of CDs that aim to bring you the best of contemporary authors reading their own work; and about bloody time. It has to be said that "contemporary" is bending the truth slightly, but when the material on offer is this good that hardly matters. Amongst the true gems in the King Mob catalogue are a recording of Black Panther Bobby Seale made by/for the Pope of US counter culture William S. Burroughs in 1968; a double CD of Charles Bukowski reading his poems in some LA shithole – complete with frequent beer breaks and swipes at his landlord – which was originally recorded by Bukowski for Apple Records way back when and never released.

Moving in to the twenty-first century, King Mob have released a CD of Stewart Home reading from his first novel, PURE MANIA, which captures all of the furious-hilarious energy of Home's live readings, but without the inevitable parade of arseholes who line up like lambs to the slaughter at all of his gigs. At last, then, here is their chance to heckle the man who has redefined the term "motor-mouth", without the very real fear of his embarassing them in front of their mates. Also available are Iain Sinclair reading from DOWN-

THE BLACK BOX: COCKPIT VOICE RECORDER ACCOUNTS OF IN-FLIGHT ACCIDENTS
Edited by Malcolm MacPherson
(Harper Collins £8.99)

The Black Box came out a year or so ago, but it didn't get any reviews at the time – which seems crazy to me, because it's a great book. Admittedly, not one to read on the plane, unless you're seriously constipated, but ideal in the safety of your own home. Most of these transcripts end with someone-or-other in the cockpit saying "Shit!" (though, on 1986's ill-fated Space Shuttle Challenger flight it was "Uh-oh"), and taken collectively, in spite of everything, these horror stories become – dare I say it – quite funny: flight crews bickering about soft drinks; air traffic controllers refusing to believe that all four engines are down; a "relaxed" (i.e. pissed) Captain chatting up the flight attendant with his feet up on the console; a French air crew showing off in a new Airbus during a low fly-by at an air show (famous last words: "We will do two fly-overs to demonstrate the quality of French aviation") – they hit the pylons at the end of the runway. But there are also

RIVER, Michael Moorcock reading from MOTHER LONDON and KING OF THE CITY, and Ken Campbell doing for Pidgin English what Linguaphone have been trying to do for French since the invention of the "compact cassette".

Most surprising is the two-lecture CD by Nick Cave. Commissioned for the Vienna Poetry Festival and BBC Radio 3 Religious Services respectively, these recordings show Cave in a new light. At one point he describes sitting in, as a child, on one of his teacher father's lectures and deciding that whatever he does with his life he'd better not turn out like him. Cave is aware of the irony in this, but he is a good teacher. These lectures are both entertaining and informative (now I know what "erotographomania" means), and not just for ageing Birthday Party fans. Throughout, Cave displays a warmth and wit which belie his inevitable talk of pain, ugliness, death and, yes, Kylie Minogue.

THE SECRET LIFE OF THE LOVE SONG by Nick Cave, and all other King Mob titles, are available in a book or record shop near you now

incredibly moving tales of "true heroism TM" where crews battle against the odds to bring their crippled planes back in one piece ("OK, somebody can kiss me and tell me I'm still here...") that are all the more gripping for the fact that MacPherson has made no attempt to embellish these stark transcripts. This is the most effective orchestration of schadenfreude since THE CHEATED, Australian crime-writer Louis Nowra's long out-of-print encyclopaedia of macabre newspaper clippings. The book's a favourite of the early Nineties house act of the same name, and, of course, our mates Black Box Recorder.

MUSIC

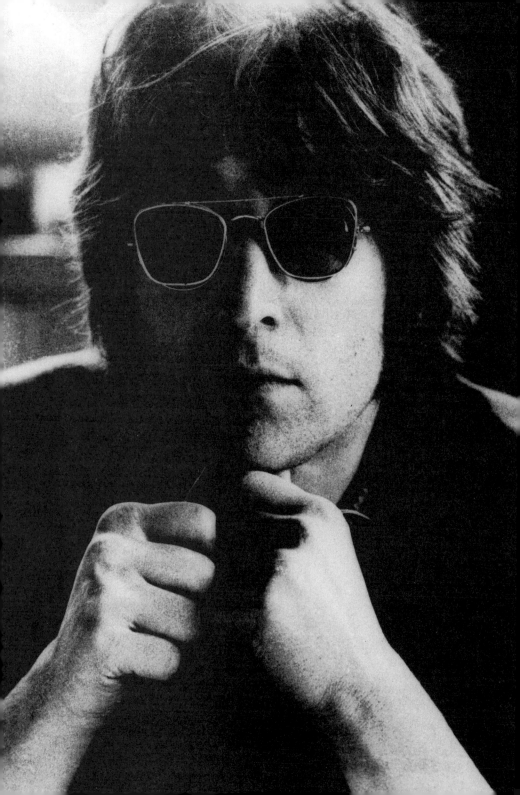

APPLE OF HIS EYE

Questions of childhood and childish idealism are provoked by the fall of Apple, The Beatles' failed artistic utopia. By ANDREW MALE

My parents kept the family photos in a silver biscuit tin at the bottom of the wardrobe. Amongst the family snaps and scraps of faded memorabilia were a series of pictures from the summer of1970 — a wild-haired eighteen year old brother in a cheesecloth shirt and heavy denim flares, a twelve year old sister posing for Nova-style fashion pics by the rose bushes and me, three and a half years old, sporting some pop-art Elton John sunglasses. I look pretty good. I even appear to be clutching my groin in some eerie prediction of the Michael Jackson/gangsta rap style, still some years in the future. Filed alongside these pictures was a black-and-white photograph of John Lennon. Smiling at the camera in the middle of a parched summer field, John Lennon is attempting to feed a large pig some unappetising food pellets.

Those in the know will instantly recognise the photo as a promotional postcard given away free with initial copies of Lennon's IMAGINE (Apple 1971) as a comic riposte to the cover of Paul McCartney's RAM album. However, my brother told me that he'd taken this photo of John Lennon in our back garden and that John Lennon was one of his mates.

In Merseyside in the early Seventies it was easy for an impressionable four-year-old to believe such an outright lie. The Beatles were everywhere, and everywhere I heard them, people seemed to be having the kind of innocent fun that a four-year-old could understand perfectly. Our neighbours, the Millers, always seemed to be having wild parties which ended with a few drunken choruses of "Yellow Submarine" and a fight in the front garden. Christmas at my Uncle Sid's

FOUR YEAR OLD ANDREW MALE IN GANGSTA POSE

wasn't complete without Auntie Netta doling out egg flip and lemonade cocktails ("snow-balls") before leading the kids through an off-colour version of "Octopus's Garden". If The Beatles seemed completely attuned to the naive, game-playing, be-here-now world of your average four-year-old, that's because they'd spent the last four years working bloody hard at getting there.

John Lennon had first taken LSD in 1966, the year of my birth. His head filled with a rag-bag of half-baked notions filched from THE TIBETAN BOOK OF THE DEAD, Aldous Huxley and the teachings of "unconventional" Harvard psychologist Timothy Leary, Lennon embarked on a mystical mental excursion into the his own inner child. The other three and, subsequently, the rest of London hippie culture, soon followed him into an ego-less "Swinging Sixties" soup of collective consciousness. As I pedalled along in my blue go-kart, sporting protective a yellow duck helmet, the youth of Britain battled the uptight capitalist machine by trying to get back to a metaphorical childhood of peace, flowers, love and having a laugh. For the Beatles, the result, alongside "Tomorrow Never Knows", "Strawberry Fields Forever" and "A Day In The Life", was such whimsical flights of immature fancy as "Magical Mystery Tour", The Maharishi Mahesh Yogi holiday camp and Apple Corps Ltd.

During that glorious July of 1970 while I was running around the garden in just shorts and Elton John shades, a journalist called Anne Nightingale was writing an article entitled "Apple coming apart at the core" for THE DAILY SKETCH. In it, she claimed that Apple Corps, which had been founded by The Beatles in February 1968 as a foundation for underprivileged artists, was finished — an empty series of offices in London's Saville Row where a skeleton staff with

THE YOUTH OF BRITAIN BATTLED THE UPTIGHT CAPITALIST MACHINE BY TRYING TO GET BACK TO A METAPHORICAL CHILDHOOD OF PEACE, FLOWERS, LOVE AND HAVING A LAUGH

nothing to do sat around, got stoned, listened to Quicksilver Messenger Service and waited for the The Fab Four to close the whole ruined enterprise.

I didn't hear about the dark side of the Beatles until 1976 when, on the way to school one summer morning, Barrie Hudson told me that the Beatles split up because Ringo Starr was gay, that he'd lived with a gay man in the Sixties and had then killed him. That gay man was, of course, Brian Epstein. Back in 1967, after the death of Brian Epstein, the Beatles had no one to run their affairs. They had also discovered that unless a certain amount of their huge income was spent on "significant ventures" they'd receive a massive bill from the taxman. As a result, on May 15 1968, Lennon and McCartney announced the formation of Apple Corps as a means of funding various late-Sixties business ventures. It was, as John Lennon put it, "an attempt to end artistic suppression and tyranny" or, as Paul put it, "a controlled weirdness... a kind of Western communism"; a JIM'LL FIX IT for hippie poets, dreamers and inventors.

In essence, this creative foundation for young people, represented by the iconic, innocent image of the single apple, wasn't a bad idea. John, Paul, George and Ringo all had projects they wanted to be involved in. George was interested in the Hare Krishna movement and experiments with electronic music. Ringo wanted to be a film star. Back in 1968, McCartney thought that demob suits might take off as the next fashion statement and wanted Apple to invest in them, while Lennon initially blew thousands on supporting children's puppet shows on Brighton beach.

Of course, I didn't know all this in 1976. So when Barry Hudson told me all about Apple Studios, how he'd been there on a family visit to London and how George Harrison was still operating the lifts, I believed him. However, his entirely made-up portrait of Apple – as a small, insular near-comic organisation where the Beatles all worked, wasn't too far from the truth.

The most striking thing about Apple was the naivety with which it approached matters of business and finance. One of the driving influences on Apple was the late Sixties acid-drenched philosophy of ego-death, where certainty and order and rules should be relinquished in favour of innocence, chance and poetry, believing that, like, everything, you know, meant something so why, erm, plan things.

Along with The Fab Four the key players at Apple included Neil Aspinall, 26, ex-Beatles road manager and now MD of Apple and Derek Taylor, 36, ex-Beatles press officer and now Apple publicist. The Apple mother company was split into various sub-divisions which included Apple Electronics, Apple Films, Apple Music Publishing, Apple Wholesale and Apple Records. The utopian Apple ideal is probably best illustrated by the works of Apple Electronics. Devised and directed by a twenty seven year old Greek named Alex Mardas – "Magic Alex" to his friends – who Lennon had met on an acid trip, Apple Electronics spent tens of thousands of pounds devising such essentials as the Electric Apple – which pulsated light and played music with no visible power source –

speakers made from wallpaper, paint that made things disappear and the Nothing Box. The Nothing Box featured a series of twelve flashing lights, ran for five years and, apart from that, did absolutely nothing. None of his products ever reached the marketplace. Alex's main project was constructing the Beatles new 72-track recording studios at Apple. It was terrible. He'd put in an eight-track tape recorder with no mixing desk, no sound-proofing and no holes in the wall to get cables from the studio to the control room. His efforts were sold off for scrap. It was later revealed that Alex's previous electronic experience had been as a TV repairman.

Apart from Magic Alex, one of Apple's first charges were a group of young Dutch clothing designers – Simon Posthuma, Josje Leeger and Marijke Koger – who called themselves The Fool. The Fool had first won favour with the Beatles after being hired to paint psychedelic designs on Lennon's new grand piano and design a fireplace for George Harrison. On such flimsy credentials The Beatles gave The Fool £400,000 to open the Apple Boutique at 94 Baker Street. As Derek Taylor puts it in Peter McCabe's APPLE TO THE CORE: "After the summer of 1967 with all that good weather and good acid, [the Beatles] opened a store while this feeling was still in existence. As soon as the summer was over the shop didn't make sense..." The designs at the Apple Boutique were wild, original, outlandish and, for the most part, unwearable. The Boutique began by losing around £50 a week just to petty pilfering. In seven months, the novelty of a Beatles store had already worn off. Punters stopped turning up and in July 1968 the Beatles made the decision to close the store and give away the final £20,000 worth of clothing. The first thing they did, however, was arrange a private visit to the Boutique and take all the best clothes for themselves.

The next project they concentrated on was Apple Music. A poster was designed showing a London busker below the headline "This Man Has Talent". The poster's explanation of Apple's business practices ended with the line "This man now owns a Bentley". The poster basically implied that anyone with the modicum of ability could become a millionaire through Apple. Four hundred tapes arrived in the first fortnight after the poster went up. Their first signings included American singer-songwriter James Taylor, fey Welsh folkie Mary Hopkin and Beatles soundalikes The Iveys (later to become Badfinger). These are the memorable ones. Others included The Black Dyke Mills Brass Band (signed because Paul thought brass bands were "coming back") and a bunch of psychedelic weirdos called Contact who believed they were alien representatives living on earth (signed because George didn't want to be caught out if they just happened to be right).

Pretty soon every would-be singer-songwriter, fast buck artist and fried outcast of the hippie underground was turning up at the Apple offices hoping for a free hand-out. The arrival of such ne'er-do-wells surely had something to do with the manner in which Apple was conducting its business in 1968.

One of the first appointments made by the company was a young American by the name of David DiLello who was employed as "the house hippie". Then, a strange individual called Caleb was appointed as the Apple astrologer, his days would be spent sitting on top of filing cabinets making business forecasts based on the I-Ching. On 15th June Lennon set up a plan through Apple to plant acorns for peace but most of the acorns went unplanted and were left to rot in the Apple Offices.

From July 1968, Derek Taylor appointed

STAFF WOULD BREAKFAST ON CHAMPAGNE AND PANADEINE AND BUY EACH OTHER DONKEYS AS PRESENTS

Jeremy Banks as photographic director of Apple and the company moved from their Oxford Street Offices to new premises on Saville Row. With Banks at the helm things took on a more chemical aspect. Staff would consume acid and vodka in huge quantities, breakfast on champagne and Panadeine in a state of permanent celebration, buy each other donkeys as presents and consume vast quantities of dope. Christmas at Apple that year was spent with a small California chapter of the Hell's Angels who, at the behest of George Harrison, had stopped over in England before going over to Czechoslovakia to "sort out the political troubles there" that year. The visitors were led by two dangerous-looking individuals named Frisco Pete and Billy Tumbleweed. They had joined up with a near-naked travelling medicine show of damaged acid freaks called Emily's Family whose various members were planning to a) fuck George Harrison and b) kidnap John and Yoko and take them to an idyllic commune in the Fiji Islands. The party featured vast quantities of scotch, coke, hash, ice cream, cake and sausage rolls. John and Yoko dressed as Santa for the kids, Brian Jones turned up and the Angels threatened to attack Derek Taylor with a knife if he didn't serve them the 43 pound turkey, like, immediately. It would be the best year of Apple Corps short and troubled life.

The disastrous recording of LET IT BE kicked off 1969, and was accompanied by some serious financial wranglings. In a bid for complete control of their own finances, the Beatles brought in city brokers Triumph Investment to buy out the 25% of their income still owned by Brian Epstein's NEMS company. Also, it came to light that — throughout 1968 — thefts from the Apple premises had amounted to four television sets plus numerous record players, electric typewriters, adding machines, cases of wine, wage packets, movie cameras, speakers and fan heaters plus an electric skillet from the kitchen and all the lead off the roof. The Beatles themselves had stopped turning up. In the first month they'd all turned up and Paul McCartney was there every day, checking on the amount of toilet paper used. Then John stopped coming, then Ringo, then George until finally even Paul couldn't be arsed. But the business carried on. A spoken word label, Zapple, was set up and Ken Kesey was commissioned to record an album. He arrived in London and started patrolling the streets with a tape recorder. On March 12th, Paul McCartney and Linda Eastman were married. The next day George was arrested for possession of cannabis. March also saw John and Yoko embark upon their campaigns for world peace, the bed-in and bagism. The thefts continued, the most serious being the tapes of Ken Kesey's spoken word album, stolen from the Apple reception. In an American interview John Lennon likened Apple to a big black hole, sucking up all his money.

Clearly, this innocent, nay, childish approach to money couldn't last. In February 1969, Lennon, Harrison and Starr asked the Rolling Stones manager Allen Klein to take over the Beatles' affairs while McCartney opted for Linda Eastman's family firm of management consultants, resulting in a court battle that long outlasted the career of the band.

Meanwhile, the Apple offices were becoming a miserable place, where the order of the day appeared to be comforting the nutters in the foyer who wanted to have their third eye massaged by George, or ejecting foul-smelling "poets" who wanted John Lennon to publish their work, or dealing with whatever Apple business was left over and then getting stoned. In August of 1969, during the recording sessions for Abbey Road, there were a series of mass resignations from Apple. One of the last signings to the label were the Radha Krishna Temple who George had heard singing "hare krishna" chants on Oxford Street. It was not a signing that inspired anyone.

The final Beatle single, "Let It Be" was released on March 14, 1970 followed by solo releases from Ringo (SENTIMENTAL JOURNEY) and Paul McCartney (MCCARTNEY). On 10th April 1970 Paul McCartney announced that the Beatles no longer existed. On August 4 1970 Apple Corps was closed down and on 31 December McCartney instituted court action to dissolve The Beatles partnership.

Back in 1976 the story of The Beatles split, as told to me by Barry Hudson, was rendered somewhat differently: "The Beatles split up after a big fight," he said, "they all hated the fact that John was with Yoko so they had a big fight in a garden and Ringo broke John's nose. My mum said that they let everybody down."

I eventually fell out with Barry Hudson after he wrote on the back of his English note-book that I looked like ET but I always wanted to tell him how accurate he and his mum were about the demise of Apple and the Beatles. They had a big fight and they let everybody down. Or, as Derek Taylor put it:

"I thought they were saviours, so did a lot of people but we over-estimated them. They were just ordinary human beings."

And I still want to believe that John Lennon fed a pig in our garden. 🗨

A BUTTERFLY IN THE GARDEN

The story behind proto-metal band Iron Butterfly's "In-A-Gadda-Da-Vida", the serial killer's tune of choice. By ANDREW MALE

"If one does what God does, often enough, one becomes as God is."
Hannibal Lektor in Manhunter (He was later renamed "Lecter")
"In-A-Gadda-Da-Vida, honey, don't you know that I love you?"
Iron Butterfly

What drives a man to kill? In the first volume of his best-selling Hannibal Lecter trilogy, RED DRAGON, author Thomas Harris addresses the issue in his character portrait of the novel's chief serial killer, Francis "Tooth Fairy" Dollarhyde. Dollarhyde's soulmate on all his killing sprees is the romantic visionary and mystic, William Blake. The Blake etching which inspires Dollarhyde to kill is "The Great Red Dragon and the Woman Clothed In The Rays Of The Sun". In the picture a mythological blood-red dragon hovers over what appears to be a supine woman in the throes of some strange ecstasy. The killer's violent interpretation of this painting is that Blake is telling him to transform outward creation into religious vision – to transform a Gomorragh back into an Eden by Swedenborgian metamorphosis. He turns the women into the dragon. As a portrait of the serial killer's mind there's none better but when director Michael Mann made RED DRAGON into the 1991 movie MAN-HUNTER, he had bigger things on his mind. How would a naive Blakean serial killer live and, more importantly, what music would he listen to?

Well, he'd reside in a hip designer flat out in the middle of the Everglades with wall-height prints of the planet Mars, abstract designer furniture and nothing in the kitchen but some big knives. And when Dollarhyde (Tom Noonan) takes a young blind lady (Joan Allen) back to his pad for that final delusional Blakeian sacrifice what does he play on his Centrex eight-track cartridge player but the full-volume, full-length 17 minute version of Iron Butterfly's "In-A-Gadda-Da-Vida".

"You're scaring me with this music!"

IRON BUTTERFLY PERFORM THEIR 17-MINUTE ROCK EPIC

screams his captive, "Why are you doing this. It's ugly." Boy, is she right. If ever we were unconvinced of Dollarhyde's evil and insanity, this is the clincher.

Only a maniac would choose to listen to the full length version of "In-a-Gadda-Da-Vida". Mann's implication is also that this music has led Dollarhyde to his fate. On paper, it looks like such an innocent little song. These are the lyrics: IN-A-GADDA-DA-VIDA, HONEY/DON'T YOU KNOW THAT I LOVE YOU?/IN-A-GADDA-DA-VIDA, BABY/DON'T YOU KNOW THAT I'LL ALWAYS BE TRUE/OH, WON'T YOU COME WITH ME/AND TAKE MY HAND?/OH, WON'T YOU COME WITH ME/AND WALK THIS LAND?/PLEASE TAKE MY HAND! After that the lyric sheet just says "Repeat" and, ominously, "Solos". A sudden, grinding needle-sharp metal riff ushers the song in. "In-A-Gada-da-Vida" is heavy metal made by the devil himself, taking an innocent little tale of Edenic innocence (In-A-Gadda-Da-Vida = In the Garden of Eden. Duh) and corrupting its very soul. Unfortunately, the album that contains this meisterwork, also called IN-A-GADDA-DA-VIDA offers no clues to such devilry. The first side of the album is filled with naive bubblegum psychedelia about groovy girls, with titles such as "Flowers And Beads" and "My Mirage", all seemingly played by drunken hippies wearing boxing gloves and the worst drummer in the world.

Ironically, the song's origins are far removed from the crypto-blasphemist metal beast it became. "In-A-Gadda-Da-Vida" was written by the Iron Butterfly's lead singer and keyboard player Doug Ingle. Ingle, the son of a church organist, had originally written it as a short little country folk song called "In the Garden of Eden".

"'In-A-Gadda-Da-Vida' was like a country ballad when we first heard it," says Lee Dorman, "but by the time the band got done with it... well, you can see what happened."

Dorman and Bushy had gone to Ingle's house to hear this little religio-country track but, as Dorman puts it, "Doug had been up for a day and a half. Plus he had been drinking some wine."

As to the magik corruption of "In The Garden of Eden", Ron Bushy lays claim to that: "I was supporting the band by making pizza," he says. "I came home at three in the morning from working one night and Doug played me a song he was writing. He polished off a whole gallon of Red Mountain Wine as the evening wore on. He played this song on the keyboard and he was so drunk that it came out as 'in-a-gadda-da-vida.' I thought it was real catchy so I just wrote it down phonetically. The next morning we woke up, looked at the writing, 'In-A-Gadda-Da-Vida,' and decided to keep the title." As the group became more comfortable with the song and its concept, it grew longer and longer in performance.

"We were about eight minutes into it," recalls Dorman, "Then we got an opportunity to go on the road with the Jefferson Airplane, and by that time, "Vida", which we called it, was up to ten, eleven, twelve minutes and moving along. When the tour got to New York, it was time to record.

"The song then took on a life of its own," says Dorman.

Although the album's production was credited to Jim Hilton, it was veteran engineer Don Casale (The Rascals, Vanilla Fudge) who actually recorded the date.

"I had a good half reel of tape left," recalls Casale, "and Ingle said, 'You'd better get another reel of tape.' I said, 'I've got plenty left.' He said, 'Trust me, you're gonna need a new reel.'"

Executives were wary of putting a 17-minute song on an album. They wanted pop songs. "We said, 'What are you going to cut out?'" says Dorman. "There's only about a minute and a half of lyrics, the rest is instrumental. No way. It was like a sonata, if you will. It's an expression of the music."

Vida would never would have succeeded without the help of FM radio, whose free-form stoner "Ten records back-to-back for all you heads out there!" style had just taken off. The track became an "underground" sensation with the kinds of DJs and kids who thought they were smashing the system by listening to a song that was longer than three minutes. The album IN-A-GADDA-DA-VIDA eventually stayed on the Billboard chart for 140 weeks, including 81 weeks in the Top 10. It became the first album certified as a Platinum Record for sales of more than a million copies. To date, it has sold over 25 million copies worldwide.

The pressures of playing "Vida" every night soon took its toll. "It was pressure, pressure, pressure and we were just burned out," said Dorman. "Doug was burnt, Ron was burnt. We quit out of our own volition."

Doug went off to write ballads while Rhino and Dorman went even heavier with Captain Beyond, one of America's loudest bands.

"We lost a lot of money," said Dorman. "Three Dog Night lost a lot. The Monkees lost a fortune. Nobody knew any better."

Although there were subsequent reformations and line-up changes, nothing recorded by Iron Butterfly ever approached the devilish depths of "Vida". For the curious, a recent reissue of the IN-A-GADDA-DA-VIDA album contains a live eighteen minute version and an extra five minute single version in addition to the 17:05 minute original. However, if you really want to go over the edge, into serial killer territory, then there was this recent advert on the internet from one-time Butterfly member Mike Pinera: "'In-A-Gadda-Da-Vida' has inspired Mike Pinera to explore the deeper mysterious meanings of this multi-platinum song. His many years performing with Iron Butterfly gives him special inside knowledge of the hauntingly melodic music. Join him as he takes you through the many moods, seasons, and life-times that come to us all." Of the tracks listed, one in particular intrigues. It's called "Trilogy" and features three sections: "In the Garden", "In A Gadda Da Vida Revisited" and "In the Garden of Eden". You have been warned. ◉

VISIONS OF ALBION

From the Kinks (left) to Van Morrison, pop music occasionally tries
to reach an essential truth about England. By RICHARD VINE

When you're away from home, the heart does funny things. You're much more likely to hear English people in a heated debate about England when they're sitting in a bar in Abu Dhabi than you are in Richmond or Milton Keynes. Geography stretches our sense of what's good, what's great, until you'd be forgiven for thinking that the most patriotic citizens are the ones who haven't been home in years.

As a teenager growing up in Hong Kong, I felt none of this. Any sense of Englishness I might have quickly disappeared as my accent floated into the lazy drawl of Tom Wolfe's Trans Atlantic Man; thoughts of Home were clouded with, well, clouds, and my sympathies lay more with a lone piece of half-joking "Brits Out" graffiti on the way to school than any desire to play cricket in downtown Kowloon. Holidays back to England were

merely vinyl collection excursions, a rabid foray into the unknown zone, where bands with ridiculously long names could be found without hunting through stacks of Anita Mui records. This seemed to be England's prime and sole reason for existing to a teenage mind pumped full of dim sum and sunshine. Music was the connection. But in the Eighties, there didn't seem to be much to connect music to the country. Radio fodder like the Duran Duran opus "Seven And The Ragged Tiger" said little, and even less about UK life. Hearing The Cult's "She Sells Sanctuary" or The Jesus And Mary Chain's "Never Understand" for the first time were both moments of primary joy, but it was more to do with the thrill of noise than any sense of place. The music that mattered to me made Britain seem cool only by association; there was nothing in the music itself that made the

country seem any less of a magnet for drizzle. Back among the expatriate community in Hong Kong there were traces of indigenous English music that wanted to celebrate, or talk about, some sense of Englishness, but the Arran-sweaterness of folk passed me by, and the insanity of Morris Dancing and its attendant curious soundtrack have not been able to attract anyone in search of teenage kicks since 843AD.

Revelation came with a song about trains. Not the smokestack lightning express of a thousand grizzly twelve bar blues, but a song about Hampshire trains, sung in a defiantly English accent:

"I often dream of trains when I'm alone. I ride on them into another zone. I dream of them constantly, heading for paradise, or Basingstoke or Reading."

The title track from Robyn Hitchcock's 1984 low-key gem holds a strange promise, offering the commuter belt as an alternative to paradise. Of course, there's a finely tuned sense of the absurd being played here, but

at the same time, there's genuine affection for these most prosaic of towns.

A track on a later album, ELEMENT OF LIGHT, describes how "in Winchester, there's nowhere at all" and again, there's a way in which the music allows the "water meadows curling round the hills" to rise out of the mundanity of suburbia, to create a picture that speaks volumes about the way England's small towns can be beautiful, while at the same time acknowledging how it can seem like there's little there but memories.

One of the most developed visions of an idyllic England comes, oddly enough, from a band better known as the kings of Sixties Carnaby cool, The Kinks. Retreating from their familiar London streets (in their minds at least), they created what was essentially a fantasy of the countryside, nostalgia for memories none of them could have had. 1968's THE KINKS ARE THE VILLAGE GREEN PRESERVATION SOCIETY is a concept album that used the indulgence of the format to celebrate the joys of tradition at the height of psychedelic madness, talking about being old in the middle of a global youth revolution. No wonder it flopped.

"We are the Village Green Preservation Society. God save strawberry jam and all the different varieties. Preserving the old ways from being abused, protecting the new ways for me and for you," sang Ray Davies, before going on to declare that The Village Green Preservation Society was also strongly in favour of Desperate Dan, Sherlock Holmes, Tudor houses, draught beer, custard pies, antique tables, billiards, vaudeville, little shops, china cups and the George Cross. Not exactly rock and roll.

Maybe that's the problem. Talking about the pastoral, entering into the romance of the countryside, or just singing about England has never really been that cool when compared to songs about America. San Francisco or Stevenage? LA or Littlehampton? Chicago or Chippenham? It always seems out of step with the agendas of rock somehow; you either start garbling about elves and Faerie Queens, or hedge a little too close for comfort to John Major's warm beer manifestos.

Look at what happens when those Kinks wannabes, Blur, try to emulate their heroes' sense of place – we end up with the mockney mishmash of "Country House", or the cynicism of "Parklife". When an attempt is made to find a local Route 66, you get Kula Shaker's 303, not, as you might assume, an ode to the classic drum machine, but a homage to the A303 ("In the land of summer sun, we have just begun. Riding out with my friends in a Mercedes Benz. You can find your way home on the 303...") which just so happens to be the road that takes traffic jams full of caravanning families past Stonehenge every summer. Like, deep.

Aside from The Fall's outstanding collaboration with William Blake, "Dog Is

THE VILLAGE GREEN PRESERVATION SOCIETY WAS STRONGLY IN FAVOUR OF DESPERATE DAN, SHERLOCK HOLMES, TUDOR HOUSES AND THE GEORGE CROSS

Life/Jerusalem" ("I will not rest until Jerusalem is built in England's green and pleasant land... It was the fault of the government."), the most successful song to conjure up everything that's great about being out in the English countryside is probably Van Morrison's "Summertime In England", recorded, appropriately enough, in the south of France.

As well as finding time during its 15.34 duration to set out one of the central tenants of his gruff Zen philosophy ("It ain't why, it just is"), he summons forth Blake, TS Eliot, Yeats, Coleridge and Wordsworth to make the case. With former JB's sax player Pee Wee Ellis on board, it's a riotously joyous celebration that feels like the perfect summer's day: "Take a walk with me, down by Avalon, and I will show you, it ain't why, why, why, it just is... TS Eliot chose England... Did you ever hear about Wordsworth and Coleridge? They were smoking by the lakeside. We'll go ridin' down by Avalon. In the country, in the summertime... Can you feel the light in England?"

Maybe that's the point. We can't – there just isn't enough light for most of the year. Summers seem to bring rain, and the winter is shrouded in a neverending grey. But when, on those rare, near mythical days, the sun does come out, and you're floating far from the 303's of the world, up by one of Van's lakes, maybe there is paradise to be found here after all. ☺

OUR CONTRIBUTORS

Matthew De Abaitua's latest short story is published in the Serpent's Tail anthology *Retro Retro* and his four-part documentary on British science fiction will be shown later in the year on Channel 4

Sarah Ainslie is a photojournalist currently working on a project on pub strippers to be shown at The Clerks House, Shoreditch

Marc Atkins has lived and worked in Europe and North America and has exhibited in Paris and NY

Steve Aylett is the author of several novels including *The Inflatable Volunteer* and *Slaughtermatic* and the short story collection *Toxicology* (Orion)

Babzotica runs her own label of swinging exotic wear and is a member of the Diabolics

Steve Beard is the author of the novel *Digital Leatherette* (Codex). A collection of his journalism, *Logic Bomb: Transmissions from the Edge of Style Culture*, is published by Serpent's Tail

Nicholas Blincoe is a novelist and his latest book is *The Dope Priest*

Dick Bradsell is a cocktail mixologist with his own TV series, *Dick's Bar*

Adam Broomberg and Oliver Chanarin are photographers whose book *Trust* will be published in October by WestZone. Their solo show is on at the Hasselblad Centre in Göteborg, Sweden

Adam Buxton is Adam from Adam and Joe

Lewis Chamberlain is an artist who has been working on a pencil drawing of a mannequin for four years. He plans to finish it this week

Jonathan Coe's novels include *What A Carve Up!*, *The House of Sleep* and *The Dwarves of Death*, now a film starring Max Beesley and Ray Winstone

Josh Collins does set design and wild stuff

Andrew Copeman is a writer and performer

Joe Cornish is Joe from Adam and Joe

Francoise La Croix has lived and worked in the UK and France. For the last four years she has been photographing solitary journeys along the English coast

Brian Dean is editor of the brilliant zine *Anxiety Culture*

Chris Draper is an illustratator who regularly contributes to *New Scientist* and the *Independent*

Bill Drummond is a serial father

Hannah Dyson draws anthropomorphic creatures and other beings

Jeremy Dyson is one of the League of Gentlemen. *Never Trust a Rabbit*, a collection of his short stories, is published by Duck Editions

Uri Geller is a mystic and spoon-bender

Joshua Glenn edits *Hermenaut* magazine and is at josh@hermenaut.com

Charles Glover specialises in portrait photography

Jonny Halifax is a director of General Lighting and Power, the creative agency

Julia Hember is a photographer who does location advertising and design work but will also do pets

NJ Hodgkinson is a fashion journalist and stylist

Will Hodgkinson is the editor's brother and writes for the Guardian

Stewart Home's *Cunt* is published by the Do Not Press. *Confusion Incorporated: A Collection of Lies, Hoaxes and Hidden Truths* is published by Codex

Alex James is a gentleman musician

James Jarvis is a master of illustration

Mark Manning now has two books out – *Crucify Me Again* (Codex) and *Get Your Cock Out* (Attack)

Andrew Male is features editor on *Mojo* magazine

Edwin Marney is an illustrator who does work for dull computer, medical and business magazine

John Michel is a mystic and a gentleman

Jonathan Moberly is publishing publican at The Foundry and Ellipsis

John Moore had a hit record with Black Box Recorder

Robert Newman is a comedian and writer

John Nicholson is an alternative historian and occasional model

Marcus Oakley is an illustrator who lives in Brixton and likes garibaldi biscuits

Magnea Orvarsdottir is an Icelandic journalist

James Parker is the film critic for *Esquire* and is writing a novel

Chris Petit's film *Asylum* is now being screened

Max Reeves is a photographer. His "Hyde Park" project begins in July at The Foundry, Shoreditch

Tim Richardson edits *New Eden*, the lovely gardens magazine

Greg Rowland plays keyboards and is on gregory@easynet.co.uk

Mark Ryden is a Tiki artist who did the cover. He's based on the West Coast

Jock Scot is Jock Scot

Shag's real name is Josh Hagel. He's a graphic artist at the forefront of the Tiki movement

Frank Skelton is a civil servant

David Solomons specialises in portraits, humour and street photography

Louis Theroux is a journalist

Tim Twelves lives and works in Echo Park, East LA and can be reached at mysteriouse@hotmail.com

Gwyn Vaughn Roberts lives in Cambridge

Richard Vine works at the *Guardian*

Watts is well known for his hot rod pinstriping

Chris Watson is an illustrator whose site www.cwinc.co.uk is coming soon

Raymond Weekes's work has appeared in *New Eden* and *Time Out*. He's on raymondweekes@hotmail.com

Ged Wells is Insane. See him at www.insane.org.uk

Tony White is the author of three novels including, most recently, *Charlieunclenorfolktango* (Codex)